MW01484777

Foundations of Social Work Research

FOUNDATIONS OF SOCIAL WORK RESEARCH

REBECCA L. MAULDIN

MAXINE DAVIS, GENEVIEVE GRAF, RICHARD HOEFER, CATHERINE LABRENZ, KATHY LEE, DIANE MITSCHKE, ERIN ROARK MURPHY, DIANA PADILLA-MEDINA, SARAH R. ROBINSON, HOLLI SLATER, BROOKE TROUTMAN, RACHEL VOTH SCHRAG, AND LING XU

Mavs Open Press

Arlington

Foundations of Social Work Research by Rebecca L. Mauldin is licensed under a Creative Commons Attribution-NonCommercial-ShareAlike 4.0 International License, except where otherwise noted.

This open textbook is based on the open textbook *Scientific Inquiry in Social Work* by Matthew DeCarlo.

ISBN 13: 978-0-98988-788-5

4750 Venture Drive, Suite 400
Ann Arbor, MI 48108
800-562-2147
www.xanedu.com

CONTENTS

ABOUT THE PUBLISHER

ABOUT MAVS OPEN PRESS

Creation of this resource was supported by Mavs Open Press, operated by the University of Texas at Arlington Libraries (UTA Libraries). Mavs Open Press offers no-cost services for UTA faculty, staff, and students who wish to openly publish their scholarship. The Libraries' program provides human and technological resources that empower our communities to publish new open access journals, to convert traditional print journals to open access publications, and to create or adapt open educational resources (OER). Resources published by Mavs Open Press are openly licensed using Creative Commons licenses and are offered in various e-book formats free of charge. Optional print copies may be available through the UTA Bookstore or can be purchased through print-on-demand services, such as Lulu.com.

ABOUT OER

OER are free teaching and learning materials that are licensed to allow for revision and reuse. They can be fully self-contained textbooks, videos, quizzes, learning modules, and more. OER are distinct from public resources in that they permit others to use, copy, distribute, modify, or reuse the content. The legal permission to modify and customize OER to meet the specific learning objectives of a particular course make them a useful pedagogical tool.

ABOUT PRESSBOOKS

Pressbooks is a web-based authoring tool based on WordPress, and it is the primary tool that Mavs Open Press (in addition to many other open textbook publishers) uses to create and adapt open textbooks. In May 2018, Pressbooks announced their *Accessibility Policy*, which outlines their efforts and commitment to making their software accessible. Please note that Pressbooks no longer supports use on Internet Explorer as there are important features in Pressbooks that Internet Explorer doesn't support.

The following browsers are best to use for Pressbooks:

- Firefox
- Chrome
- Safari
- Edge

ABOUT THE PRINT VERSION

This publication was designed to work best online and features a number of hyperlinks in the text. We have retained the blue font for hyperlinks in the print version to make it easier to find the URL in the "Links by Chapter" section at the back of the book.

CONTACT US

Information about open education at UTA is available online. If you are an instructor who is using this OER for a course, please let us know by filling out our OER Adoption Form. Contact us at oer@uta.edu for other inquires related to UTA Libraries publishing services.

ABOUT THIS PROJECT

OVERVIEW

This textbook was created to provide an introduction to research methods for BSW and MSW students, with particular emphasis on research and practice relevant to students at the University of Texas at Arlington. It provides an introduction to social work students to help evaluate research for evidence-based practice and design social work research projects. It can be used with its companion, *A Guidebook for Social Work Literature Reviews and Research Questions* by Rebecca L. Mauldin and Matthew DeCarlo, or as a stand alone textbook.

CREATION PROCESS

In the summer of 2019, Dr. Rebecca L. Mauldin of the University of Texas at Arlington's School of Social Work coordinated a project to adopt an Open Educational Resource textbook for the School of Social Work's Research Methods courses across the BSW and MSW programs. *Scientific Inquiry in Social Work* by Matthew DeCarlo was used as a primary source text. In the creation of this text, Dr. Mauldin worked with Amanda Steed, MSW Graduate Student Research Assistant, and Brooke Troutman, Assistant Librarian to incorporate and revise the source material, locate additional OER material for the book, solicit contributions from faculty members, and write additional material for the text book.

ABOUT THE AUTHOR

Rebecca L. Mauldin is an assistant professor at the University of Texas at Arlington's School of Social Work. Dr. Mauldin's research interests include social networks, social support, gerontology, and generosity. Her research focuses on the role of social relationships in the health and well-being of older adults. She examines the resources and benefits associated with relationships among residents of long-term care facilities, older immigrants, and older adults aging in place. Collaborative in nature, Dr. Mauldin enjoys community practice, program development, and coalition building. She thrives in teaching environments and brings forth others' strengths in her practice, scholarship, and teaching.

ACKNOWLEDGMENTS

UTA CARES GRANT PROGRAM

Creation of this OER was funded by the UTA CARES Grant Program, which is sponsored by UTA Libraries. Under the auspices of UTA's Coalition for Alternative Resources in Education for Students (CARES), the grant program supports educators interested in practicing open education through the adoption of OER and, when no suitable open resource is available, through the creation of new OER or the adoption of library-licensed or other free content. Additionally, the program promotes innovation in teaching and learning through the exploration of open educational practices, such as collaborating with students to produce educational content of value to a wider community. Information about the grant program and funded projects is available online.

AUTHOR'S NOTE

This guidebook to writing literature reviews would not be possible without the source material. Dr. DeCarlo's textbook is a comprehensive introduction to social work research methods. I am grateful to him for his generosity and support. I would like to thank Michelle Reed of the UTA Libraries for sharing their extensive knowledge and their guidance in compiling this guide. Also from the UTA Libraries, Brooke Troutman also provided guidance and contributed material. Amanda Steed worked many hours to assist in this book's creation and offered incisive insights to make this guide as useful to students as possible. My appreciation also goes out to Teresa McIntyre, Diane Mitschke, and Regina Praetorius, three faculty members at the UTA School of Social Work, who reviewed the original source material for this guidebook and offered their suggestions for this guide. I thank faculty contributors from the UTA School of Social Work: Maxine Davis, Genevieve Graf, Noelle Fields, Aaron Hagedorn, Richard Hoefer, Catherine LaBrenz, Kathy Lee, Diane Mitschke, Diana Padilla-Medina, Holli Slater, Rachel Voth Schrag, and Ling Xu for contributing material to the guidebook. Finally, I wish to acknowledge Ruben Espricueta of the School of Social Work for his assistance with graphics and photography.

PROJECT LEAD

Rebecca L. Mauldin – Assistant Professor, University of Texas at Arlington

CONTRIBUTING AUTHORS

Chapter 1: Richard Hoefer, Professor, School of Social Work, University of Texas at Arlington

Chapter 2: Catherine LaBrenz, Assistant Professor, School of Social Work, University of Texas at Arlington

Chapter 4: Aaron Hagedorn, Assistant Dean of Research and Faculty Affairs, School of Social Work, University of Texas at Arlington

Chapter 5: Ling Xu and Noelle Fields, Assistant Professors, School of Social Work, University of Texas at Arlington

Chapter 7: Diana Padilla-Medina, Asssistant Professor, School of Social Work, University of Texas at Arlington

Chapter 8: Diane Mitschke, Associate Professor, and Holli Slater, Assistant Dean for Academic and Student Affairs, School of Social Work, University of Texas at Arlington

Chapter 9: Genevieve Graf, Assistant Professor, School of Social Work, University of Texas at Arlington; Erin Roark Murphy, MSW, School of Social Work, University of Texas at Arlington

Chapter 10: Kathy Lee, Assistant Professor, School of Social Work, University of Texas at Arlington

Chapter 11: Maxine Davis, Assistant Professor, School of Social Work, University of Texas at Arlington; Sarah R. Robinson, LMSW, School of Social Work, University of Texas at Arlington

Chapter 12: Rachel Voth Schrag, Assistant Professor, School of Social Work, University of Texas at Arlington

ABOUT THE COVER

Brittany Griffiths, UTA Libraries' Publishing Specialist, designed the cover for this OER. The images used were taken by Ruben Espiricueta and were used with his permission.

CHAPTER ONE: INTRODUCTION TO RESEARCH

How do social workers know the right thing to do? It's an important question. Incorrect social work actions may actively harm clients and communities. Timely and effective social work interventions further social justice and promote individual change. To do make the right choices, we must have a basis of knowledge, the skills to understand it, and the commitment to growing that knowledge. The source of social work knowledge is social science and this book is about how to understand and apply it to social work practice.

CHAPTER OUTLINE

- 1.1 How do social workers know what to do?
- 1.2 Science and social work
- 1.3 Why should we care?
- 1.4 Understanding research

CONTENT ADVISORY

This chapter discusses or mentions the following topics: stereotypes of people on welfare, sexual harassment and sexist job discrimination, sexism, poverty, homelessness, mental illness, substance abuse, and child maltreatment.

1.1 HOW DO SOCIAL WORKERS KNOW WHAT TO DO?

Learning Objectives

- Reflect on how we know what to do as social workers
- Differentiate between micro-, meso-, and macro-level analysis
- Describe intuition, its purpose in social work, and its limitations
- Identify specific types of cognitive biases and how the influence thought
- Define scientific inquiry

WHAT WOULD YOU DO?

Imagine you are a clinical social worker at a children's mental health agency. Today, you receive a referral from your town's middle school about a client who often skips school, gets into fights, and is disruptive in class. The school has suspended him and met with the parents multiple times, who say they practice strict discipline at home. Yet, the client's behavior only gotten worse. When you arrive at the school to meet with the boy, you notice he has difficulty maintaining eye contact with you, appears distracted, and has a few bruises on his legs. At the same time, he is also a gifted artist, and you two spend the hour in which you assess him painting and drawing.

- *Given the strengths and challenges you notice, what interventions would you select for this client and how would you know your interventions worked?*

Imagine you are a social worker in an urban food desert, a geographic area in which there is no grocery store that sells fresh food. Many of your low-income clients rely on food from the dollar store or convenience stores in order to live or simply order takeout. You are becoming concerned about your clients' health, as many of them are obese and say they are unable to buy fresh food. Because convenience stores are more expensive and your clients mostly survive on minimum wage jobs or Supplemental Nutrition Assistance Program (SNAP) benefits, they often have to rely on food pantries towards the end of the month once their money runs out. You have spent the past month building a coalition composed of members from your community, including non-profit agencies, religious groups, and healthcare workers to lobby your city council.

- *How should your group address the issue of food deserts in your community? What intervention do you suggest? How would you know if your intervention worked?*

You are a social worker working at a public policy center focused on homelessness. Your city is seeking a large federal grant to address the growing problem of homelessness in your city and has hired you as a consultant to work on the grant proposal. After conducting a needs assessment in collaboration with local social service agencies and interviewing people who are homeless, you meet with city councilmembers to talk about your options to create a program. Local agencies want to spend the money to build additional capacity at existing shelters in the community. They also want to create a transitional housing program at an unused apartment complex where people can live after the shelter and learn independent living skills. On the other hand, the clients you interview want to receive housing vouchers so they can rent an apartment from a landlord in the community. They also fear the agencies running the shelter and transitional housing program would dictate how to live their lives and impose unnecessary rules, like restrictions on guests or quiet hours. When you ask the agencies about client feedback, they state that clients could not be trusted to manage in their own apartments and need the structure and supervision provided by agency support workers.

- *What kind of program should your city choose to implement? Which program is most likely to be effective?*

Assuming you've taken a social work course before, you will notice that the case studies cover different levels of analysis in the social ecosystem—micro, meso, and macro. At the **micro-level**, social workers examine the smallest levels of interaction; even in some cases, just "the self" alone. That is our child in case 1. When social workers investigate groups and communities, such as our food desert in case 2, their inquiry is at the **meso-level**. At the **macro-level**, social workers examine social structures and institutions. Research at the macro-level examines large-scale patterns, including culture and government policy, as in case 3. These domains interact with each other, and it is common for a social work research project to address more than one level of analysis. Moreover, research that occurs on one level is likely to have implications at the other levels of analysis.

HOW DO SOCIAL WORKERS KNOW WHAT TO DO?

Welcome to social work research. This chapter begins with three problems that social workers might face in practice and three questions about what a social worker should do next. If you haven't already, spend a minute or two thinking about how you would respond to each case and jot down some notes. How would you respond to each of these cases?

For many of you this textbook will likely come at an early point in your social work education, so it may seem unfair to ask you what the right answers are. And to disappoint you further, this course will not teach you the right answer to these questions. It will, however, teach you how to answer these questions for yourself. Social workers must learn how to examine the literature on a topic, come to a reasoned conclusion, and use that knowledge in their practice.

Similarly, social workers engage in research to make sure their interventions are helping, not harming, clients and to contribute to social science as well as social justice.

Again, assuming you did not have advanced knowledge of the topics in the case studies, when you thought about what you might do in those practice situations, you were likely using **intuition** (Cheung, 2016). Intuition is a way of knowing that is mostly unconscious. You simply have a gut feeling about what you should do. As you think about a problem such as those in the case studies, you notice certain details and ignore others. Using your past experiences, you apply knowledge that seems to be relevant and make predictions about what might be true.

In this way, intuition is based on **direct experience**. Many of us know things simply because we've experienced them directly. For example, you would know that electric fences can be pretty dangerous and painful if you touched one while standing in a puddle of water. We all probably have times we can recall when we learned something because we experienced it. If you grew up in Minnesota, you would observe plenty of kids learning each winter that it really is true that your tongue will stick to metal if it's very cold outside. Similarly, if you passed a police officer on a two-lane highway while driving 20 miles over the speed limit, you would probably learn that that's a good way to earn a traffic ticket.

Intuition and direct experience are powerful forces. Uniquely, social work is a discipline that values intuition, though it will take quite a while for you to develop what social workers refer to as **practice wisdom**. Practice wisdom is the "learning by doing" that develops as one practices social work over a period of time. Social workers also reflect on their practice, independently and with colleagues, which sharpens their intuitions and opens their mind to other viewpoints. While your direct experience in social work may be limited at this point, feel confident that through reflective practice you will attain practice wisdom.

However, it's important to note that intuitions are not always correct. Think back to the first case study. What might be your novice diagnosis for this child's behavior? Does he have attention deficit hyperactivity disorder (ADHD) because he is distractible and getting into trouble at school? Or are those symptoms of autism spectrum disorder or an attachment disorder? Are the bruises on his legs an indicator of ADHD, or do they indicate possible physical abuse at home? Even if you arrived at an accurate assessment of the situation, you would still need to figure out what kind of intervention to use with the client. If he has a mental health issue, you might say, "give him therapy." Well…what kind of therapy? Should we use cognitive-behavioral therapy, play therapy, art therapy, family therapy, or animal assisted therapy? Should we try a combination of therapy and medication prescribed by a psychiatrist?

We could guess which intervention would be best...but in practice, that would be highly unethical. If we guessed wrong, we could be wasting time, or worse, actively harming a client. We need to ground our social work interventions with clients and systems with something more secure than our intuition and experience.

COGNITIVE BIASES

Although the human mind is a marvel of observation and data analysis, there are universal flaws in thinking that must be overcome. We all rely on mental shortcuts to help us make sense of a continuous stream of new information. All people, including me and you, must train our minds to be aware of predictable flaws in thinking, termed **cognitive biases**. Here is a link to the Wikipedia entry on cognitive biases. As you can see, it is quite long. We will review some of the most important ones here, but take a minute and browse around to get a sense of how baked-in cognitive biases are to how humans think.

The most important cognitive bias for social scientists to be aware of is **confirmation bias**. Confirmation bias involves observing and analyzing information in a way that confirms what you already think is true. No person is a blank slate. We all arrive at each moment with a set of beliefs, experiences, and models of how the world works that we develop over time. Often, these are grounded in our own personal experiences. Confirmation bias assumes these intuitions are correct and ignores or manipulates new information order to avoid challenging what we already believe to be true.

Confirmation bias can be seen in many ways. Sometimes, people will only pay attention to the information that fits their preconceived ideas and ignore information that does not fit. This is called **selective observation**. Other times, people will make hasty conclusions about a broad pattern based on only a few observations. This is called **overgeneralization**. Let's walk through an example and see how they each would function.

In our second case study, we are trying to figure out how to help people who receive SNAP (formerly Food Stamps) who live in a food desert. Let's say that we have arrived at a solution and are now lobbying the city council to implement it. There are many people who have negative beliefs about people who are "on welfare." These people believe individuals who receive social welfare benefits spend their money irresponsibly, are too lazy to get a job, and manipulate the system to maintain or increase their government payout. People expressing this belief may provide an example like Louis Cuff, who bought steak and lobster with his SNAP benefits and resold them for a profit.

City council members who hold these beliefs may ignore the truth about your client population—that people experiencing poverty usually spend their money responsibly and genuinely need help accessing fresh and healthy food. This would be an example of selective observation, only looking at the cases that confirm their biased beliefs about people in poverty and ignoring evidence that challenges that perspective. Likely, these are grounded in overgeneralization, in which one example, like Mr. Cuff, is applied broadly to the population of people using social welfare programs. Social workers in this situation would have to hope that city council members are open to another perspective and can be swayed by evidence that challenges their beliefs. Otherwise, they will continue to rely on a biased view of people in poverty when they create policies.

But where do these beliefs and biases come from? Perhaps, someone who the person considers an authority told them that people in poverty are lazy and manipulative. Naively relying on **authority** can take many forms. We might rely on our parents, friends, or religious leaders as authorities on a topic. We might consult someone who identifies as an expert in the field and simply follow what they say. We might hop aboard a "bandwagon" and adopt the fashionable ideas and theories of our peers and friends.

Now, it is important to note that experts in the field should generally be trusted to provide well-informed answers on a topic, though that knowledge should be receptive to skeptical critique and will develop over time as more scholars study the topic. There are limits to skepticism, however. Disagreeing with experts about global warming, the shape of the earth, or the efficacy and safety of vaccines does not make one free of cognitive biases. On the contrary, it is likely that the person is falling victim to the **Dunning-Kruger effect**, in which unskilled people overestimate their ability to find the truth. As this comic illustrates, they are at the top of Mount Stupid. Only through rigorous, scientific inquiry can they progress down the back slope and hope to increase their depth of knowledge about a topic.

SCIENTIFIC INQUIRY

Cognitive biases are most often expressed when people are using informal observation. Until you read the question at the beginning of this chapter, you may have had little reason to formally observe and make sense of information about children's mental health, food deserts, or homelessness policy. Because you engaged in informal observation, it is more likely that you will express cognitive biases in your responses. The problem with informal observation is that sometimes it is right, and sometimes it is wrong. And without any systematic process for observing or assessing the accuracy of our observations, we can never really be sure that our informal observations are accurate. In order to minimize the effect of cognitive biases and come up with the truest understanding of a topic, we must apply a systematic framework for understanding what we observe.

The opposite of informal observation is scientific inquiry, used interchangeably with the term **research methods** in this text. These terms refer to an organized, logical way of knowing that involves both theory and observation. Science accounts for the limitations of cognitive biases—not perfectly, though—by ensuring observations are done rigorously, following a prescribed set of steps. Scientists clearly describe the methods they use to conduct observations and create theories about the social world. Theories are tested by observing the social world, and they can be shown to be false or incomplete. In short, scientists try to learn the truth. Social workers use scientific truths in their practice and conduct research to revise and extend our understanding of what is true in the social world. Social workers who ignore science and act based on biased or informal observation may actively harm clients.

Key Takeaways
• Social work research occurs on the micro-, meso-, and macro-level.
• Intuition is a power, though woefully incomplete, guide to action in social work.
• All human thought is subject to cognitive biases.

- Scientific inquiry accounts for cognitive biases by applying an organized, logical way of observing and theorizing about the world.

Glossary

- Authority- learning by listening to what people in authority say is true
- Cognitive biases- predictable flaws in thinking
- Confirmation bias- observing and analyzing information in a way that confirms what you already think is true
- Direct experience- learning through informal observation
- Dunning-Kruger effect- when unskilled people overestimate their ability and knowledge (and experts underestimate their ability and knowledge)
- Intuition- your "gut feeling" about what to do
- Macro-level- examining social structures and institutions
- Meso-level- examining interaction between groups
- Micro-level- examining the smallest levels of interaction, usually individuals
- Overgeneralization- using limited observations to make assumptions about broad patterns
- Practice wisdom- "learning by doing" that guides social work intervention and increases over time
- Research methods- an organized, logical way of knowing based on theory and observation

Image Attributions

Thinking woman by Free-Photos via Pixabay CC-0

Light bulb by MasterTux via Pixabay CC-0

1.2 SCIENCE AND SOCIAL WORK

Learning Objectives

- Define science
- Describe the the difference between objective and subjective truth(s)
- Describe the role of ontology and epistemology in scientific inquiry

SCIENCE AND SOCIAL WORK

Science is a particular way of knowing that attempts to systematically collect and categorize facts or truths. A key word here is systematically–conducting science is a deliberate process. Scientists gather information about facts in a way that is organized and intentional, usually following a set of predetermined steps. More specifically, social work is informed by social science, the science of humanity, social interactions, and social structures. In other words, social work research uses organized and intentional procedures to uncover facts or truths about the social world. And social workers rely on social scientific research to promote individual and social change.

PHILOSOPHY OF SOCIAL SCIENCE

This approach to finding truth probably sounds similar to something you heard in your middle school science classes. When you learned about the gravitational force or the mitochondria of a cell, you were learning about the theories and observations that make up our understanding of the physical world. These theories rely on an **ontology**, or a set of assumptions about what is real. We assume that gravity is real and that the mitochondria of a cell are real. Mitochondria are easy to spot with a powerful enough microscope and we can observe and theorize about their function in a cell. The gravitational force is invisible, but clearly apparent from observable facts, like watching an apple fall. The theories about gravity have changed over the years, but improvements in theory were made when observations could not be correctly interpreted using existing theories.

If we weren't able to perceive mitochondria or gravity, they would still be there, doing their thing because they exist independent of our observation of them. This is a philosophical idea called *realism,* and it simply means that the concepts we talk about in science really and truly exist. Ontology in physics and biology is focused on **objective truth**. Chances are you've heard of "being objective" before. It involves observing and thinking with an open mind, pushing aside anything that might bias your perspective. Objectivity also means we want to find what is true for everyone, not just what is true for one person. Certainly, gravity is true for everyone and everywhere. Let's consider a social work example, though. It is objectively true that children who are subjected to severely traumatic experiences will experience negative mental health effects afterwards. A diagnosis of post-traumatic stress disorder (PTSD) is considered to be objective, referring to a real mental health issue that exists independent of the social worker observing it and that is highly similar in its presentation with our client as it would be with other clients.

So, an objective ontological perspective means that what we observe is true for everyone and true even when we aren't there to observe it. How do we come to know objective truths like these? This is the study of **epistemology**, or our assumptions about how we come to know what is real and true. The most relevant epistemological question in the social sciences is whether truth is better accessed using numbers or words. Generally, scientists approaching research with an objective ontology and epistemology will use **quantitative methods** to arrive at scientific truth. Quantitative methods examine numerical data to precisely describe and predict elements of the social world. This is due to the epistemological assumption that mathematics can represent the phenomena and relationships we observe in the social world.

Mathematical relationships are uniquely useful, in that they allow comparisons across individuals as well as across time and space. For example, while people can have different definitions for poverty, an objective measurement such as an annual income of less than $25,100 for a family of four provides (1) a precise measurement, (2) that can be compared to incomes from all other people in any society from any time period, (3) and refer to real quantities of money that exist in the world. In this book, we will review survey and experimental methods, which are the most common designs that use quantitative methods to answer research questions.

It may surprise you to learn that objective facts, such as income or age, are not the only facts in the social sciences. Indeed, social science is not only concerned with objective truth. Social science also describes **subjective truth**, or the truths that are unique to individuals, groups, and contexts. Unlike objective truth, which is true for all people, subjective truths will vary based on who you are observing and the context in which you are observing them. The beliefs, opinions, and preferences of people are actually truths that social scientists measure and describe. Additionally, subjective truths do not exist independent of human observation because they are the product of the human mind. We negotiate what is true in the social world through language, arriving at a consensus and engaging in debate.

Epistemologically, a scientist seeking subjective truth assumes that truth lies in what people say, their words. A scientist uses **qualitative methods** to analyze words or other media to understand their meaning. Humans are social creatures, and we give meaning to our thoughts and feelings through language. Linguistic communication is unique. We share ideas with each other at a remarkable rate. In so doing, ideas come into and out of existence in a spontaneous and emergent fashion. Words are given a meaning by their creator. But anyone who receives that communication can absorb, amplify, and even change its original intent. Because social science studies human interaction, subjectivists argue that language is the best way to understand the world.

This epistemology is based on some interesting ontological assumptions. What happens when someone incorrectly interprets a situation? While their interpretation may be wrong, it is certainly true *to them* that they are right. Furthermore, they act on the assumption that they are right. In this sense, even incorrect interpretations are truths, even though they are only true to one person. This leads us to question whether the social concepts we think about really exist. They might only exist in our heads, unlike concepts from the natural sciences which exist independent of our thoughts. For example, if everyone ceased to believe in gravity, we wouldn't all float away. It has an existence independent of human thought.

Let's think through an example. In the Diagnositic and Statistical Manual (DSM) classification of mental health disorders, there is a list of culture-bound syndromes which only appear in certain cultures. For example, *susto* describes a unique cluster of symptoms experienced by people in Latin American cultures after a traumatic event that focus on the body. Indeed, many of these syndromes do not fit within a Western conceptualization of mental health because they differentiate less between the mind and body. To a Western scientist, *susto* may seem less real than PTSD. To someone from Latin America, their symptoms may not fit neatly into the PTSD framework developed within Western society. This conflict raises the question–do either *susto* or PTSD really exist at all? If your answer is "no," you are adopting the ontology of *anti-realism*, that social concepts do not have an existence apart from human thought. Unlike the realists who seek a single, universal truth, the anti-realists see a sea of truths, created and shared within a social and cultural environment.

Let's consider another example: *manels* or all-male panel discussions at conferences and conventions. Check out this National Public Radio article for some hilarious examples, ironically including panels about diversity and gender representation. Manels are a problem in academic gatherings, Comic-Cons, and other large group events. A holdover of sexist stereotypes and gender-based privilege, manels perpetuate the sexist idea that men are the experts who deserve to be listened to by other, less important and knowledgeable people. At least, that's what we've come to recognize over the past few decades thanks to feminist critique. However, let's take the perspective of a few different participants at a hypothetical conference and examine their individual, subjective truths.

When the conference schedule is announced, we see that of the ten panel discussions announced, there are only two that contain women. Pamela, an expert on the neurobiology of child abuse, thinks that this is unfair and as she was excluded from a panel on her specialty. Marco, an event organizer, feels that since the organizers simply went with who was most qualified to speak and did not consider gender, the results could not be sexist. Dionne, a professor who specializes in queer theory and indigenous social work, agrees with Pamela that manels are sexist but also feels that the focus on gender excludes and overlooks the problems with race, disability, sexual and gender identity, and social class among the conference panel members. Given these differing interpretations, how can we come to know what is true about this situation?

Honestly, there are a lot of truths here, not just one truth. Clearly, Pamela's truth is that manels are sexist. Marco's truth is that they are not necessarily sexist, as long as they were chosen in a sex-blind manner. While none of these statements is objectively true—a single truth for everyone, in all possible circumstances—they are subjectively true to the people who thought them up. Subjective truth consists of the the different meanings, understandings, and interpretations created by people and communicated throughout society. The communication of ideas is important, as it is how people come to a consensus on how to interpret a situation, negotiating the meaning of events, and informing how people act. Thus, as feminist critiques of society become more accepted, people will behave in less sexist ways. From a subjective perspective, there is no magical number of female panelists conferences much reach to be sufficiently non-sexist. Instead, we should investigate using language how people interpret the gender issues at the event, analyzing them within a historical and cultural context. But how do we find truth when everyone had their own unique interpretation? By finding patterns.

SCIENCE MEANS FINDING PATTERNS IN DATA

Regardless of whether you are seeking objective truth or subjective truths, research and scientific inquiry aim to find and explain patterns. Most of the time, a pattern will not explain every single person's experience, a fact about social science that is both fascinating and frustrating. Even individuals who do not know each other and do not coordinate in any deliberate way can create patterns that persist over time. Those new to social science may find these patterns frustrating because they may believe that the patterns that describe their gender, age, or some other facet of their lives don't really represent their experience. It's true. A pattern can exist among your cohort without your individual participation in it. There is diversity within diversity.

Let's consider some specific examples. One area that social workers commonly investigate is the impact of a person's social class background on their experiences and lot in life. You probably wouldn't be surprised to learn that a person's social class background has an impact on their educational attainment and achievement. In fact, one group of researchers (Ellwood

& Kane, 2000) in the early 1990s found that the percentage of children who did not receive any postsecondary schooling was four times greater among those in the lowest quartile (25%) income bracket than those in the upper quartile of income earners (i.e., children from high-income families were far more likely than low-income children to go on to college). Another recent study found that having more liquid wealth that can be easily converted into cash actually seems to predict children's math and reading achievement (Elliott, Jung, Kim, & Chowa, 2010).

These findings—that wealth and income shape a child's educational experiences—are probably not that shocking to any of us. Yet, some of us may know someone who may be an exception to the rule. Sometimes the patterns that social scientists observe fit our commonly held beliefs about the way the world works. When this happens, we don't tend to take issue with the fact that patterns don't necessarily represent all people's experiences. But what happens when the patterns disrupt our assumptions?

For example, did you know that teachers are far more likely to encourage boys to think critically in school by asking them to expand on answers they give in class and by commenting on boys' remarks and observations? When girls speak up in class, teachers are more likely to simply nod and move on. The pattern of teachers engaging in more complex interactions with boys means that boys and girls do not receive the same educational experience in school (Sadker & Sadker, 1994). You and your classmates, of all genders, may find this news upsetting.

People who object to these findings tend to cite evidence from their own personal experience, refuting that the pattern actually exists. However, the problem with this response is that objecting to a social pattern on the grounds that it doesn't match one's individual experience misses the point about patterns. Patterns don't perfectly predict what will happen to an individual person. Yet, they are a reasonable guide that, when systematically observed, can help guide social work thought and action.

A FINAL NOTE ON QUALITATIVE AND QUANTITATIVE METHODS

There is no one superior way to find patterns that help us understand the world. There are multiple philosophical, theoretical, and methodological ways to approach uncovering scientific truths. Qualitative methods aim to provide an in-depth understanding of a relatively small number of cases. Quantitative methods offer less depth on each case but can say more about broad patterns in society because they typically focus on a much larger number of cases. A researcher should approach the process of scientific inquiry by formulating a clear research question and conducting research using the methodological tools best suited to that question.

Believe it or not, there are still significant methodological battles being waged in the academic literature on objective vs. subjective social science. Usually, quantitative methods are viewed as "more scientific" and qualitative methods are viewed as "less scientific." Part of this battle is historical. As the social sciences developed, they were compared with the natural sciences, especially physics, which rely on mathematics and statistics to find truth. It is a hotly debated topic whether social science should adopt the philosophical assumptions of the natural sciences—with its emphasis on prediction, mathematics, and objectivity—or use a different set of tools—understanding, language, and subjectivity—to find scientific truth.

You are fortunate to be in a profession that values multiple scientific ways of knowing. The qualitative/quantitative debate is fueled by researchers who may prefer one approach over another, either because their own research questions are better suited to one particular approach or because they happened to have been trained in one specific method. In this textbook, we'll operate from the perspective that qualitative and quantitative methods are complementary rather than competing. While these two methodological approaches certainly differ, the main point is that they simply have different goals, strengths, and weaknesses. A social work researcher should choose the methods that best match with the question they are asking.

Key Takeaways

- Social work is informed by science.
- Social science is concerns with both objective and subjective knowledge.
- Social science research aims to understand patterns in the social world.
- Social scientists use both qualitative and quantitative methods. While different, these methods are often complementary.

Glossary

- Epistemology- a set of assumptions about how we come to know what is real and true

- Objective truth- a single truth, observed without bias, that is universally applicable
- Ontology- a set of assumptions about what is real
- Qualitative methods- examine words or other media to understand their meaning
- Quantitative methods- examine numerical data to precisely describe and predict elements of the social world
- Science- a particular way of knowing that attempts to systematically collect and categorize facts or truth
- Subjective truth- one truth among many, bound within a social and cultural context

Image Attributions

Science and Technology by Petr Kratochvil CC-0

Abstract art blur bright by Pixabay CC-0

1.3 WHY SHOULD WE CARE?

<table>
<tr><td colspan="1">Learning Objectives</td></tr>
</table>

- Describe and discuss four important reasons why students should care about social scientific research methods
- Identify how social workers use research as part of evidence-based practice

At this point, you may be wondering about the relevance of research methods to your life. Whether or not you choose to become a social worker, you should care about research methods for two basic reasons: (1) research methods are regularly applied to solve social problems and issues that shape how our society is organized, thus you have to live with the results of research methods every day of your life, and (2) understanding research methods will help you evaluate the effectiveness of social work interventions, an important skill for future employment.

CONSUMING RESEARCH AND LIVING WITH ITS RESULTS

Another *New Yorker* cartoon depicts two men chatting with each other at a bar. One is saying to the other, "Are you just pissing and moaning, or can you verify what you're saying with data?" Which would you rather be, just a complainer or someone who can actually verify what you're saying? Understanding research methods and how they work can help position you to actually do more than just complain. Further, whether you know it or not, research probably has some impact on your life each and every day. Many of our laws, social policies, and court proceedings are grounded in some degree of empirical research and evidence (Jenkins & Kroll-Smith, 1996). That's not to say that all laws and social policies are good or make sense. However, you can't have an informed opinion about any of them without understanding where they come from, how they were formed, and what their evidence base is. All social workers, from micro to macro, need to understand the root causes and policy solutions to social problems that their clients are experiencing.

A recent lawsuit against Walmart provides an example of social science research in action. A sociologist named Professor William Bielby was enlisted by plaintiffs in the suit to conduct an analysis of Walmart's personnel policies in order to support their claim that Walmart engages in gender discriminatory practices. Bielby's analysis shows that Walmart's compensation and promotion decisions may indeed have been vulnerable to gender bias. In June 2011, the United States Supreme Court decided against allowing the case to proceed as a class-action lawsuit (*Wal-Mart Stores, Inc. v. Dukes*, 2011). While a class-action suit was not pursued in this case, consider the impact that such a suit against one of our nation's largest employers could have on companies and their employees around the country and perhaps even on your individual experience as a consumer.

In addition to having to live with laws and policies that have been crafted based on social science research, you are also a consumer of all kinds of research, and understanding methods can help you be a smarter consumer. Ever notice the magazine headlines that peer out at you while you are waiting in line to pay for your groceries? They are geared toward piquing your interest and making you believe that you will learn a great deal if you follow the advice in a particular article. However, since you would have no way of knowing whether the magazine's editors had gathered their data from a representative sample of people like you and your friends, you would have no reason to believe that the advice would be worthwhile. By having some understanding of research methods, you can avoid wasting your money by buying the magazine and wasting your time by following inappropriate advice.

Pick up or log on to the website for just about any magazine or newspaper, or turn on just about any news broadcast, and chances are you'll hear something about some new and exciting research results. Understanding research methods will help you read past any hype and ask good questions about what you see and hear. In other words, research methods can help you become a more responsible consumer of public and popular information. And who wouldn't want to be more responsible?

EVIDENCE-BASED PRACTICE

Probably the most asked questions, though seldom asked directly, are "Why am I in this class?" or "When will I ever use this information?" While it may seem strange, the answer is "pretty often." Social work supervisors and administrators at agency-based settings will likely have to demonstrate that their agency's programs are effective at achieving their goals. Most private and public grants will require evidence of effectiveness in order to continue receiving money and keep the programs running. Social workers at community-based organization commonly use research methods to target their interventions to the needs of their service area. Clinical social workers must also make sure that the interventions they use in practice are effective and not harmful to clients. Social workers may also want to track client progress on goals, help clients gather data about their clinical issues, or use data to advocate for change. All social workers in all practice situations must also remain current on the scientific literature to ensure competent and ethical practice.

In all of these cases, a social worker needs to be able to understand and evaluate scientific information. **Evidence-based practice** (EBP) for social workers involves making decisions on how to help clients based on the best available evidence. A social worker must examine the literature, understanding both the theory and evidence relevant to the practice situation. According to Rubin and Babbie (2017), EBP also involves understanding client characteristics, using practice wisdom and existing resources, and adapting to environmental context. Plainly said, EBP consists of four main components: **(1) the best evidence available for the practice-related question or concern, (2) client values and preferences, (3) practitioner expertise, and (4) client circumstances**.

EBP is not simply "doing what the literature says," but rather a process by which practitioners examine the literature, client, self, and context to inform interventions with clients and systems. As we discussed in Section 1.2, the patterns discovered by scientific research are not perfectly applicable to all situations. Instead, we rely on the critical thinking of social workers to apply scientific knowledge to real-world situations. Social workers apply their critical thinking to the process of EBP by starting with a question about their practice, seeking evidence to answer the question, critically reviewing the evidence they find, making and implementing a decision based on the four components of EBP, and then evaluating the outcome of the decision. EBP is a continual process in which new practice questions continually arise.

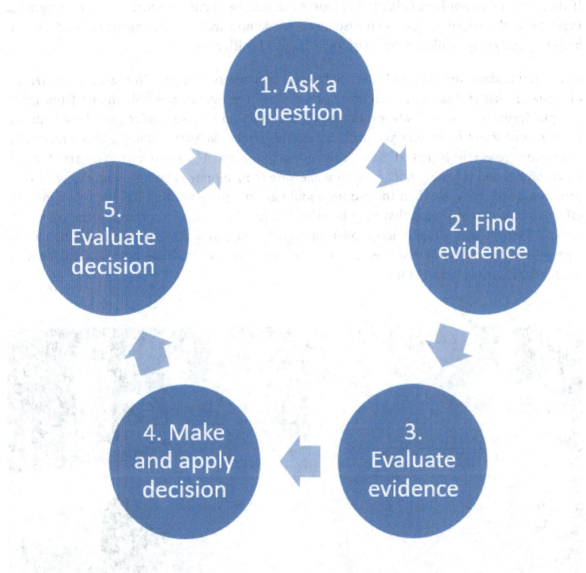

Figure 1.1. The steps of the evidence-based practice process.

Let's consider an example of a social work administrator at a children's mental health agency. The agency uses private grant funds to fund a program that provides low-income children with bicycles, teaches the children how to repair and care for their bicycles, and leads group bicycle outings after school. Physical activity has been shown to improve mental health outcomes in scientific studies, but is this social worker's program improving mental health in their clients? Ethically, the social worker should make sure that the program is achieving its goals.

If the program is not beneficial, the resources should be spent on more effective programs. Practically, the social worker will also need to demonstrate to the agency's funders that bicycling truly helps children deal with their mental health concerns.

The example above demonstrates the need for social workers to engage in **evaluation research** or research that evaluates the outcomes of a policy or program. She will choose from many acceptable ways to investigate program effectiveness, and those choices are based on the principles of scientific inquiry you will learn in this textbook. As the example above mentions, evaluation research is baked into how nonprofit human service agencies are funded. Government and private grants need to make sure their money is being spent wisely. If your program does not work, then the money should go to a program that has been shown to be effective or a new program that may be effective. Just because a program has the right goal doesn't mean it will actually accomplish that goal. Grant reporting is an important part of agency-based social work practice. Agencies, in a very important sense, help us discover what approaches actually help clients.

In addition to engaging in evaluation research to satisfy the requirements of a grant, your agency may engage in evaluation research for the purposes of validating a new approach to treatment. Innovation in social work is incredibly important. Sam Tsemberis relates an "aha" moment from his practice in this Ted talk on homelessness. A faculty member at the New York University School of Medicine, he noticed a problem with people cycling in and out of the local psychiatric hospital wards. Clients would arrive in psychiatric crisis, stabilize under medical supervision in the hospital, and end up back at the hospital back in psychiatric crisis shortly after discharge. When he asked the clients what their issues were, they said they were unable to participate in homelessness programs because they were not always compliant with medication for their mental health diagnosis and they continued to use drugs and alcohol. Collaboratively, the problem facing these clients was defined as a homelessness service system that was unable to meet clients where they were. Clients who were unwilling to remain completely abstinent from drugs and alcohol or who did not want to take psychiatric medications were simply cycling in and out of psychiatric crisis, moving from the hospital to the street and back to the hospital.

The solution that Sam Tsemberis implemented and popularized was called Housing First, and it is an approach to homelessness prevention that starts by, you guessed it, providing people with housing first. Similar to an approach to child and family homelessness created by Tanya Tull, Tsemberis created a model of addressing chronic homelessness with people with co-occurring disorders (substance abuse and mental illness). The Housing First model holds that housing is a human right, one that should not be denied based on substance use or mental health diagnosis. Clients are given housing as soon as possible. The Housing First agency provides wraparound treatment from an interdisciplinary team, including social workers, nurses, psychiatrists, and former clients who are in recovery. Over the past few decades, this program has gone from one program in New York City to the program of choice for federal, state, and local governments seeking to address homelessness in their communities.

The main idea behind Housing First is that once clients have an apartment of their own, they are better able to engage in mental health and substance abuse treatment. While this approach may seem logical to you, it is backwards from the traditional homelessness treatment model. The traditional approach began with the client stopping drug and alcohol use and taking prescribed medication. Only after clients achieved these goals were they offered group housing. If the client remained sober and medication compliant, they could then graduate towards less restrictive individual housing.

Evaluation research helps practitioners establish that their innovation is better than the alternatives and should be implemented more broadly. By comparing clients who were served through Housing First and traditional treatment, Tsemberis could establish that Housing First was more effective at keeping people housed and progressing on mental health and substance abuse goals. Starting first with smaller studies and graduating to much larger ones, Housing First built a reputation as an effective approach to addressing homelessness. When President Bush created the Collaborative Initiative to Help End Chronic Homelessness in 2003, Housing First was used in a majority of the interventions and demonstrated its effectiveness on a national scale. In 2007, it was acknowledged as an evidence-based practice in the Substance Abuse and Mental Health Services Administration's (SAMHSA) National Registry of Evidence-Based Programs and Policies (NREPP).

Try browsing around the NREPP website and looking for interventions on topics that interest you. Other sources of evidence-based practices include the Cochrane Reviews digital library and Campbell Collaboration. The use of systematic reviews, meta-analyses, and randomized controlled trials are particularly important in this regard.

So why share the story of Housing First? Well, it may help you think about what you hope to contribute to our knowledge on social work practice. What is your bright idea and how can it change the world? Practitioners innovate all the time, often incorporating those innovations into their agency's approach and mission. Through the use of research methods, agency-based social workers can demonstrate to policymakers and other social workers that their innovations should be more widely used. Without this wellspring of new ideas, social services would not be able to adapt to the changing needs of clients. Social workers in agency-based practice may also participate in research projects happening at their agency. Partnerships between schools of social work and agencies are a common way of testing and implementing innovations in social work. Clinicians receive specialized training, clients receive additional services, agencies gain prestige, and researchers can study how an intervention works in the real world.

While you may not become a scientist in the sense of wearing a lab coat and using a microscope, social workers must understand science in order to engage in ethical practice. In this section, we reviewed many ways in which research is a part of social work practice, including:

- Determining the best intervention for a client or system
- Ensuring existing services are accomplishing their goals
- Satisfying requirements to receive funding from private agencies and government grants
- Testing a new idea and demonstrating that it should be more widely implemented

SPOTLIGHT ON UTA SCHOOL OF SOCIAL WORK

AN EVIDENCE-BASED PROGRAM TO PREVENT CHILD MALTREATMENT

We all know that preventing a problem is better than trying to fix the effects afterwards. Child maltreatment is a problem that social workers often encounter—wouldn't it be wonderful if we could keep it from happening? Is there an effective intervention for parents who are feeling overwhelmed and are perhaps on the edge of maltreating their children? University of Texas at Arlington's Dr. Richard Hoefer and (at the time Ph.D. student) Dante Bryant conducted a program evaluation to find out if that is possible. While more research is needed to verify the findings, their work points out a possible way of preventing child maltreatment for some families.

A private nonprofit received a grant to develop and test the "Multi-disciplinary Approach to Prevention Services" program (MAPS). Program staff worked with parents at-risk of committing acts of maltreatment. The overall evaluation question was whether the program had a positive impact.

Before evaluators answer an outcome question like this, they must understand the logic behind a program and test whether that model is correct. In this program, developers believed that parents at-risk of maltreating their children did not have the knowledge and skills needed to be successful parents. Thus, parents were frustrated and unhappy with their children and their own parenting. This leads to a higher risk of maltreatment.

The program's logic was that if the parents learned and applied skills of effective parenting, positive changes would ensue. Parents' perception of their children's behavior would improve, their dissatisfaction would decrease, and maltreatment would not occur. In the longer term, parents would not be involved with Child Protective Services and money would be saved. The program was thus implemented to reduce the need for Child Protective Services (with its costs) by targeting negative parental behavior, strengthening parent-child relations, improving the family environment, and keeping families together.

The evaluation of MAPS answered these questions: (1) Did program participants increase their resource engagement? (2) Did program participants improve parenting knowledge, skills and satisfaction? (3) Did program participants report additional involvement with CPS?

The authors used a one group pretest-posttest design (which you will learn about later in this textbook) to assess program outcomes and achievement levels. Questionnaires were administered as a during the client intake and assessment process; the same questions were later used after the program as a posttest. Hoefer and Bryant (2017) used the Parenting Scale (Arnold, O'Leary, Wolff, & Acker, 1993) to measure actual parental behavior, the Eyberg Child Behavior Inventory (Burns & Patterson, 1990) to measure both the children's behavior and how parents perceived it (how much they were bothered by what the child did), and the Kansas Parental Satisfaction scale (James, Schumm, Kennedy, Grigsby, & Shectman, 1985) to understand how parents felt about their own parenting.

At the end of the program, Hoefer and Bryant used data from 64 families to determine results. Parents did receive more resources (primarily parenting skills classes) than they had before the program. All measures of parenting knowledge, skills and satisfaction showed positive changes at a statistically significant level, when comparing pretests and post-tests. Importantly, by the end of the program, only one family of the 64 in the program was further involved with Child Protective Services.

We need more research, though, because the one-group pre-test/post-test design of the evaluation cannot show a causal relationship for the outcomes. In addition, this evaluation was not able to follow families beyond the program's end to look at long-term effects. Still, along with other research on the efficacy of improving parenting skills to reduce child maltreatment, it builds on a good case to use such interventions on a widespread basis to reduce harm to children.

Key Takeaways

- Whether we know it or not, our everyday lives are shaped by social scientific research.
- Understanding research methods is important for competent and ethical social work practice.
- Understanding social science and research methods can help us become more astute and more responsible consumers of information.
- Knowledge about social scientific research methods is important for ethical practice, as it ensures interventions are based on evidence.

Glossary

- Evaluation research- research that evaluates the outcomes of a policy or program
- Evidence-based practice- making decisions on how to help clients based on the best available evidence

Image Attributions

A peer counselor with mother by US Department of Agriculture CC-BY-2.0

Homeless man in New York 2008 by JMSuarez CC-BY-2.0

1.4 UNDERSTANDING RESEARCH

Learning Objectives

- Describe common barriers to engaging with social work research
- Identify alternative ways to thinking about research methods

Sometimes students struggle to see the connection between research and social work practice. Most students enjoy a social work theory class because they can better understand the world around them. Students also like practice because it shows them how to conduct clinical work with clients—i.e., what most social work students want to do. It can be helpful to look critically at the potential barriers to embracing the study of social work. Most student barriers to research come from the following beliefs:

RESEARCH IS USELESS!

Students who say that research methods is not a useful class to them are saying something important. As a scholar (or student), your most valuable asset is your time. You give your time to the subjects you consider important to you and your future practice. Because most social workers don't become researchers or practitioner-researchers, students feel like a research methods class is a waste of time.

Our discussion of evidence-based practice and the ways in which social workers use research methods in practice brought home the idea that social workers play an important role in creating new knowledge about social services. On a more immediate level, research methods will also help you become a stronger social work student. Upcoming chapters of this textbook will review how to search for literature on a topic and write a literature review. These skills are relevant in every classroom during your academic career. The rest of the textbook will help you understand the mechanics of research methods so you can better understand the content of those pesky journal articles your professors force you to cite in your papers.

RESEARCH IS TOO HARD!

Research methods involves a lot of terminology that is entirely new to social workers. Other domains of social work, such as practice, are easier to apply your intuition towards. You understand how to be an empathetic person, and your experiences in life can help guide you through a practice situation or even theoretical or conceptual question. Research may seem like a totally new area in which you have no previous experience. It can seem like a lot to learn. In addition to the normal memorization and application of terms, research methods also has wrong answers. There are certain combinations of methods that just don't work together.

The fear is entirely understandable. Research is not straightforward. As Figure 1.1 shows, it is a process that is non-linear, involving multiple revisions, wrong turns, and dead ends before you figure out the best question and research approach. You may have to go back to chapters after having read them or even peek ahead at chapters your class hasn't covered yet.

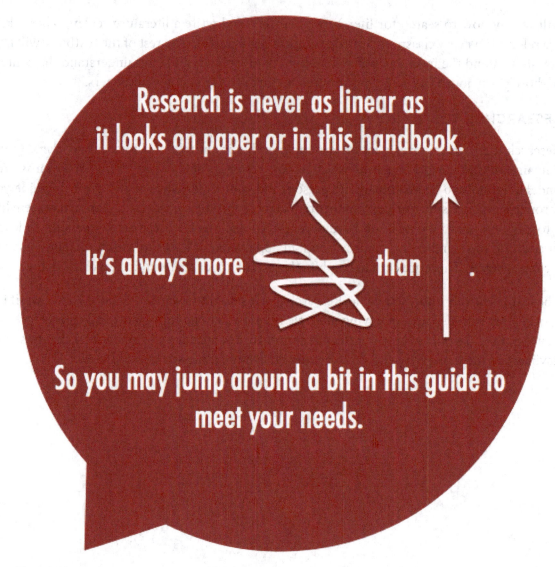

Figure 1.1 Research as a non-linear process (Ohio State University Libraries CC-BY 4.0)

Moreover, research is something you learn by doing…and stumbling a few times. It's an iterative process, or one that requires lots of tries to get right. There isn't a shortcut for learning research, but hopefully your research methods class is one in which your research project is broken down into smaller parts and you get consistent feedback throughout the process. No one just *knows* research. It's something you pick up by doing it, reflecting on the experiences and results, redoing your work, and revising it in consultation with your professor.

RESEARCH IS BORING!

Research methods is sometimes seen as a boring topic by many students. Practice knowledge and even theory are fun to learn because they are easy to apply and give you insight into the world around you. Research just seems like its own weird, remote thing.

Your social work education will present some generalist material, which is applicable to nearly all social work practice situations, and some applied material, which is applicable to specific social work practice situations. However, no education will provide you with everything you need to know. And certainly, no education will tell you what will be discovered over the next few decades of your practice. Our exploration of research methods will help you further understand how the theories, practice models, and techniques you learn in your other classes are created and tested scientifically. The material you learn in research class will allow you to think critically about material throughout your entire program and into your social work career.

GET OUT OF YOUR OWN WAY

Together, the beliefs of "research is useless, boring, and hard" can create a self-fulfilling prophecy for students. If you believe research is boring, you won't find it interesting. If you believe research is hard, you will struggle more with assignments. If you believe research is useless, you won't see its utility. Let's provide some reframing of how you might think about research using these touchstones:

- All social workers rely on social science research to engage in competent practice.
- No one *already* knows research. It's something I'll learn through practice. And it's challenging for everyone.
- Research is relevant to me because it allows me to figure out what is known about any topic I want to study.
- If the topic I choose to study is important to me, I will be more interested in research.

STRUCTURE OF THIS TEXTBOOK

While you may not have chosen this course, by reframing your approach to it, you increase the likelihood of getting a lot out of it. To that end, here is the structure of this book:

In Chapters 2-5, you'll learn about how research informs and tests theory. We'll discuss how to conduct research in an ethical manner, create research questions, and measure concepts in the social world.

Chapters 6-10 will describe how to conduct research, whether it's a quantitative survey or experiment, or alternately, a qualitative interview or focus group. We'll also review how to analyze data that someone else has already collected.

Finally, Chapters 11 and 12 will review the types of research most commonly used in social work practice, including evaluation research and action research, and how to report the results of your research to various audiences.

Key Takeaways

- Anxiety about research methods is a common experience for students.
- Research methods will help you become a better scholar and practitioner.

Image Attributions

Untitled image by Ohio State University Libraries CC-BY 4.0

CHAPTER TWO: LINKING METHODS WITH THEORY

In this chapter, we'll explore the connections between paradigms, social theories, and social scientific research methods. We'll also consider how our analytic, paradigmatic, and theoretical perspective might shape or be shaped by our methodological choices. In short, we'll answer the question of what theory has to do with research methods.

CHAPTER OUTLINE

- 2.1 Micro, meso, and macro approaches
- 2.2 Paradigms, theories, and how they shape a researcher's approach
- 2.3 Inductive and deductive reasoning

CONTENT ADVISORY

This chapter discusses or mentions the following topics: suicide; policing; teen dating violence; laws regulating rape, sodomy, and child sexual abuse; gang communication styles; racism, policing, and lynching; domestic violence and sexual harassment; substance abuse; and child maltreatment, neglect, and family reunification.

2.1 MICRO, MESO, AND MACRO APPROACHES

Learning Objectives

- Describe a micro-level approach to research, and provide an example of a micro-level study
- Describe a meso-level approach to research, and provide an example of a meso-level study
- Describe a macro-level approach to research, and provide an example of a macro-level study

In Chapter 1, we reviewed the micro, meso, and macro framework that social workers use to understand the world. As you'll recall, micro-level research studies individuals and one-on-one interactions, meso-level research studies groups, and macro-level research studies institutions and policies. Let's take a closer look at some specific examples of social work research to better understand each of the three levels of inquiry described previously. Some topics are best suited to be examined at one specific level, while other topics can be studied at each of the three different levels. The particular level of inquiry might shape a social worker's questions about the topic, or a social scientist might view the topic from different angles depending on the level of inquiry being employed.

First, let's consider some suitable examples of different topics for a particular level of inquiry. Work by Philip Baiden and Eusebius Small at the University of Texas at Arlington's School of Social Workoffers an excellent example of research at the micro-level. In one study, Baiden, Mengo, Boateng, and Small (2018) use prior micro-level theories to study the association between age at first alcohol use and suicidal ideation among high school students. In this study, the researchers found that age at first alcohol use has been linked with a number of mental health problems among adolescents. Additionally, adolescents who started having alcohol before age 13 were more likely to experience suicidal ideation. In another study, Baiden, Stewart, and Fallon (2017) examined the role of adverse childhood experiences as determinants of non-suicidal self-injury among children that were referred to mental health treatment facilities. They found that 29% of children in these programs did engage in non-suicidal self-harm. These findings were consistent with previous studies and theories. Both of these studies fall within the category of micro-level analysis.

At the meso-level, social scientists tend to study the experiences of groups and the interactions between groups. In a study conducted by UTA's Anne Nordberg and Regina Praetorius, young people from minority groups and their interactions with police and law enforcement were explored (Nordberg, Crawford, Praetorius, & Hatcher, 2016). The researchers found 4 themes in the data related the interactions between young people and law enforcement: dangerous, controlling, prejudiced, and ineffective interactions. This research offers social workers a better insight into what minority youth often experience when they encounter law enforcement. In a different study of group-level interactions, John R. Gallagher and Anne Nordberg (2016) conducted research comparing and contrasting the different experiences of White and African American participants in the drug court system. The objective was to compare the lived experiences each group had when they interacted with the system of drug court judicial representatives. They found that the graduation rate for White participants was much higher than that of African Americans. However, the majority of both White and African American participants reported reasonably high levels of understanding and compassion by the drug court officials (Gallagher & Nordberg, 2016). This study focused on group-level interactions with systems in a community, a meso-level focus.

Social workers who conduct macro-level research study interactions at the broadest level, such as interactions between and across nations, states, or cultural systems. One example of macro-level research can be seen in an article by UTA's Richard Hoefer and colleagues (Hoefer, Black, & Ricard, 2015). These researchers examined the impact of state policy on teen dating violence prevalence. By comparing laws across a number of states, Hoefer, Black, and Ricard learned that states with higher median income in 2009 had a significantly lower incidence of teen dating violence than states with lower median income. Findings from the study suggest that addressing poverty and economic issues within a state may impact the prevalence of teen dating violence. In another macro-level study, Hoefer and Shannon Silva (2010) studied the private nonprofit sector in the United States and its substantial expansion in the last several years. The study addressed the growing national shortage of suitable nonprofit managers. It aimed to develop and introduce a new process for assessing administration skills and improving leadership skills in nonprofit workers.

While it is true that some topics lend themselves to a particular level of inquiry, there are many topics that could be studied from any of the three levels. The choice depends on the specific interest of the researcher, the approach she would like to take and the sorts of questions she wants to be able to answer about the topic.

Let's look at an example. Gang activity has been a topic of interest to social workers for many years and has been studied from each of the levels of inquiry described here. At the micro-level, social workers might study the inner workings of a specific gang, communication styles, and what everyday life is like for gang members. Though not written by a social worker, one example of a micro-level analysis of gang activity can be found in Sanyika Shakur's 1993 autobiography, *Monster*. In his book, Shakur describes his former day-to-day life as a member of the Crips in South-Central Los Angeles. Shakur's recounting of his experiences highlights micro-level interactions between himself, fellow Crips members, and other gangs.

At the meso-level, social workers are likely to examine interactions between gangs or perhaps how different branches of the same gang vary from one area to the next. At the macro-level, we could compare the impact of gang activity across communities or examine the economic impact of gangs on nations. Excellent examples of gang research at all three levels of analysis can be found in the *Journal of Gang Research* published by the National Gang Crime Research Center (NGCRC). Sudhir Venkatesh's (2008) study, *Gang Leader for a Day*, is an example of research on gangs that utilizes all three levels of analysis. Venkatesh conducted participant observation with a gang in Chicago. He learned about the everyday lives of gang members (micro) and how the gang he studied interacted with and fit within the landscape of other gang "franchises" (meso). In addition, Venkatesh described the impact of the gang on the broader community and economy (macro).

Key Takeaways

- Social work research can occur at any of the following three analytical levels: micro, meso, or macro.
- Some topics lend themselves to one particular analytical level, while others could be studied from any, or all, of the three levels of analysis.

2.2 PARADIGMS, THEORIES, AND HOW THEY SHAPE A RESEARCHER'S APPROACH

Learning Objectives

- Define paradigm, and describe the significance of paradigms
- Identify and describe the four predominant paradigms found in the social sciences
- Define theory
- Describe the role that theory plays in social work research

The terms paradigm and theory are often used interchangeably in social science, although social scientists do not always agree whether these are identical or distinct concepts. This text makes a clear distinction between the two ideas because thinking about each concept as analytically distinct provides a useful framework for understanding the connections between research methods and social scientific ways of thinking.

PARADIGMS IN SOCIAL SCIENCE

For our purposes, we'll define **paradigm** as a way of viewing the world (or "analytic lens" akin to a set of glasses) and a framework from which to understand the human experience (Kuhn, 1962). It can be difficult to fully grasp the idea of paradigmatic assumptions because we are very ingrained in our own, personal everyday way of thinking. For example, let's look at people's views on abortion. To some, abortion is a medical procedure that should be undertaken at the discretion of each individual woman. To others, abortion is murder and members of society should collectively have the right to decide when, if at all, abortion should be undertaken.

Chances are, if you have an opinion about this topic, you are pretty certain about the veracity of your perspective. Then again, the person who sits next to you in class may have a very different opinion and yet be equally confident about the truth of their perspective. Who is correct?

You are each operating under a set of assumptions about the way the world does—or at least should—work. Perhaps your assumptions come from your political perspective, which helps shape your view on a variety of social issues, or perhaps your assumptions are based on what you learned from your parents or in church. In any case, there is a paradigm that shapes your stance on the issue. Those paradigms are a set of assumptions. Your classmate might assume that life begins at conception and the fetus' life should be at the center of moral analysis. Conversely, you may assume that life begins when the fetus is viable outside the womb and that a mother's choice is more important than a fetus's life. There is no way to scientifically test when life begins, whose interests are more important, or the value of choice. They are merely philosophical assumptions or beliefs. Thus, a pro-life paradigm may rest in part on a belief in divine morality and fetal rights. A pro-choice paradigm may rest on a mother's self-determination and a belief that the positive consequences of abortion outweigh the negative ones. These beliefs and assumptions influence how we think about any aspect of the issue.

In Chapter 1, we discussed the various ways that we know what we know. Paradigms are a way of framing what we know, what we can know, and how we can know it. In social science, there are several predominant paradigms, each with its own unique ontological and epistemological perspective. Recall that ontology is the study of what is real, and epistemology is the study of how we come to know what is real. Let's look at four of the most common social scientific paradigms that might guide you as you begin to think about conducting research.

The first paradigm we'll consider, called positivism, is the framework that likely comes to mind for many of you when you think of science. **Positivism** is guided by the principles of objectivity, knowability, and deductive logic. Deductive logic is discussed in more detail in next section of this chapter. The positivist framework operates from the assumption that society can and should be studied empirically and scientifically. Positivism also calls for a value-free science, one in which researchers aim to abandon their biases and values in a quest for objective, empirical, and knowable truth.

Another predominant paradigm in social work is **social constructionism**. Peter Berger and Thomas Luckman (1966) are credited by many for having developed this perspective in sociology. While positivists seek "the truth," the social constructionist framework posits that "truth" varies. Truth is different based on who you ask, and people change their definitions of truth all the time based on their interactions with other people. This is because we, according to this paradigm, create reality ourselves (as opposed to it simply existing and us working to discover it) through our interactions and our interpretations of those interactions. Key to the social constructionist perspective is the idea that social context and interaction frame our realities.

Researchers operating within this framework take keen interest in how people come to socially agree, or disagree, about what is real and true. Consideration of how meanings of different hand gestures vary across different regions of the world aptly demonstrates that meanings are constructed socially and collectively. Think about what it means to you when you see a person raise their middle finger. In the United States, people probably understand that person isn't very happy (nor is the person to whom the finger is being directed). In some societies, it is another gesture, such as the thumbs up gesture, that raises eyebrows. While the thumbs up gesture may have a particular meaning in North American culture, that meaning is not shared across cultures (Wong, 2007). So, what is the "truth" of the middle finger or thumbs up? It depends on what the person giving it intended, how the person receiving it interpreted it, and the social context in which the action occurred.

It would be a mistake to think of the social constructionist perspective as only individualistic. While individuals may construct their own realities, groups—from a small one such as a married couple to large ones such as nations—often agree on notions of what is true and what "is." In other words, the meanings that we construct have power beyond the individual people who create them. Therefore, the ways that people and communities work to create and change such meanings is of as much interest to social constructionists as how they were created in the first place.

A third paradigm is the **critical** paradigm. At its core, the critical paradigm is focused on power, inequality, and social change. Although some rather diverse perspectives are included here, the critical paradigm, in general, includes ideas developed by early social theorists, such as Max Horkheimer (Calhoun, Gerteis, Moody, Pfaff, & Virk, 2007), and later works developed by feminist scholars, such as Nancy Fraser (1989). Unlike the positivist paradigm, the critical paradigm posits that social science can never be truly objective or value-free. Further, this paradigm operates from the perspective that scientific investigation should be conducted with the express goal of social change in mind. Researchers in the critical paradigm might start with the knowledge that systems are biased against, for example, women or ethnic minorities. Moreover, their research projects are designed not only to collect data, but also change the participants in the research as well as the systems being studied. The critical paradigm not only studies power imbalances but seeks to change those power imbalances.

Finally, **postmodernism** is a paradigm that challenges almost every way of knowing that many social scientists take for granted (Best & Kellner, 1991). While positivists claim that there is an objective, knowable truth, postmodernists would say that there is not. While social constructionists may argue that truth is in the eye of the beholder (or in the eye of the group that agrees on it), postmodernists may claim that we can never really know such truth because, in the studying and reporting of others' truths, the researcher stamps their own truth on the investigation. Finally, while the critical paradigm may argue that power, inequality, and change shape reality and truth, a postmodernist may in turn ask whose power, whose inequality, whose change, whose reality, and whose truth. As you might imagine, the postmodernist paradigm poses quite a challenge for researchers. How do you study something that may or may not be real or that is only real in your current and unique experience of it? This fascinating question is worth pondering as you begin to think about conducting your own research. Part of the value of the postmodern paradigm is its emphasis on the limitations of human knowledge. Table 2.1 summarizes each of the paradigms discussed here.

Table 2.1 Four social science paradigms

Paradigm	Emphasis	Assumption
Positivism	Objectivity, knowability, and deductive logic	Society can and should be studied empirically and scientifically.
Social Constructionism	Truth as varying, socially constructed, and ever-changing	Reality is created collectively. Social context and interaction frame our realities.
Critical	Power, inequality, and social change	Social science can never be truly value-free and should be conducted with the express goal of social change in mind.
Postmodernism	Inherent problems with previous paradigms.	Truth is always bound within historical and cultural context. There are no universally true explanations.

Let's work through an example. If we are examining a problem like substance abuse, what would a social scientific investigation look like in each paradigm? A positivist study may focus on precisely measuring substance abuse and finding out the key causes of substance abuse during adolescence. Forgoing the *objectivity* of precisely measuring substance abuse, social constructionist study might focus on how people who abuse substances understand their lives and relationships with various drugs of abuse. In so doing, it seeks out the *subjective* truth of each participant in the study. A study from the critical paradigm would investigate how people who have substance abuse problems are an oppressed group in society and seek to liberate them from external sources of oppression, like punitive drug laws, and internal sources of oppression, like internalized fear and shame. A postmodern study may involve one person's self-reported journey into substance abuse and changes that occurred in their self-perception that accompanied their transition from recreational to problematic drug use. These examples should illustrate how one topic can be investigated across each paradigm.

SOCIAL SCIENCE THEORIES

Much like paradigms, theories provide a way of looking at the world and of understanding human interaction. Paradigms are grounded in big assumptions about the world—what is real, how do we create knowledge—whereas theories describe more specific phenomena. A common definition for **theory** in social work is "a systematic set of interrelated statements intended to explain some aspect of social life" (Rubin & Babbie, 2017, p. 615). At their core, theories can be used to provide explanations of any number or variety of phenomena. They help us answer the "why" questions we often have about the patterns we observe in social life. Theories also often help us answer our "how" questions. While paradigms may point us in a particular direction with respect to our "why" questions, theories more specifically map out the explanation, or the "how," behind the "why."

Introductory social work textbooks introduce students to the major theories in social work—conflict theory, symbolic interactionism, social exchange theory, and systems theory. As social workers study longer, they are introduced to more specific theories in their area of focus, as well as perspectives and models (e.g., the strengths perspective), which provide more practice-focused approaches to understanding social work.

As you may recall from a class on social work theory, systems theorists view all parts of society as interconnected and focus on the relationships, boundaries, and flows of energy between these systems and subsystems (Schriver, 2011). Conflict theorists are interested in questions of power and who wins and who loses based on the way that society is organized. Symbolic interactionists focus on how meaning is created and negotiated through meaningful (i.e., symbolic) interactions. Finally, social exchange theorists examine how human beings base their behavior on a rational calculation of rewards and costs.

Just as researchers might examine the same topic from different levels of inquiry or paradigms, they could also investigate the same topic from different theoretical perspectives. In this case, even their research questions could be the same, but the way they make sense of whatever phenomenon it is they are investigating will be shaped in large part by theory. Table 2.2 summarizes the major points of focus for four major theories and outlines how a researcher might approach the study of the same topic, in this case the study of substance abuse, from each of the perspectives.

Table 2.2 Four social work theories as related to the study of substance abuse

Theory	Focuses on	A study of substance abuse might examine
Systems	Interrelations between parts of society; how parts work together	How a lack of employment opportunities might impact rates of substance abuse in an area
Conflict	Who wins and who loses based on the way that society is organized	How the War on Drugs has impacted minority communities
Symbolic interactionism	How meaning is created and negotiated though interactions	How people's self-definitions as "addicts" helps or hurts their ability to remain sober
Utility theory	How behavior is influenced by costs and rewards	Whether increased distribution of anti-overdose medications makes overdose more or less likely

Within each area of specialization in social work, there are many other theories that aim to explain more specific types of interactions. For example, within the study of sexual harassment, different theories posit different explanations for why harassment occurs. One theory, first developed by criminologists, is called routine activities theory. It posits that sexual harassment is most likely to occur when a workplace lacks unified groups and when potentially vulnerable targets and motivated offenders are both present (DeCoster, Estes, & Mueller, 1999). Other theories of sexual harassment, called relational theories, suggest that a person's relationships, such as their marriages or friendships, are the key to understanding why and how workplace sexual harassment occurs and how people will respond to it when it does occur (Morgan,

1999). Relational theories focus on the power that different social relationships provide (e.g., married people who have supportive partners at home might be more likely than those who lack support at home to report sexual harassment when it occurs). Finally, feminist theories of sexual harassment take a different stance. These theories posit that the way our current gender system is organized, where those who are the most masculine have the most power, best explains why and how workplace sexual harassment occurs (MacKinnon, 1979). As you might imagine, which theory a researcher applies to examine the topic of sexual harassment will shape the questions the researcher asks about harassment. It will also shape the explanations the researcher provides for why harassment occurs.

For an undergraduate student beginning their study of a new topic, it may be intimidating to learn that there are so many theories beyond what you've learned in your theory classes. What's worse is that there is no central database of different theories on your topic. However, as you review the literature in your topic area, you will learn more about the theories that scientists have created to explain how your topic works in the real world. In addition to peer-reviewed journal articles, another good source of theories is a book about your topic. Books often contain works of theoretical and philosophical importance that are beyond the scope of an academic journal.

PARADIGM AND THEORY IN SOCIAL WORK

Theories, paradigms, levels of analysis, and the order in which one proceeds in the research process all play an important role in shaping what we ask about the social world, how we ask it, and in some cases, even what we are likely to find. A micro-level study of gangs will look much different than a macro-level study of gangs. In some cases, you could apply multiple levels of analysis to your investigation, but doing so isn't always practical or feasible. Therefore, understanding the different levels of analysis and being aware of which level you happen to be employing is crucial. One's theoretical perspective will also shape a study. In particular, the theory invoked will likely shape not only the way a question about a topic is asked but also which topic gets investigated in the first place. Further, if you find yourself especially committed to one theory over another, it may limit the kinds of questions you pose. As a result, you may miss other possible explanations.

The limitations of paradigms and theories do not mean that social science is fundamentally biased. At the same time, we can never claim to be entirely value free. Social constructionists and postmodernists might point out that bias is always a part of research to at least some degree. Our job as researchers is to recognize and address our biases as part of the research process, if an imperfect part. We all use our own approaches, be they theories, levels of analysis, or temporal processes, to frame and conduct our work. Understanding those frames and approaches is crucial not only for successfully embarking upon and completing any research-based investigation, but also for responsibly reading and understanding others' work.

SPOTLIGHT ON UTA SCHOOL OF SOCIAL WORK

CATHERINE LABRENZ CONNECTS SOCIAL THEORY AND CHILD WELFARE RESEARCH

When Catherine LaBrenz, an assistant professor at the University of Texas at Arlington's School of Social Work was a child welfare practitioner, she noticed that several children who had reunified with their biological parents from the foster care system were re-entering care because of continued exposure to child maltreatment. As she observed the challenging behaviors these children often presented, she wondered how the agency might better support families to prevent children from re-entering foster care after permanence. In her doctoral studies, she used her practice experience to form a research project with the goal of better understanding how agencies could better support families post-reunification.

From a *critical* paradigm, Dr. LaBrenz approached this question with the understanding that families that come into contact with child welfare systems often experience disadvantage and are subjected to unequal power distributions when accessing services, going to court, and participating in case decision-making (LaBrenz & Fong, 2016). Furthermore, the goal of this research was to change some of the aspects of the child welfare system, particularly within the practitioner's agency, to better support families.

To better understand *why* some families may be more at-risk for multiple entries into foster care, Dr. LaBrenz began with an extensive literature review that identified diverse theories that explained factors at the *child, family,* and *system-* level that could impact post-permanence success. Figure 2.1 displays the micro-, meso-, and macro-level theories that she and her research team identified and decided to explore further.

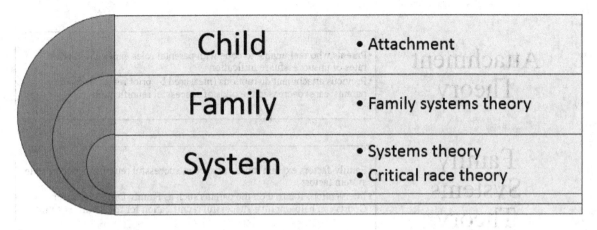

Figure 2.1. Micro-, Meso-, and Macro- Theories of Child Maltreatment

At the child-level, Attachment theory posits that consistent, stable nurturing during infancy impacts children's ability to form relationships with others throughout their life (Ainsworth, Blehar, Waters, & Wall, 1978; Bowlby, 1969). At the family-level, Family systems theory posits that family interactions impact functioning among all members of a family unit (Broderick 1971). At the macro-level, Critical race theory (Delgado & Stefancic, 2001) can help understand racial disparities in child welfare systems. Moreover, Systems theory (Bronfenbrenner, 1986) can help examine interactions among the micro-, meso- and macro-levels to assess diverse systems that impact families involved in child welfare services.

In the next step of the project, national datasets were used to examine child-, family-, and system- factors that impacted rates of successful reunification, or reunification with no future re-entries into foster care. Then, a systematic review of the literature was conducted to determine what evidence existed for interventions to increase rates of successful reunification. Finally, a different national dataset was used to examine how effective diverse interventions were for specific groups of families, such as those with infants and toddlers.

Figure 2.2 displays the principal findings from the research project and connects each main finding to one of the theoretical frameworks.

Attachment Theory	• Parents who feel unable to cope with parental roles experience higher rates of unsuccessful reunification • Previous attachment disruptions (measured by prior removals from parents' care) decreased the odds of successful reunification
Family Systems Theory	• Family-factors explain more variance in successful reunification than state system factors • Interventions focused on the parents such as Family Drug Treatment Courts can help improve successful reunification for the family as a unit
Systems Theory	• Although the majority of variance is at the family-level, the impact of state system factors such as poverty rates and average time to reunify impact successful reunification rates • Interventions that integrate multiple systems, such as child welfare and substance use through Family Drug Treatment Courts, or Recovery Coaches
Critical Race Theory	• Overall, African American and Latino families have higher rates of successful reunification than White families • However, this relationship varies significantly by **state,** a finding that needs to be explored in future research

Figure 2.2 Findings of Factors and Interventions Associated with Reunification Success and Theories

The first part of the research project found parents who felt unable to cope with their parental role, and families with previous attachment disruptions, to have higher rates of re-entry into foster care. This connects with Attachment theory, in that families with more instability and inconsistency in caregiving felt less able to fulfill their parental roles, which in turn led to further disruption in the child's attachment.

With regards to family-level theories, Dr. LaBrenz found that family-level risk and protective factors were more predictive of re-entry to foster care than child- or agency-level factors. The systematic review also found that interventions that targeted parents, such as Family Drug

Treatment Courts, led to better outcomes for children and families. This aligns with Family systems theory in that family-centered interventions and targeting the entire family leads to better family functioning and fewer re-entries into foster care.

In parallel, the systematic review concluded that interventions that integrated multiple systems, such as child welfare and substance use, increased the likelihood of successful reunification. This supports Systems theory, in that multiple systems can be engaged to provide ongoing support for families in child welfare systems (Trucco, 2012). Furthermore, the results from the analyses of the national datasets found that rates of re-entry into foster care for African American and Latino families varied significantly by state. Thus, racial and ethnic disparities remained in some, but not all, state child welfare systems.

Overall, the findings from the research project supported Attachment theory, Family systems theory, Systems theory, and Critical race theory as guiding explanations for *why* some children and families experience foster care re-entry while others do not. Dr. LaBrenz was able to present these findings and connect them to direct implications for practices and policies that could support attachment, multi-system collaborations, and family-centered practices.

Key Takeaways

- Paradigms shape our everyday view of the world.
- Researchers use theory to help frame their research questions and to help them make sense of the answers to those questions.
- Applying the four key theories of social work is a good start, but you will likely have to look for more specific theories about your topic.

Glossary

- Critical paradigm- a paradigm in social science research focused on power, inequality, and social change
- Paradigm- a way of viewing the world and a framework from which to understand the human

experience

- Positivism- a paradigm guided by the principles of objectivity, knowability, and deductive logic
- Postmodernism- a paradigm focused on the historical and contextual embeddedness of scientific knowledge and a skepticism towards certainty and grand explanations in social science
- Social constructionism- a paradigm based on the idea that social context and interaction frame our realities
- Theory- "a systematic set of interrelated statements intended to explain some aspect of social life" (Rubin & Babbie, 2017, p. 615)

Image attributions

point mold and cloud mold by tasaikensuke CC-0

why by GDJ CC-0

2.3 INDUCTIVE AND DEDUCTIVE REASONING

Learning Objectives

- Describe the inductive approach to research, and provide examples of inductive research
- Describe the deductive approach to research, and provide examples of deductive research
- Describe the ways that inductive and deductive approaches may be complementary

Theories structure and inform social work research. So, too, does research structure and inform theory. The reciprocal relationship between theory and research often becomes evident to students new to these topics when they consider the relationships between theory and research in inductive and deductive approaches to research. In both cases, theory is crucial. But the relationship between theory and research differs for each approach.

Inductive and deductive approaches to research are quite different, but they can also be complementary. Let's start by looking at each one and how they differ from one another. Then we'll move on to thinking about how they complement one another.

INDUCTIVE APPROACHES AND SOME EXAMPLES

In an **inductive approach** to research, a researcher begins by collecting data that is relevant to her topic of interest. Once a substantial amount of data have been collected, the researcher will then take a breather from data collection, stepping back to get a bird's eye view of their data. At this stage, the researcher looks for patterns in the data, working to develop a theory that could explain those patterns. Thus, when researchers take an inductive approach, they start with a set of observations and then they move from those particular experiences to a more general set of propositions about those experiences. In other words, they move from data to theory, or from the specific to the general. Figure 6.1 outlines the steps involved with an inductive approach to research.

Figure 6.1 Inductive research

There are many good examples of inductive research, but we'll look at just a few here. One fascinating study in which the researchers took an inductive approach is Katherine Allen, Christine Kaestle, and Abbie Goldberg's (2011) study of how boys and young men learn about menstruation. To understand this process, Allen and her colleagues analyzed the written narratives of 23 young men in which the men described how they learned about menstruation, what they thought of it when they first learned about it, and what they think of it now. By looking for patterns across all 23 men's narratives, the researchers were able to develop a general theory of how boys and young men learn about this aspect of girls' and women's biology. They conclude that sisters play an important role in boys' early understanding of menstruation, that menstruation makes boys feel somewhat separated from girls, and that as they enter young adulthood and form romantic relationships, young men develop more mature attitudes about menstruation. Note how this study began with the data—men's narratives of learning about menstruation—and tried to develop a theory.

In another inductive study, Kristin Ferguson and colleagues (Ferguson, Kim, & McCoy, 2011) analyzed empirical data to better understand how best to meet the needs of young people who are homeless. The authors analyzed data from focus groups with 20 young people at a homeless shelter. From these data they developed a set of recommendations for those interested in applied interventions that serve homeless youth. The researchers also developed hypotheses for people who might wish to conduct further investigation of the topic. Though Ferguson and her colleagues did not test the hypotheses that they developed from their analysis, their study ends where most deductive investigations begin: with a theory and a hypothesis derived from that theory.

DEDUCTIVE APPROACHES AND SOME EXAMPLES

Researchers taking a **deductive approach** take the steps described earlier for inductive research and reverse their order. They start with a social theory that they find compelling and then test its implications with data. That is, they move from a more general level to a more specific one. A deductive approach to research is the one that people typically associate with scientific investigation. The researcher studies what others have done, reads existing theories of whatever phenomenon she is studying, and then tests hypotheses that emerge from those theories. Figure 2.2 outlines the steps involved with a deductive approach to research.

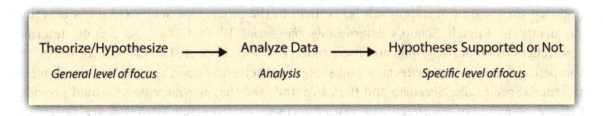

Figure 2.2 Deductive research

While not all researchers follow a deductive approach, as you have seen in the preceding discussion, many do, and there are a number of excellent recent examples of deductive research. We'll take a look at a couple of those next.

In a study of United States law enforcement responses to hate crimes, Ryan King and colleagues (King, Messner, & Baller, 2009) hypothesized that law enforcement's response would be less vigorous in areas of the country that had a stronger history of racial violence. The authors developed their hypothesis from their reading of prior research and theories on the topic. They tested the hypothesis by analyzing data on states' lynching histories and hate crime responses. Overall, the authors found support for their hypothesis. One might associate this research with critical theory.

In another recent deductive study, Melissa Milkie and Catharine Warner (2011) studied the effects of different classroom environments on first graders' mental health. Based on prior research and theory, Milkie and Warner hypothesized that negative classroom features, such as a lack of basic supplies and even heat, would be associated with emotional and behavioral problems in children. One might associate this research with systems theory. The researchers found support for their hypothesis, demonstrating that policymakers should probably be paying more attention to the mental health outcomes of children's school experiences, just as they track academic outcomes (American Sociological Association, 2011).

COMPLEMENTARY APPROACHES

While inductive and deductive approaches to research seem quite different, they can actually be rather complementary. In some cases, researchers will plan for their study to include multiple components, one inductive and the other deductive. In other cases, a researcher might begin a study with the plan to only conduct either inductive or deductive research, but then discovers along the way that the other approach is needed to help illuminate findings.

Researchers may not always set out to employ both approaches in their work but sometimes find that their use of one approach leads them to the other. One such example is described eloquently in Russell Schutt's *Investigating the Social World* (2006). As Schutt describes, researchers Lawrence Sherman and Richard Berk (1984) conducted an experiment to test two competing theories of the effects of punishment on deterring deviance (in this case, domestic violence). Specifically, Sherman and Berk hypothesized that *deterrence theory* would provide a better explanation of the effects of arresting accused batterers than *labeling theory*. Deterrence theory predicts that arresting an accused spouse batterer will *reduce* future incidents of violence. Conversely, labeling theory predicts that arresting accused spouse batterers will *increase* future incidents. Figure 2.3 summarizes the two competing theories and the predictions that Sherman and Berk set out to test.

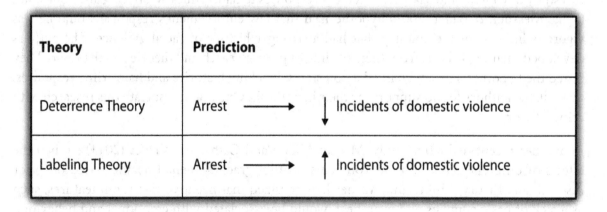

Figure 2.3 Predicting the effects of arrest on future spouse battery

Sherman and Berk found, after conducting an experiment with the help of local police in one city, that arrest did in fact deter future incidents of violence, thus supporting their hypothesis that deterrence theory would better predict the effect of arrest. After conducting this research, they and other researchers did what is called replication and went on to conduct similar experiments in six additional cities (Berk, Campbell, Klap, & Western, 1992; Pate & Hamilton, 1992; Sherman & Smith, 1992). Results from these follow-up studies were mixed. In some cases, arrest deterred future incidents of violence. In other cases, it did not. This left the researchers with new data that they needed to explain. The researchers therefore took an inductive approach in an effort to make sense of their latest empirical observations. The new studies revealed that arrest seemed to have a deterrent effect for those who were married and employed, but that it led to increased offenses for those who were unmarried and unemployed. Researchers thus turned to control theory, which predicts that having some stake in conformity through the social ties provided by marriage and employment, as the better explanation.

What the Sherman and Berk research, along with the follow-up studies, shows us is that we might start with a deductive approach to research, but then, if confronted by new data that we must make sense of, we may move to an inductive approach.

Theory	Prediction
~~Deterrence Theory~~	~~Arrest ⟶ ↓ Incidents of domestic violence~~
~~Labeling Theory~~	~~Arrest ⟶ ↑ Incidents of domestic violence~~
Control Theory	Arrest ⟶ ↓ Incidents of domestic violence for the married and employed
	Arrest ⟶ ↑ Incidents of domestic violence for the unmarried and unemployed

Figure 2.4 Predicting the effects of arrest on future spouse battery: A new theory

Key Takeaways

- The inductive approach begins with a set of empirical observations, seeking patterns in those observations, and then theorizing about those patterns.
- The deductive approach begins with a theory, developing hypotheses from that theory, and then collecting and analyzing data to test those hypotheses.
- Inductive and deductive approaches to research can be employed together for a more complete understanding of the topic that a researcher is studying.
- Though researchers don't always set out to use both inductive and deductive strategies in their work, they sometimes find that new questions arise in the course of an investigation that can best be answered by employing both approaches.

Glossary

- Deductive approach- study what others have done, reads existing theories of whatever phenomenon she is studying, and then tests hypotheses that emerge from those theories
- Inductive approach- start with a set of observations and then move from particular experiences to a more general set of propositions about those experiences

Image Attributions

All figures in this section are copied from Blackstone, A. (2012) Principles of sociological inquiry: Qualitative and quantitative methods. Saylor Foundation. Retrieved from: https://saylordotorg.github.io/text_principles-of-sociological-inquiry-qualitative-and-quantitative-methods/ Shared under CC-BY-NC-SA 3.0 License

FOR A LOOK INSIDE PLEASE SCAN OR VISIT

CHAPTER THREE: ETHICS IN SOCIAL WORK RESEARCH

Would it surprise you learn that scientists who conduct research may withhold effective treatments from individuals with diseases? Perhaps it wouldn't surprise you, since you may have heard of the Tuskegee Syphilis Experiment, in which treatments for syphilis were knowingly withheld from African-American participants for decades. Would it surprise you to learn that the practice of withholding treatment continues today? Multiple studies in the developing world continue to use placebo control groups in testing for cancer screenings, cancer treatments, and HIV treatments (Joffe & Miller, 2014). [1] What standards would you use to judge withholding treatment as ethical or unethical? Most importantly, how can you make sure that your study respects the human rights of your participants?

CHAPTER OUTLINE

- 3.1 Research on humans
- 3.2 Specific ethical issues to consider
- 3.3 Ethics at micro, meso, and macro levels
- 3.4 The practice of science versus the uses of science

CONTENT ADVISORY

This chapter discusses or mentions the following topics: unethical research that has occurred in the past against marginalized groups in America and during the Holocaust.

---

1. Joffe, S., & Miller, F. G. (2014). Ethics of cancer clinical trials in low-resource settings. *Journal of Clinical Oncology*, *32*(28), 3192-3196.

3.1 RESEARCH ON HUMANS

Learning Objectives

- Define human subjects research
- Describe and provide examples of nonhuman subjects that researchers might examine
- Define institutional review boards and describe their purpose
- Distinguish between the different levels of review conducted by institutional review boards

In 1998, actor Jim Carey starred in the movie *The Truman Show*. At first glance, the film appears to depict a perfect research experiment. Just imagine the possibilities if we could control every aspect of a person's life, from how and where that person lives to where they work to whom they marry. Of course, keeping someone in a bubble, controlling every aspect of their life, and sitting back and watching would be highly unethical (not to mention illegal). However, the movie clearly inspires thoughts about the differences between scientific research and research on nonhumans. One of the most exciting—and most challenging—aspects of conducting social work research is the fact that (at least much of the time) our subjects are living human beings whose free will and human rights will always have an impact on what we are able to research and how we are able to conduct that research.

HUMAN RESEARCH VERSUS NONHUMAN RESEARCH

While all research comes with its own set of ethical concerns, those associated with research conducted on human subjects vary dramatically from those of research conducted on nonliving entities. The US Department of Health and Human Services (USDHHS) defines a human subject as "a living individual about whom an investigator (whether professional or student) conducting research obtains (1) data through intervention or interaction with the individual, or (2) identifiable private information" (USDHHS, 1993, para. 1). Some researchers prefer the term participants to subjects, as it acknowledges the agency of people who participate in the study. For our purposes, we will use the two terms interchangeably.

In some states, human subjects also include deceased individuals and human fetal materials. Nonhuman research subjects, on the other hand, are objects or entities that investigators manipulate or analyze in the process of conducting research. Nonhuman research subjects typically include sources such as newspapers, historical documents, clinical notes, television shows, buildings, and even garbage (to name just a few) that are analyzed for unobtrusive research projects. Unsurprisingly, research on human subjects is regulated much more heavily than research on nonhuman subjects. However, there are ethical considerations that all researchers must consider regardless of their research subject. We'll discuss those considerations in addition to concerns that are unique to research on human subjects.

A HISTORICAL LOOK AT RESEARCH ON HUMANS

Research on humans hasn't always been regulated in the way that it is today. The earliest documented cases of research using human subjects are of medical vaccination trials (Rothman, 1987). One such case took place in the late 1700s, when scientist Edward Jenner exposed an 8-year-old boy to smallpox in order to identify a vaccine for the devastating disease. Medical research on human subjects continued without much law or policy intervention until the mid-1900s when, at the end of World War II, a number of Nazi doctors and scientists were put on trial for conducting human experimentation during the course of which they tortured and murdered many concentration camp inmates (Faden & Beauchamp, 1986). One little-known fact, as described by Faden and Beauchamp in their 1986 book, is that at the very time that the Nazis conducted their horrendous experiments, Germany did actually have written regulations specifying that human subjects must clearly and willingly consent to their participation in medical research. Obviously these regulations were completely disregarded by the Nazi experimenters, but the fact that they existed suggests that efforts to regulate the ethical conduct of research, while necessary, are certainly not sufficient for ensuring that human subjects' rights will be honored. The trials, conducted in Nuremberg, Germany, resulted in the creation of the **Nuremberg Code**, a 10-point set of research principles designed to guide doctors and scientists who conduct research on human subjects. Today, the Nuremberg Code guides medical and other research conducted on human subjects, including social science research.

Medical scientists are not the only researchers who have conducted questionable research on humans. In the 1960s, psychologist Stanley Milgram (1974) conducted a series of experiments designed to understand obedience to authority in which he tricked subjects into believing they were administering an electric shock to other subjects. In fact, the shocks weren't real at all, but some, though not many, of Milgram's research participants experienced extreme emotional distress after the experiment (Ogden, 2008). A reaction of emotional distress is understandable. The realization that you are willing to administer painful shocks to another human being just because someone who looks authoritative has told you to do so might indeed be traumatizing—even if you later learn that the shocks weren't real.

Around the same time that Milgram conducted his experiments, sociology graduate student Laud Humphreys (1970) was collecting data for his dissertation research on the tearoom trade, which was the practice of men engaging in anonymous sexual encounters in public restrooms. Humphreys wished to understand who these men were and why they participated in the trade. To conduct his research, Humphreys offered to serve as a "watch queen," who is the person who keeps an eye out for police and gets the benefit of being able to watch the sexual encounters, in a local park restroom where the tearoom trade was known to occur. What Humphreys did not do was identify himself as a researcher to his research subjects. Instead, he watched his subjects for several months, getting to know several of them, learning more about the tearoom trade practice and, without the knowledge of his research subjects, jotting down their license plate numbers as they pulled into or out of the parking lot near the restroom.

Sometime after participating as a watch queen, with the help of several insiders who had access to motor vehicle registration information, Humphreys used those license plate numbers to obtain the names and home addresses of his research subjects. Then, disguised as a public health researcher, Humphreys visited his subjects in their homes and interviewed them about their lives and their health. Humphreys' research dispelled a good number of myths and stereotypes about the tearoom trade and its participants. He learned, for example, that over half of his subjects were married to women and many of them did not identify as gay or bisexual. [1]

1. Humphreys's research is still relevant today. In fact, as the 2007 arrest of Idaho Senator Larry Craig in a public restroom at the Minneapolis–St. Paul airport attests, undercover police operations targeting tearoom activities still

Once Humphreys' work became public, the result was some major controversy at his home university (e.g., the chancellor tried to have his degree revoked), among scientists in general, and among members of the public, as it raised public concerns about the purpose and conduct of social science research. In addition, the *Washington Post* journalist Nicholas von Hoffman wrote the following warning about "sociological snoopers":

> We're so preoccupied with defending our privacy against insurance investigators, dope sleuths, counterespionage men, divorce detectives and credit checkers, that we overlook the social scientists behind the hunting blinds who're also peeping into what we thought were our most private and secret lives. But they are there, studying us, taking notes, getting to know us, as indifferent as everybody else to the feeling that to be a complete human involves having an aspect of ourselves that's unknown (von Hoffman, 1970).

In the original version of his report, Humphreys defended the ethics of his actions. In 2008, years after Humphreys' death, his book was reprinted with the addition of a retrospect on the ethical implications of his work. In his written reflections on his research and the fallout from it, Humphreys maintained that his tearoom observations constituted ethical research on the grounds that those interactions occurred in public places. But Humphreys added that he would conduct the second part of his research differently. Rather than trace license numbers and interview unwitting tearoom participants in their homes under the guise of public health research, Humphreys instead would spend more time in the field and work to cultivate a pool of informants. Those informants would know that he was a researcher and would be able to fully consent to being interviewed. In the end, Humphreys concluded "there is no reason to believe that any research subjects have suffered because of my efforts, or that the resultant demystification of impersonal sex has harmed society" (Humphreys, 2008, p. 231).

Today, given increasing regulation of social scientific research, chances are slim that a researcher would be allowed to conduct a project similar to Humphreys'. Some argue that Humphreys' research was deceptive, put his subjects at risk of losing their families and their positions in society, and was therefore unethical (Warwick, 1973; Warwick, 1982). Others suggest that Humphreys' research "did not violate any premise of either beneficence or the sociological interest in social justice" and that the benefits of Humphreys' research, namely the dissolution of myths about the tearoom trade specifically and human sexual practice more generally, outweigh the potential risks associated with the work (Lenza, 2004, p. 23).[2] What do you think, and why?

occur, more than 40 years after Humphreys conducted his research. Humphreys's research is also frequently cited by attorneys who represent clients arrested for lewd behavior in public restrooms.

2. See also Nardi, P. M. (1995). "The breastplate of righteousness": Twenty-five years after Laud Humphreys' *Tearoom trade: Impersonal sex in public places. Journal of Homosexuality, 30,* 1–10.

In addition to these studies, other research like the Tuskegee Syphilis Experiment led to increasing public awareness of and concern about research on human subjects (Reverby, 2009). The Tuskegee Syphilis Experiment was conducted in Alabama from the 1930s to the 1970s. The goal of the study was to understand the natural progression of syphilis in human beings. Investigators working for the Public Health Service enrolled hundreds of poor African American men in the study, some of whom had been diagnosed with syphilis and others who had not. Even after effective syphilis treatment was identified in the 1940s, research participants were denied treatment so that researchers could continue to observe the progression of the disease. The study came to an end in 1972 after knowledge of the experiment became public. In 1997, President Clinton publicly apologized on behalf of the American people for the study.

In 1974, the US Congress enacted the National Research Act, which created the National Commission for the Protection of Human Subjects in Biomedical and Behavioral Research. The commission produced *The Belmont Report*, a document outlining basic ethical principles for research on human subjects (National Commission for the Protection of Human Subjects in Biomedical and Behavioral Research, 1979). The National Research Act of 1974 also required that all institutions receiving federal support establish institutional review boards (IRBs) to protect the rights of human research subjects. Since that time, many organizations that do not receive federal support but where research is conducted have also established review boards to evaluate the ethics of the research they conduct.

INSTITUTIONAL REVIEW BOARDS (IRBS)

Institutional Review Boards, or IRBs, are tasked with ensuring that the rights and welfare of human research subjects will be protected at all institutions, including universities, hospitals, nonprofit research institutions, and other organizations, that receive federal support for research. IRBs typically consist of members from a variety of disciplines, such as sociology, economics, education, social work, and communications (to name a few). Most IRBs also include representatives from the community in which they reside. For example, representatives from nearby prisons, hospitals, or treatment centers might sit on the IRBs of university campuses near them. The diversity of membership helps to ensure that the many and complex ethical issues that may arise from human subjects research will be considered fully and by a knowledgeable and experienced panel. Investigators conducting research on human subjects are required to submit proposals outlining their research plans to IRBs for review and approval prior to beginning their research. Even students who conduct research on human subjects must have their proposed work reviewed and approved by the IRB before beginning any research (though, on some campuses, some exceptions are made for classroom projects that will not be shared outside of the classroom).

The IRB has three levels of review, defined in statute by the USDHHS. **Exempt review** is the lowest level of review. Studies that are considered exempt expose participants to the least potential for harm and often involves little participation by human subjects. In social work, exempt studies often examine data that is publicly available or secondary data from another researcher that has been de-identified by the person who collected it. **Expedited review** is the middle level of review. Studies considered under expedited review do not have to go before the full IRB board because they expose participants to minimal risk. However, the studies must be thoroughly reviewed by a member of the IRB committee. While there are many types of studies that qualify for expedited review, the most relevant to social workers include the use of existing medical records, recordings (such as interviews) gathered for research purposes, and research on individual group characteristics or behavior. Finally, the highest level of review is called a **full board review**. A full board review will involve multiple members of the IRB evaluating your proposal. When researchers submit a proposal under full board review, the full IRB board will meet, discuss any questions or concerns with the study, invite the researcher to answer questions and defend their proposal, and vote to approve the study or send it back for revision. Full board proposals pose greater than minimal risk to participants. They may also involve the participation of **vulnerable populations**, or people who need additional protection from the IRB. Vulnerable populations include pregnant women, prisoners, children, people with cognitive impairments, people with physical disabilities, employees, and students. While some of these populations can fall under expedited review, they will usually require the full IRB to approve their study.

It may surprise you to hear that IRBs are not always popular or appreciated by researchers. Who wouldn't want to conduct ethical research, you ask? In some cases, the concern is that IRBs are most well-versed in reviewing biomedical and experimental research, neither of which is particularly common within social work. Much social work research, especially qualitative research, is open ended in nature, a fact that can be problematic for IRBs. The members of IRBs often want to know in advance exactly who will be observed, where, when, and for how long, whether and how they will be approached, exactly what questions they will be asked, and what predictions the researcher has for her findings. Providing this level of detail for a year-long participant observation within an activist group of 200-plus members, for example, would be extraordinarily frustrating for the researcher in the best case and most likely would prove to be impossible. Of course, IRBs do not intend to have researchers avoid studying controversial topics or avoid using certain methodologically sound data collection techniques, but unfortunately, that is sometimes the result. The solution is not to do away with review boards, which serve a necessary and important function, but instead to help educate IRB members about the variety of social scientific research methods and topics covered by social workers and other social scientists.

Key Takeaways

- Research on human subjects presents a unique set of challenges and opportunities when it comes to conducting ethical research.
- Research on human subjects has not always been regulated to the extent that it is today.
- All institutions receiving federal support for research must have an IRB. Organizations that do not receive federal support but where research is conducted also often include IRBs as part of their organizational structure.
- Researchers submit studies for IRB review at one of three different levels, depending on the level of harm the study may cause.

Glossary

- Exempt review- lowest level of IRB review, for studies for studies with minimal risk or human subject involvement
- Expedited review- middle level of IRB review, for studies with minimal risk but greater human subject involvement
- Full board review- highest level of IRB, for studies with greater than minimal risk to participants
- Vulnerable populations- groups of people who receive additional protection during IRB review

Image attributions

ethics by Tumisu CC-0

roundtable meeting by Debora Cartagena CC-0

3.2 SPECIFIC ETHICAL ISSUES TO CONSIDER

Learning Objectives

- Define informed consent, and describe how it works
- Identify the unique concerns related to the study of vulnerable populations
- Differentiate between anonymity and confidentiality
- Explain the ethical responsibilities of social workers conducting research
- Identify the unique ethical concern posed by internet research

As should be clear by now, conducting research on humans presents a number of unique ethical considerations. Human research subjects must be given the opportunity to consent to their participation in research, fully informed of the study's risks, benefits, and purpose. Further, subjects' identities and the information they share should be protected by researchers. Of course, how consent and identity protection are defined may vary by individual researcher, institution, or academic discipline. In section 3.1, we examined the role that institutions play in shaping research ethics. In this section, we'll take a look at a few specific topics that individual researchers and social workers in general must consider before embarking on research with human subjects.

INFORMED CONSENT

A norm of voluntary participation is presumed in all social work research projects. In other words, we cannot force anyone to participate in our research without that person's knowledge or consent (so much for that *Truman Show* experiment). Researchers must therefore design procedures to obtain subjects' informed consent to participate in their research. **Informed consent** is defined as a subject's voluntary agreement to participate in research based on a full understanding of the research and of the possible risks and benefits involved. Although it sounds simple, ensuring that one has actually obtained informed consent is a much more complex process than you might initially presume.

The first requirement is that, in giving their informed consent, subjects may neither waive nor even *appear* to waive any of their legal rights. Subjects also cannot release a researcher, her sponsor, or institution from any legal liability should something go wrong during the course of their participation in the research (USDHHS,2009). [1] Because social work research does not typically involve asking subjects to place themselves at risk of physical harm by, for example, taking untested drugs or consenting to new medical procedures, social work researchers do

---

1. The full set of requirements for informed consent can be read online at the Office for Human Research Protections.

not often worry about potential liability associated with their research projects. However, their research may involve other types of risks.

For example, what if a social work researcher fails to sufficiently conceal the identity of a subject who admits to participating in a local swinger's club? In this case, a violation of confidentiality may negatively affect the participant's social standing, marriage, custody rights, or employment. Social work research may also involve asking about intimately personal topics, such as trauma or suicide that may be difficult for participants to discuss. Participants may re-experience traumatic events and symptoms when they participate in a study. Even if you are careful to fully inform your participants of all risks before they consent to the research process, you can probably empathize with participants thinking they could bear talking about a difficult topic and then finding it too overwhelming once they start. In cases like these, it is important for a social work researcher to have a plan to provide supports. This may mean providing referrals to counseling supports in the community or even calling the police if the participant is an imminent danger to themselves or others.

It is vital that social work researchers explain their mandatory reporting duties in the consent form and ensure participants understand them before they participate. Researchers should also emphasize to participants that they can stop the research process at any time or decide to withdraw from the research study for any reason. Importantly, it is not the job of the social work researcher to act as a clinician to the participant. While a supportive role is certainly appropriate for someone experiencing a mental health crisis, social workers must ethically avoid dual roles. Referring a participant in crisis to other mental health professionals who may be better able to help them is preferred.

Beyond the legal issues, most IRBs require researchers to share some details about the purpose of the research, possible benefits of participation, and, most importantly, possible risks associated with participating in that research with their subjects. In addition, researchers must describe how they will protect subjects' identities; how, where, and for how long any data collected will be stored; and whom to contact for additional information about the study or about subjects' rights. All this information is typically shared in an informed consent form that researchers provide to subjects. In some cases, subjects are asked to sign the consent form indicating that they have read it and fully understand its contents. In other cases, subjects are simply provided a copy of the consent form and researchers are responsible for making sure that subjects have read and understand the form before proceeding with any kind of data collection. Figure 3.1 showcases a sample informed consent form from a research project on child-free adults. Note that this consent form describes a risk that may be unique to the particular method of data collection being employed: focus groups.

INFORMED CONSENT FORM: FOCUS GROUPS

You are invited to participate in a research project being conducted by Dr. Amy Blackstone, a faculty member in the Department of Sociology at the University of Maine. The purpose of the research is to understand the processes by which adults without children decide to not have children and the social responses to their choice.

What Will You Be Asked to Do?
If you decide to participate, you will be asked to respond to questions about your decision to not have children. Specific questions include the following: Why did you make the decision to remain childfree? What do you most enjoy about your childfree lifestyle? What are some of the drawbacks of your childfree lifestyle? How have others responded to your decision? What role does your status as married or single play in people's responses? What role does your identity as heterosexual or homosexual play in people's responses? What does the word "family" mean to you? It will take between 75 and 115 minutes to participate.

Risks
- In addition to your time and inconvenience, there is the possibility that you may become uncomfortable answering the questions.
- Due to the focus group format, it is possible the confidentiality of your responses will not be maintained by other focus group participants.

Benefits
- Except for the compensation you will receive (see below), there are no other benefits to you from participating in this study.
- While this study will have no direct benefit to you, this research will help us learn more about the processes by which some adults choose not to rear children. This population has been understudied in sociological research.

Compensation
You will receive $20 for participating in a focus group.

Confidentiality
Your name will not be kept on any documents except a participant key (see below). A pseudonym will be used to protect your identity. The focus group will be tape recorded and then transcribed. Recordings will be stored in a locked file cabinet inside Dr. Blackstone's locked office and destroyed after data analysis is complete (by or before August 2010). Research assistant Alyssa Radmore will have access to the data in Dr. Blackstone's office when Dr. Blackstone is present. Your name or other identifying information will not be reported in any publications. The key linking your name to the data will be destroyed after data analysis is complete. Written focus group transcripts will be kept indefinitely in Dr. Blackstone's locked office. These transcripts will not contain any identifying information such as your name. Because individuals in addition to the researchers will be present during the focus group, your confidentiality cannot be guaranteed.

Voluntary
Participation is voluntary. If you choose to take part in this study, you may stop at any time during the study. Stopping the study will not alter the compensation you will receive. You may skip any questions you do not wish to answer. Skipping questions will not alter the compensation you will receive.

Contact Information
If you have any questions about this study, please contact me by phone (207-581-2392), e-mail (amy.blackstone@umit.maine.edu), or mail (University of Maine Department of Sociology, 5728 Fernald Hall, Orono, ME 04469). If you have any questions about your rights as a research participant, please contact Gayle Anderson, Assistant to the University of Maine's Protection of Human Subjects Review Board, at 207-581-1498 (or e-mail gayle.anderson@umit.maine.edu).

Figure 3.1 Sample informed consent form

One last point to consider when preparing to obtain informed consent is that not all potential research subjects are considered equally competent or legally allowed to consent to participate in research. Subjects from vulnerable populations may be at risk of experiencing undue influence or coercion.[2] The rules for consent are more stringent for vulnerable populations. For example, minors must have the consent of a legal guardian in order to participate in research. In some cases, the minors themselves are also asked to participate in the consent process by signing special, age-appropriate "assent" forms designed specifically for them. Prisoners and parolees also qualify as vulnerable populations. Concern about the vulnerability of these subjects comes from the very real possibility that prisoners and parolees could perceive that they will receive some highly desired reward, such as early release, if they participate in research. Another potential concern regarding vulnerable populations is that they may be underrepresented in research, and even denied potential benefits of participation in research, specifically because of concerns about their ability to consent. So, on the one hand, researchers must take extra care to ensure that their procedures for obtaining consent from vulnerable populations are not coercive. The procedures for receiving approval to conduct research on these groups may be more rigorous than that for non-vulnerable populations. On the other hand, researchers must work to avoid excluding members of vulnerable populations from participation simply on the grounds that they are vulnerable or that obtaining their consent may be more complex. While there is no easy solution to this double-edged sword, an awareness of the potential concerns associated with research on vulnerable populations is important for identifying whatever solution is most appropriate for a specific case.

PROTECTION OF IDENTITIES

As mentioned earlier, the informed consent process includes the requirement that researchers outline how they will protect the identities of subjects. This aspect of the process, however, is one of the most commonly misunderstood aspects of research.

In protecting subjects' identities, researchers typically promise to maintain either the anonymity or confidentiality of their research subjects. Anonymity is the more stringent of the two. When a researcher promises **anonymity** to participants, not even the researcher is able to link participants' data with their identities. Anonymity may be impossible for some social work researchers to promise because several of the modes of data collection that social workers employ. Face-to-face interviewing means that subjects will be visible to researchers and will

---

2. The guidelines on vulnerable populations can be read online at the the US Department of Health and Human Services'.

hold a conversation, making anonymity impossible. In other cases, the researcher may have a signed consent form or obtain personal information on a survey and will therefore know the identities of their research participants. In these cases, a researcher should be able to at least promise confidentiality to participants.

Offering **confidentiality** means that some identifying information on one's subjects is known and may be kept, but only the researcher can link participants with their data and she promises not to do so publicly. Confidentiality in research is quite similar to confidentiality in clinical practice. You know who your clients are, but others do not. You agree to keep their information and identity private. As you can see under the "Risks" section of the consent form in Figure 3.1, sometimes it is not even possible to promise that a subject's confidentiality will be maintained. This is the case if data are collected in public or in the presence of other research participants (e.g., in the course of a focus group). Participants who social work researchers deem to be of imminent danger to self or others or those that disclose abuse of children and other vulnerable populations fall under a social worker's duty to report. Researchers must then violate confidentiality to fulfill their legal obligations.

Protecting research participants' identities is not always a simple prospect, especially for those conducting research on stigmatized groups or illegal behaviors. Sociologist Scott DeMuth learned that all too well when conducting his dissertation research on a group of animal rights activists. As a participant observer, DeMuth knew the identities of his research subjects. So when some of his research subjects vandalized facilities and removed animals from several research labs at the University of Iowa, a grand jury called on Mr. DeMuth to reveal the identities of the participants in the raid. When DeMuth refused to do so, he was jailed briefly and then charged with conspiracy to commit animal enterprise terrorism and cause damage to the animal enterprise (Jaschik, 2009).

Publicly, DeMuth's case raised many of the same questions as Laud Humphreys' work 40 years earlier. What do social scientists owe the public? Is DeMuth, by protecting his research subjects, harming those whose labs were vandalized? Is he harming the taxpayers who funded those labs? Or is it more important that DeMuth emphasize what he owes his research subjects, who were told their identities would be protected? DeMuth's case also sparked controversy among academics, some of whom thought that as an academic himself, DeMuth should have been more sympathetic to the plight of the faculty and students who lost years of research as a result of the attack on their labs. Many others stood by DeMuth, arguing that the personal and academic freedom of scholars must be protected whether we support their research topics and subjects or not. DeMuth's academic adviser even created a new group, Scholars for Academic Justice, to support DeMuth and other academics who face persecution or prosecution as a result of the research they conduct. What do you think? Should DeMuth have revealed the identities of his research subjects? Why or why not?

SOCIAL WORK ETHICS AND RESEARCH

Often times, specific disciplines will provide their own set of guidelines for protecting research subjects and, more generally, for conducting ethical research. For social workers, the National Association of Social Workers (NASW) Code of Ethics section 5.02 describes the responsibilities of social workers in conducting research. Summarized below, these responsibilities are framed as part of a social worker's responsibility to the profession. As representative of the social work profession, it is your responsibility to conduct and use research in an ethical manner.

A social worker should:

- Monitor and evaluate policies, programs, and practice interventions
- Contribute to the development of knowledge through research
- Keep current with the best available research evidence to inform practice
- Ensure voluntary and fully informed consent of all participants
- Not engage in any deception in the research process
- Allow participants to withdraw from the study at any time
- Provide access for participants to appropriate supportive services
- Protect research participants from harm
- Maintain confidentiality
- Report findings accurately
- Disclose any conflicts of interest

INTERNET RESEARCH

It is increasingly common for the internet to be used as a tool for conducting research and as a source of data such as the content of websites, blogs, or discussion boards. Research ethical principles apply to internet research, but there are ethical considerations that are unique to internet research.

Some of the major tensions and considerations of internet research include defining human subjects, differentiating between what is public and what is private, and making appropriate distinctions between individuals and data. These tensions lead to new concerns about informed consent, confidentiality, privacy, and harm when conducting internet research. These are important considerations because they link to the fundamental ethical principle of minimizing harm. Does the connection between one's online data and his or her physical person enable psychological, economic, or physical, harm?

- *Defining Human Subjects:* In internet research, "human subject" has never been a good fit for describing many internet-based research environments. For example, should authors of web content be considered human subjects? This question is important because many regulatory bodies do not conduct ethical reviews if they determine that the research does not involve human subjects. Internet researchers have not reached a consensus about how to define the term "human subjects." In fact, some contend that defining human subjects may not be as important as defining other terms such as harm, vulnerability, personally identifiable information, and so forth.

- *Differentiating between Public and Private:* Individual and cultural definitions and expectations of privacy are ambiguous, contested, and changing. On the internet, people may operate in public spaces but maintain strong perceptions or expectations of privacy. Or, they may acknowledge that the substance of their communication is public, but that the specific context in which it appears implies restrictions on how that information is – or should be – used by other parties. For example, a user may feel comfortable broadcasting tweets to a public audience, following the norms of the Twitter community. However, to find out that these 'public' tweets had been collected within a data set and combed over by a researcher could possibly feel like an encroachment on privacy. Despite what a simplified conceptualization of "public/ private" might offer, there is no categorical way to discern all eventual harm. Data aggregators or search tools make information accessible to a wider public than what might have been originally intended. Social, academic, or regulatory delineations of public and private as a clearly recognizable binary no longer holds in everyday practice.

- *Distinctions between individuals and data:* The internet complicates the fundamental research ethics question of personhood. Is an avatar a person? Is one's digital information an extension of the self? In the U.S. regulatory system, the primary question has generally been: Are we working with human subjects or not? If information is collected directly from individuals, such as an email exchange, instant message, or an interview in a virtual world, we are likely to naturally define the research scenario as one that involves a person. If the connection between the object of research and the person who produced it is indistinct, there may be a tendency to define the research scenario as one that does not involve any persons. This may oversimplify the situation–the question of whether one is dealing with a human subject is different from the question about whether information is linked to individuals: Can we assume a person is wholly removed from large data pools? For example, a data set containing thousands of tweets or an aggregation of surfing behaviors collected from a bot is perhaps far removed from the persons who engaged in these activities. In these scenarios, it is possible to forget that there was ever a person somewhere in the process that could be directly or indirectly impacted by the research. Yet there is considerable evidence that even 'anonymized' datasets that contain enough personal information can result in individuals being identifiable. Scholars and technologists continue to wrestle with how to adequately protect individuals when analyzing such datasets (Sweeny, 2009; Narayanan & Shmatikov, 2008, 2009).

These three issues represent ongoing tensions for internet research. Although researchers might like straightforward answers to questions such as "Will capturing a person's Tweets cause them harm?" or "Is a blog a public or private space," the uniqueness and almost endless range of specific situations has defied attempts to provide universal answers. The Association of Internet Researchers (Markham & Buchanan, 2012) has created a guide called Ethical Decision-Making and Internet Research that provides a detailed discussion of these issues.

Key Takeaways
• Researchers must obtain the informed consent of the people who participate in their research.
• Social workers must take steps to minimize the harms that could arise during the research process.
• If a researcher promises anonymity, she cannot link individual participants with their data.
• If a researcher promises confidentiality, she promises not to reveal the identities of research participants, even though she can link individual participants with their data.
• The NASW Code of Ethics includes specific responsibilities for social work researchers.
• Internet research is increasingly common and has its own unique set of ethical considerations.

Glossary

- Anonymity- the identity of research participants is not known to researchers
- Confidentiality- identifying information about research participants is known to the researchers but is not divulged to anyone else
- Informed consent- a research subject's voluntary agreement to participate in a study based on a full understanding of the study and of the possible risks and benefits involved

Image attributions

consent by Catkin CC-0

Figure 3.1 is copied from Blackstone, A. (2012) Principles of sociological inquiry: Qualitative and quantitative methods. Saylor Foundation. Retrieved from: https://saylordotorg.github.io/text_principles-of-sociological-inquiry-qualitative-and-quantitative-methods/ Shared under CC-BY-NC-SA 3.0 License

Anonymous by kalhh CC-0

3.3 ETHICS AT MICRO, MESO, AND MACRO LEVELS

Learning Objectives

- Identify and distinguish between micro-, meso-, and macro-level considerations with respect to the ethical conduct of social scientific research

One useful way to think about the breadth of ethical questions that might arise out of any research project is to think about potential issues from the perspective of different analytical levels. In Chapter 1, you learned about the micro-, meso-, and macro-levels of inquiry and how a researcher's specific point of focus might vary depending on her level of inquiry. Here we'll apply this ecological framework to a discussion of research ethics. Within most research projects, there are specific questions that arise for researchers at each of these three levels.

At the micro-level, researchers must consider their own conduct and the rights of individual research participants. For example, did Stanley Milgram behave ethically when he allowed research participants to think that they were administering electronic shocks to fellow participants? Did Laud Humphreys behave ethically when he deceived his research subjects about his own identity? Were the rights of individuals in these studies protected? The questions posed here are the sort that you will want to ask yourself as a researcher when considering ethics at the micro-level.

At the meso-level, researchers should think about their duty to the community. How will the results of your study impact your target population? Ideally, your results will benefit your target population by identifying important areas for social workers to intervene. However, it is possible that your study may perpetuate negative stereotypes about your target population or damage its reputation. Indigenous people in particular have highlighted how historically social science has furthered marginalization of indigenous peoples (Smith, 2013). In addition to your target population, you must also consider your responsibilities to the profession of social work. When you engage in social work research, you stand on the reputation the profession has built for over a century. Attending to research ethics helps to fulfill your responsibilities to the profession, in addition to your target population.

Finally, at the macro-level, researchers should consider their duty to, and the expectations of, society. Perhaps the most high-profile case involving macro-level questions of research ethics comes from debates over whether to use data gathered by, or cite published studies based on data gathered from, the Nazis in the course of their unethical and horrendous experiments on humans during World War II (Moe, 1984). Some argue that because the data were gathered in such an unquestionably unethical manner, they should never be used. Further, some who argue against using the Nazi data point out that not only were the experiments immoral but the methods used to collect data were also scientifically questionable. The data, say these people, are neither valid nor reliable and should therefore not be used in any current scientific investigation (Berger, 1990).

On the other hand, some people argue that data themselves are neutral; that "information gathered is independent of the ethics of the methods and that the two are not linked together" (Pozos, 1992, p. 104). Others point out that not using the data could inadvertently strengthen the claims of those who deny that the Holocaust ever happened. In his striking statement in support of publishing the data, medical ethics professor Velvl Greene (1992) says,

> Instead of banning the Nazi data or assigning it to some archivist or custodial committee, I maintain that it be exhumed, printed, and disseminated to every medical school in the world along with the details of methodology and the names of the doctors who did it, whether or not they were indicted, acquitted, or hanged....Let the students and the residents and the young doctors know that this was not ancient history or an episode from a horror movie where the actors get up after filming and prepare for another role. It was real. It happened yesterday (p. 169–170).

While debates about the use of data collected by the Nazis are typically centered on medical scientists' use of them, there are conceivable circumstances under which these data might be used by social scientists. Perhaps, for example, a social scientist might wish to examine contemporary reactions to the experiments. Or perhaps the data could be used in a study of the sociology of science. What do you think? Should data gathered by the Nazis be used or cited today? What arguments can you make in support of your position, and how would you respond to those who disagree? Table 3.1 summarizes the key questions that researchers might ask themselves about the ethics of their research at each level of inquiry.

Table 3.1 Key ethics questions at three different levels of inquiry

Level of inquiry	Focus	Key ethics questions for researchers to ask themselves
Micro-level	Individual	Does my research impinge on the individual's right to privacy?
		Could my research offend subjects in any way?
		Could my research cause emotional distress to any of my subjects?
		Has my own conduct been ethical throughout the research process?
Meso-level	Group	Does my research follow the ethical guidelines of my profession and discipline?
		Could my research negatively impact a community?
		Have I met my duty to those who funded my research?
Macro-level	Society	Does my research meet the societal expectations of social research?
		Have I met my social responsibilities as a researcher?

Key Takeaways

- At the micro-level, researchers should consider their own conduct and the rights of individual research participants.

- At the meso-level, researchers should consider the expectations of their profession, any organizations that may have funded their research, and the communities affected by their research.

- At the macro-level, researchers should consider their duty to and the expectations of society with respect to social scientific research.

3.4 THE PRACTICE OF SCIENCE VERSUS THE USES OF SCIENCE

Learning Objectives

- Identify why researchers must provide a detailed description of methodology
- Describe what it means to use science in an ethical way

Research ethics has to do with both how research is conducted and how findings from that research are used. In this section, we'll consider research ethics from both angles.

DOING SCIENCE THE ETHICAL WAY

As you should now be aware, researchers must consider their own personal ethical principles in addition to following those of their institution, their discipline, and their community. We've already considered many of the ways that social workers strive to ensure the ethical practice of research, such as informing and protecting subjects. But the practice of ethical research doesn't end once subjects have been identified and data have been collected. Social workers must also fully disclose their research procedures and findings. This means being honest about how research subjects were identified and recruited, how exactly data were collected and analyzed, and ultimately, what findings were reached.

If researchers fully disclose how they conducted their research, then those who use their work to build research projects, create social policies, or make decisions can have confidence in the work. By sharing how research was conducted, a researcher helps assure readers she has conducted legitimate research and didn't simply come to whatever conclusions she *wanted* to find. A description or presentation of research findings that is not accompanied by information about research methodology is missing some relevant information. Sometimes methodological details are left out because there isn't time or space to share them. This is often the case with news reports of research findings. Other times, there may be a more insidious reason that that important information isn't there. This may be the case if sharing methodological details would call the legitimacy of a study into question. As researchers, it is our ethical responsibility to fully disclose our research procedures. As consumers of research, it is our ethical responsibility to pay attention to such details. We'll discuss this more in the next section.

There's a New Yorker cartoon that depicts a set of filing cabinets that aptly demonstrates what we don't want to see happen with research. Each filing cabinet drawer in the cartoon is labeled differently. The labels include such headings as, "Our Facts," "Their Facts," "Neutral Facts," "Disputable Facts," "Absolute Facts," "Bare Facts," "Unsubstantiated Facts," and "Indisputable Facts." The implication of this cartoon is that one might just choose to open the file drawer of her choice and pick whichever facts one likes best. While this may occur if we use some of the unscientific ways of knowing described in Chapter 1, it is fortunately not how the discovery of facts works in social work or in any other science for that matter. There actually is a method to this madness we call research.

Honesty in research is facilitated by the scientific principle of replication. Ideally, this means that one scientist could repeat another's study with relative ease. By replicating a study, we may become more (or less) confident in the original study's findings. Replication is far more difficult (perhaps impossible) to achieve in the case of ethnographic studies that last months or years, but it nevertheless sets an important standard for all social scientific researchers—that we provide as much detail as possible about the processes by which we reach our conclusions.

HONESTY

Full disclosure also includes the need to be honest about a study's strengths and weaknesses, both with oneself and with others. Being aware of the strengths and weaknesses of their own work can help researchers make reasonable recommendations about the next steps other researchers might consider taking in their inquiries. Awareness and disclosure of a study's strengths and weaknesses can also help highlight the theoretical or policy implications of one's work. In addition, openness about strengths and weaknesses helps those reading the research better evaluate the work and decide for themselves how or whether to rely on its findings. Finally, openness about a study's sponsors is crucial. How can we effectively evaluate research without knowing who paid the bills?

The standard of replicability along with openness about a study's strengths, weaknesses, and funders enable those who read the research to evaluate it fairly and completely. Knowledge of funding sources is often raised as an issue in medical research. Understandably, independent studies of new drugs may be more compelling to the Food and Drug Administration (FDA) than studies touting the virtues of a new drug that happen to have been funded by the company who created that drug. But medical researchers aren't the only ones who need to be honest about their funding. If we know, for example, that a political think tank with ties to a particular party has funded some research, we can take that knowledge into consideration when reviewing the study's findings and stated policy implications. Lastly, and related to this point, we must consider how, by whom, and for what purpose research may be used.

USING SCIENCE THE ETHICAL WAY

Science has many uses. Here, the word "use" means the ways that science is understood and applied (as opposed to the way it is conducted). Some use science to create laws and social policies; others use it to understand themselves and those around them. Some people rely on science to improve their life conditions or those of other people, while still others use it to improve their businesses or other undertakings. In each case, the most ethical way for us to use science is to educate ourselves about the design and purpose of any studies we may wish to use or apply, to recognize our limitations in terms of scientific and methodological knowledge and how those limitations may impact our understanding of research, and to apply the findings of scientific investigation only in cases or to populations for which they are actually relevant.

Social scientists who conduct research on behalf of organizations and agencies may face additional ethical questions about the use of their research, particularly when the organization for which a study is conducted controls the final report and the publicity it receives. There is a potential conflict of interest for evaluation researchers who are employees of the agency being evaluated. A similar conflict of interest might exist between independent researchers whose work is being funded by some government agency or private foundation.

So who decides what constitutes ethical conduct or use of research? Perhaps we all do. What qualifies as ethical research may shift over time and across cultures as individual researchers; disciplinary organizations; members of society; and regulatory entities, such as institutional review boards, courts, and lawmakers all work to define the boundaries between ethical and unethical research.

Key Takeaways

- Conducting research ethically requires that researchers be ethical not only in their data collection procedures but also in reporting their methods and findings.
- The ethical use of research requires an effort to understand research, an awareness of your own limitations in terms of knowledge and understanding, and the honest application of research findings.

Image attributions

honesty by GDJ CC-0

CHAPTER FOUR: DESIGN AND CAUSALITY

Chapter 2 oriented you to the theories relevant to your topic area; the macro, meso, or micro levels of analysis; and the assumptions or paradigms of research. This chapter will use these elements to help you conceptualize and design your research project. You will make specific choices about the purpose of your research, quantitative or qualitative methods, and establishing causality. You'll also learn how and why researchers use both qualitative and quantitative methods in the same study.

CHAPTER OUTLINE

- 4.1 Types of research
- 4.2 Causality
- 4.3 Unit of analysis and unit of observation
- 4.4 Mixed methods

CONTENT ADVISORY

This chapter discusses or mentions the following topics: child neglect and abuse, sexual harassment, the criminal justice system, homelessness, sexual and domestic violence, depression, and substance abuse.

4.1 TYPES OF RESEARCH

Learning Objectives

- Differentiate between exploratory, descriptive, and explanatory research

A recent news story about college students' addictions to electronic gadgets (Lisk, 2011) describes findings from some research by Professor Susan Moeller and colleagues from the University of Maryland. The story raises a number of interesting questions. Just what sorts of gadgets are students addicted to? How do these addictions work? Why do they exist, and who is most likely to experience them?

Social science research is great for answering just these sorts of questions. But in order to answer our questions well, we must take care in designing our research projects. In this chapter, we'll consider what aspects of a research project should be considered at the beginning, including specifying the goals of the research, the components that are common across most research projects, and a few other considerations.

DESIGN

One of the first things to think about when designing a research project is what you hope to accomplish, in very general terms, by conducting the research. What do you hope to be able to say about your topic? Do you hope to gain a deep understanding of whatever phenomenon it is that you're studying, or would you rather have a broad, but perhaps less deep, understanding? Do you want your research to be used by policymakers or others to shape social life, or is this project more about exploring your curiosities? Your answers to each of these questions will shape your research design.

EXPLORATION, DESCRIPTION, AND EXPLANATION

You'll need to decide in the beginning phases whether your research will be exploratory, descriptive, or explanatory. Each has a different purpose, so how you design your research project will be determined in part by this decision.

Researchers conducting **exploratory research** are typically at the early stages of examining their topics. These sorts of projects are usually conducted when a researcher wants to test the feasibility of conducting a more extensive study and to figure out the "lay of the land" with respect to the particular topic. Perhaps very little prior research has been conducted on this subject. If this is the case, a researcher may wish to do some exploratory work to learn what method to use in collecting data, how best to approach research subjects, or even what sorts of questions are reasonable to ask. A researcher wanting to simply satisfy her own curiosity about a topic could also conduct exploratory research. In the case of the study of college students' addictions to their electronic gadgets, a researcher conducting exploratory research on this topic may simply wish to learn more about students' use of these gadgets. Because these addictions seemed to be a relatively new phenomenon, an exploratory study of the topic made sense as an initial first step toward understanding it.

It is important to note that exploratory designs do not make sense for topic areas with a lot of existing research. For example, the question "What are common interventions for parents who neglect their children?" would not make much sense as a research question. One could simply look at journal articles and textbooks to see what interventions are commonly used with this population. Exploratory questions are best suited to topics that have not been studied. Students may sometimes say there is not much literature on their chosen topic, when there is in fact a large body of literature on that topic. However, that said, there are a few students each semester who pick a topic for which there is little existing research. Perhaps, if you were looking at child neglect interventions for parents who identify as transgender or parents who are refugees from the Syrian civil war, less would be known about child neglect for those specific populations. In that case, an exploratory design would make sense as there is less literature to guide your study.

Descriptive research is used to describe or define a particular phenomenon. For example, a social work researcher may want to understand what it means to be a first-generation college student or a resident in a psychiatric group home. In this case, descriptive research would be an appropriate strategy. A descriptive study of college students' addictions to their electronic gadgets, for example, might aim to describe patterns in how many hours students use gadgets or which sorts of gadgets students tend to use most regularly.

Researchers at the *Princeton Review* conduct descriptive research each year when they set out to provide students and their parents with information about colleges and universities around the United States. They describe the social life at a school, the cost of admission, and student-to-faculty ratios (to name just a few of the categories reported). Although students and parents may be able to obtain much of this information on their own, having access to the data gathered by a team of researchers is much more convenient and less time consuming.

Social workers often rely on descriptive research to tell them about their service area. Keeping track of the number of children receiving foster care services, their demographic makeup (e.g., race, gender), and length of time in care are excellent examples of descriptive research. On a more macro-level, the Centers for Disease Control provides a remarkable amount of descriptive research on mental and physical health conditions. In fact, descriptive research has many useful applications, and you probably rely on findings from descriptive research without even being aware that that is what you are doing.

Finally, social work researchers often aim to explain why particular phenomena work in the way that they do. Research that answers "why" questions is referred to as **explanatory** research. In this case, the researcher is trying to identify the causes and effects of whatever phenomenon she is studying. An explanatory study of college students' addictions to their electronic gadgets might aim to understand why students become addicted. Does it have anything to do with their family histories? With their other extracurricular hobbies and activities? With whom they spend their time? An explanatory study could answer these kinds of questions.

There are numerous examples of explanatory social scientific investigations. For example, in one study, Dominique Simons and Sandy Wurtele (2010) sought to discover whether receiving corporal punishment from parents led children to turn to violence in solving their interpersonal conflicts with other children. In their study of 102 families with children between the ages of 3 and 7, the researchers found that experiencing frequent spanking did, in fact, result in children being more likely to accept aggressive problem-solving techniques. Another example of explanatory research can be seen in Robert Faris and Diane Felmlee's (2011) research on the connections between popularity and bullying. From their study of 8th, 9th, and 10th graders in 19 North Carolina schools, they found that aggression increased as adolescents' popularity increased. (This pattern was found until adolescents reached the top 2% in the popularity ranks. After that, aggression declines).

The choice between descriptive, exploratory, and explanatory research should be made with your research question in mind. What does your question ask? Are you trying to learn the basics about a new area, establish a clear "why" relationship, or define or describe an activity or concept? In the next section, we will explore how each type of research is associated with different methods, paradigms, and forms of logic.

Key Takeaways

- Exploratory research is usually conducted when a researcher has just begun an investigation and wishes to understand the topic generally.
- Descriptive research is research that aims to describe or define the topic at hand.
- Explanatory research is research that aims to explain why particular phenomena work in the way that they do.

Glossary

- Descriptive research- research that describes or define a particular phenomenon
- Explanatory research- explains why particular phenomena work in the way that they do, answers "why" questions

- Exploratory research- conducted during the early stages of a project, usually when a researcher wants to test the feasibility of conducting a more extensive study

Image attributions

Pencil by kaboompics CC-0

Two men and one woman in a photo by Rawpixel.com CC-0

4.2 CAUSALITY

Learning Objectives

- Define and provide an example of idiographic and nomothetic causal explanations
- Describe the role of causality in quantitative research as compared to qualitative research
- Identify, define, and describe each of the main criteria for nomothetic causal explanations
- Describe the difference between and provide examples of independent, dependent, and control variables
- Define hypothesis, be able to state a clear hypothesis, and discuss the respective roles of quantitative and qualitative research when it comes to hypotheses

Most social scientific studies attempt to provide some kind of causal explanation. In other words, it is about cause and effect. A study on an intervention to prevent child abuse is trying to draw a connection between the intervention and changes in child abuse. **Causality** refers to the idea that one event, behavior, or belief will result in the occurrence of another, subsequent event, behavior, or belief. It seems simple, but you may be surprised to learn there is more than one way to explain how one thing causes another. How can that be? How could there be many ways to understand causality?

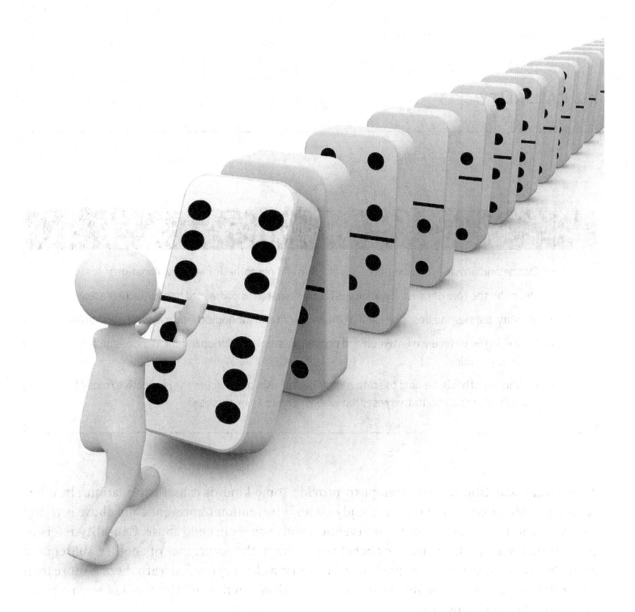

Think back to our chapter on paradigms, which were analytic lenses comprised of assumptions about the world. You'll remember the positivist paradigm as the one that believes in objectivity and social constructionist paradigm as the one that believes in subjectivity. Both paradigms are correct, though incomplete, viewpoints on the social world and social science.

A researcher operating in the social constructionist paradigm would view truth as subjective.

In causality, that means that in order to try to understand what caused what, we would need to report what people tell us. Well, that seems pretty straightforward, right? Well, what if two different people saw the same event from the exact same viewpoint and came up with two totally different explanations about what caused what? A social constructionist might say that both people are correct. There is not one singular truth that is true for everyone, but many truths created and shared by people.

When social constructionists engage in science, they are trying to establish one type of causality—idiographic causality. The word *idiographic* comes from the root word "idio" which means peculiar to one, personal, and distinct. An **idiographic causal explanation** means that you will attempt to explain or describe your phenomenon exhaustively, based on the subjective understandings of your participants. Idiographic causal explanations are intended to explain one particular context or phenomenon. These explanations are bound with the narratives people create about their lives and experience, and are embedded in a cultural, historical, and environmental context. Idiographic causal explanations are so powerful because they convey a deep understanding of a phenomenon and its context. From a social constructionist perspective, the truth is messy. Idiographic research involves finding patterns and themes in the causal themes established by your research participants.

If that doesn't sound like what you normally think of as "science," you're not alone. Although the ideas behind idiographic research are quite old in philosophy, they were only applied to the sciences at the start of the last century. If we think of famous Western scientists like Newton or Darwin, they never saw truth as subjective. They operated with the understanding there were objectively true laws of science that were applicable in all situations. In their time, another paradigm—the positivist paradigm—was dominant and continues its dominance today. When positivists try to establish causality, they are like Newton and Darwin, trying to come up with a broad, sweeping explanation that is universally true for all people. This is the hallmark of a **nomothetic causal explanation**. The word *nomothetic* is derived from the root word "nomo" which means related to a law or legislative, and "thetic" which means something that establishes. Put the root words together and it means something that is establishing a law, or in our case, a universal explanation.

Nomothetic causal explanations are incredibly powerful. They allow scientists to make predictions about what will happen in the future, with a certain margin of error. Moreover, they allow scientists to **generalize**—that is, make claims about a large population based on a smaller sample of people or items. Generalizing is important. We clearly do not have time to ask everyone their opinion on a topic, nor do we have the ability to look at every interaction in the social world. We need a type of causal explanation that helps us predict and estimate truth in all situations.

If these still seem like obscure philosophy terms, let's consider an example. Imagine you are working for a community-based non-profit agency serving people with disabilities. You are putting together a report to help lobby the state government for additional funding for community support programs, and you need to support your argument for additional funding at your agency. If you looked at nomothetic research, you might learn how previous studies have shown that, in general, community-based programs like yours are linked with better health and employment outcomes for people with disabilities. Nomothetic research seeks to explain that community-based programs are better for *everyone* with disabilities. If you looked at idiographic research, you would get stories and experiences of people in community-based programs. These individual stories are full of detail about the lived experience of being in a community-based program. Using idiographic research, you can understand what it's like to be a person with a disability and then communicate that to the state government. For example, a person might say "I feel at home when I'm at this agency because they treat me like a family member" or "this is the agency that helped me get my first paycheck."

Neither kind of causal explanation is better than the other. A decision to conduct idiographic research means that you will attempt to explain or describe your phenomenon exhaustively, attending to cultural context and subjective interpretations. A decision to conduct nomothetic research, on the other hand, means that you will try to explain what is true for everyone and predict what will be true in the future. In short, idiographic explanations have greater depth, and nomothetic explanations have greater breadth. More importantly, social workers understand the value of both approaches to understanding the social world. A social worker helping a client with substance abuse issues seeks idiographic knowledge when they ask about that client's life story, investigate their unique physical environment, or probe how they understand their addiction. At the same time, a social worker also uses nomothetic knowledge to guide their interventions. Nomothetic research may help guide them to minimize risk factors and maximize protective factors or use an evidence-based therapy, relying on knowledge about what *in general* helps people with substance abuse issues.

NOMOTHETIC CAUSAL EXPLANATIONS

If you are trying to generalize about causality, or create a nomothetic causal explanation, then the rest of these statements are likely to be true: you will use quantitative methods, reason deductively, and engage in explanatory research. How can we make that prediction? Let's take it part by part.

Because nomothetic causal explanations try to generalize, they must be able to reduce phenomena to a universal language, mathematics. Mathematics allows us to precisely measure, in universal terms, phenomena in the social world. Because explanatory researchers want a clean "x causes y" explanation, they need to use the universal language of mathematics to achieve their goal. That's why nomothetic causal explanations use quantitative methods. It's helpful to note that not all quantitative studies are explanatory. For example, a descriptive study could reveal the number of people without homes in your county, though it won't tell you why they are homeless. But nearly all explanatory studies are quantitative.

What we've been talking about here is an association between variables. When one variable precedes or predicts another, we have what researchers call independent and dependent variables. Two variables can be associated without having a causal relationship. However, when certain conditions are met (which we describe later in this chapter), the independent variable is considered as a "*cause*" of the dependent variable. For our example on spanking and aggressive behavior, spanking would be the independent variable and aggressive behavior addiction would be the dependent variable. In causal explanations, the **independent variable** is the cause, and the **dependent variable** is the effect. Dependent variables *depend* on independent variables. If all of that gets confusing, just remember this graphical depiction:

Figure 4.1 Visual representation of a nomothetic causal explanation

The strength of the association between the independent variable and dependent variable is another important factor to take into consideration when attempting to make causal claims when your research approach is nomothetic. In this context, strength refers to **statistical significance**. When the association between two variables is shown to be statistically significant, we can have greater confidence that the data from our sample reflect a true association between those variables in the target population. Statistical significance is usually represented in statistics as the ***p*-value**. Generally a *p*-value of .05 or less indicates the association between the two variables is statistically significant.

A **hypothesis** is a statement describing a researcher's expectation regarding the research findings. Hypotheses in quantitative research are nomothetic causal explanations that the researcher expects to demonstrate. Hypotheses are written to describe the expected association between the independent and dependent variables. Your prediction should be taken from a theory or model of the social world. For example, you may hypothesize that treating clinical clients with warmth and positive regard is likely to help them achieve their therapeutic goals. That hypothesis would be using the humanistic theories of Carl Rogers. Using previous theories to generate hypotheses is an example of deductive research. If Rogers' theory of unconditional positive regard is accurate, your hypothesis should be true.

Let's consider a couple of examples. In research on sexual harassment (Uggen & Blackstone, 2004), one might hypothesize, based on feminist theories of sexual harassment, that more females than males will experience specific sexually harassing behaviors. What is the causal explanation being predicted here? Which is the independent and which is the dependent variable? In this case, we hypothesized that a person's gender (independent variable) would predict their likelihood to experience sexual harassment (dependent variable).

Sometimes researchers will hypothesize that an association will take a specific direction. As a result, an increase or decrease in one area might be said to cause an increase or decrease in another. For example, you might choose to study the association between age and support for legalization of marijuana. Perhaps you've taken a sociology class and, based on the theories you've read, you hypothesize that age is negatively related to support for marijuana legalization. In fact, there are empirical data that support this hypothesis. Gallup has conducted research on this very question since the 1960s (Carroll, 2005). What have you just hypothesized? You have hypothesized that as people get older, the likelihood of their supporting marijuana legalization decreases. Thus, as age (your independent variable) moves in one direction (up), support for marijuana legalization (your dependent variable) moves in another direction (down). So, **positive associations** involve two variables going in the same direction and **negative associations** involve two variables going in opposite directions. If writing hypotheses feels tricky, it is sometimes helpful to draw them out and depict each of the two hypotheses we have just discussed.

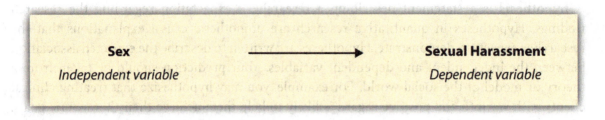

Figure 4.2 Hypothesis describing the expected association between sex and sexual harassment

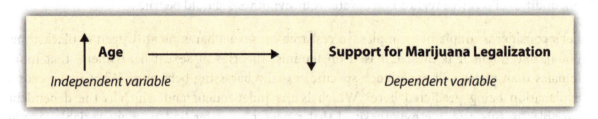

Figure 4.3 Hypothesis describing the expected direction of association between age and support for marijuana legalization

It's important to note that once a study starts, it is unethical to change your hypothesis to match the data that you found. For example, what happens if you conduct a study to test the hypothesis from Figure 4.3 on support for marijuana legalization, but you find no association between age and support for legalization? It means that your hypothesis was wrong, but that's still valuable information. It would challenge what the existing literature says on your topic, demonstrating that more research needs to be done to figure out the factors that impact support for marijuana legalization. Don't be embarrassed by negative results, and definitely don't change your hypothesis to make it appear correct all along!

ESTABLISHING CAUSALITY IN NOMOTHETIC RESEARCH

Let's say you conduct your study and you find evidence that supports your hypothesis, as age increases, support for marijuana legalization decreases. Success! Causal explanation complete, right? Not quite. You've only established one of the criteria for causality. The main criteria for causality have to do with covariation, plausibility, temporality, and spuriousness. In our example from Figure 4.3, we have established only one criteria—covariation. When variables **covary**, they vary together. Both age and support for marijuana legalization vary in our study. Our sample contains people of varying ages and varying levels of support for marijuana legalization and they vary together in a patterned way–when age increases, support for legalization decreases.

Just because there might be some correlation between two variables does not mean that a causal explanation between the two is really plausible. **Plausibility** means that in order to make the claim that one event, behavior, or belief causes another, the claim has to make sense. It makes sense that people from previous generations would have different attitudes towards marijuana than younger generations. People who grew up in the time of Reefer Madness or the hippies may hold different views than those raised in an era of legalized medicinal and recreational use of marijuana.

Once we've established that there is a plausible association between the two variables, we also need to establish that the cause happened before the effect, the criterion of **temporality**. A person's age is a quality that appears long before any opinions on drug policy, so temporally the cause comes before the effect. It wouldn't make any sense to say that support for marijuana legalization makes a person's age increase. Even if you could predict someone's age based on their support for marijuana legalization, you couldn't say someone's age was caused by their support for legalization.

Finally, scientists must establish nonspuriousness. A **spurious association** is one in which an association between two variables appears to be causal but can in fact be explained by some third variable. For example, we could point to the fact that older cohorts are less likely to have used marijuana. Maybe it is actually use of marijuana that leads people to be more open to legalization, not their age. This is often referred to as the third variable problem, where a seemingly true causal explanation is actually caused by a third variable not in the hypothesis. In this example, the association between age and support for legalization could be more about having tried marijuana than the age of the person.

Quantitative researchers are sensitive to the effects of potentially spurious associations. They are an important form of critique of scientific work. As a result, they will often measure these third variables in their study, so they can control for their effects. These are called **control variables**, and they refer to variables whose effects are controlled for mathematically in the data analysis process. Control variables can be a bit confusing, but think about it as an argument between you, the researcher, and a critic.

Researcher: "The older a person is, the less likely they are to support marijuana legalization."

Critic: "Actually, it's more about whether a person has used marijuana before. That is what truly determines whether someone supports marijuana legalization."

Researcher: "Well, I measured previous marijuana use in my study and mathematically controlled for its effects in my analysis. The association between age and support for marijuana legalization is still statistically significant and is the most important association here."

Let's consider a few additional, real-world examples of spuriousness. Did you know, for example, that high rates of ice cream sales have been shown to cause drowning? Of course, that's not really true, but there is a positive association between the two. In this case, the third variable that causes both high ice cream sales and increased deaths by drowning is time of year, as the summer season sees increases in both (Babbie, 2010). Here's another good one: it is true that as the salaries of Presbyterian ministers in Massachusetts rise, so too does the price of rum in Havana, Cuba. Well, duh, you might be saying to yourself. Everyone knows how much ministers in Massachusetts love their rum, right? Not so fast. Both salaries and rum prices have increased, true, but so has the price of just about everything else (Huff & Geis, 1993).

Finally, research shows that the more firefighters present at a fire, the more damage is done at the scene. What this statement leaves out, of course, is that as the size of a fire increases so too does the amount of damage caused as does the number of firefighters called on to help (Frankfort-Nachmias & Leon-Guerrero, 2011). In each of these examples, it is the presence of a third variable that explains the apparent association between the two original variables.

In sum, the following criteria must be met for a correlation to be considered causal:

- The two variables must vary together.
- The association must be plausible.
- The cause must precede the effect in time.
- The association must be nonspurious (not due to a third variable).

Once these criteria are met, there is a nomothetic causal explanation, one that is objectively true. However, this is difficult for researchers to achieve. You will almost never hear researchers say that they have *proven* their hypotheses. A statement that bold implies that a association has been shown to exist with absolute certainty and that there is no chance that there are conditions under which the hypothesis would not be true. Instead, researchers tend to say that their hypotheses have been supported (or not). This more cautious way of discussing findings allows for the possibility that new evidence or new ways of examining an association will be discovered. Researchers may also discuss a null hypothesis. The null hypothesis is one that predicts no association between the variables being studied. If a researcher fails to accept the null hypothesis, she is saying that the variables in question are likely to be related to one another.

IDIOGRAPHIC CAUSAL EXPLANATIONS

If you not trying to generalize, but instead are trying to establish an idiographic causal explanation, then you are likely going to use qualitative methods, reason inductively, and engage in exploratory or descriptive research. We can understand these assumptions by walking through them, one by one.

Researchers seeking idiographic causal explanation are not trying to generalize, so they have no need to reduce phenomena to mathematics. In fact, using the language of mathematics to reduce the social world down is a bad thing, as it robs the causality of its meaning and context. Idiographic causal explanations are bound within people's stories and interpretations. Usually, these are expressed through words. Not all qualitative studies analyze words, as some can use interpretations of visual or performance art, but the vast majority of social science studies do.

But wait, we predicted that an idiographic causal explanation would use descriptive or exploratory research. How can we build causality if we are just describing or exploring a topic? Wouldn't we need to do explanatory research to build any kind of causal explanation? To clarify, explanatory research attempts to establish nomothetic causal explanations—an independent variable is demonstrated to cause changes a dependent variable. Exploratory and descriptive qualitative research are actually descriptions of the causal explanations established by the participants in your study. Instead of saying "x causes y," your participants will describe their experiences with "x," which they will tell you was caused by and influenced a variety of other factors, depending on time, environment, and subjective experience. As stated before, idiographic causal explanations are messy. The job of a social science researcher is to accurately identify patterns in what participants describe.

Let's consider an example. What would you say if you were asked why you decided to become a social worker? If we interviewed many social workers about their decisions to become social workers, we might begin to notice patterns. We might find out that many social workers begin their careers based on a variety of factors, such as: personal experience with a disability or social injustice, positive experiences with social workers, or a desire to help others. No one factor is the "most important factor," like with nomothetic causal explanations. Instead, a complex web of factors, contingent on context, emerge in the dataset when you interpret what people have said.

Finding patterns in data, as you'll remember from Chapter 2, is what inductive reasoning is all about. A qualitative researcher collects data, usually words, and notices patterns. Those patterns inform the theories we use in social work. In many ways, the idiographic causal explanations created in qualitative research are like the social theories we reviewed in Chapter 2 and other theories you use in your practice and theory courses. Theories are explanations about how different concepts are associated with each other how that network of associations works in the real world. While you can think of theories like Systems Theory as Theory (with a capital "T"), inductive causality is like theory with a small "t." It may apply only to the participants, environment, and moment in time in which the data were gathered. Nevertheless, it contributes important information to the body of knowledge on the topic studied.

Unlike nomothetic causal explanations, there are no formal criteria (e.g., covariation) for establishing causality in idiographic causal explanations. In fact, some criteria like temporality and nonspuriousness may be violated. For example, if an adolescent client says, "It's hard for me to tell whether my depression began before my drinking, but both got worse when I was expelled from my first high school," they are recognizing that oftentimes it's not so simple that one thing causes another. Sometimes, there is a reciprocal association where one variable (depression) impacts another (alcohol abuse), which then feeds back into the first variable (depression) and also into other variables (school). Other criteria, such as covariation and plausibility still make sense, as the associations you highlight as part of your idiographic causal explanation should still be plausibly true and it elements should vary together.

Similarly, idiographic causal explanations differ in terms of hypotheses. If you recall from the last section, hypotheses in nomothetic causal explanations are testable predictions based on previous theory. In idiographic research, instead of predicting that "x will decrease y," researchers will use previous literature to figure out what concepts might be important to participants and how they believe participants might respond during the study. Based on an analysis of the literature a researcher may formulate a few *tentative hypotheses* about what they expect to find in their qualitative study. Unlike nomothetic hypotheses, these are likely to change during the research process. As the researcher learns more from their participants, they might introduce new concepts that participants talk about. Because the participants are the experts in idiographic causal explanation, a researcher should be open to emerging topics and shift their research questions and hypotheses accordingly.

COMPLEMENTARY APPROACHES TO CAUSALITY

Over time, as more qualitative studies are done and patterns emerge across different studies and locations, more sophisticated theories emerge that explain phenomena across multiple contexts. In this way, qualitative researchers use idiographic causal explanations for **theory building** or the creation of new theories based on inductive reasoning. Quantitative researchers, on the other hand, use nomothetic causal explanations for **theory testing**, wherein a hypothesis is created from existing theory (big T or small t) and tested mathematically (i.e., deductive reasoning). Once a theory is developed from qualitative data, a quantitative researcher can seek to test that theory. In this way, qualitatively-derived theory can inspire a hypothesis for a quantitative research project.

TWO DIFFERENT BASKETS

Idiographic and nomothetic causal explanations form the "two baskets" of research design elements pictured in Figure 4.4 below. Later on, they will also determine the sampling approach, measures, and data analysis in your study.

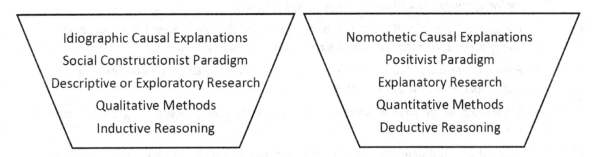

Figure 4.4: Two baskets (or approaches) to research

In most cases, mixing components from one basket with the other would not make sense. If you are using quantitative methods with an idiographic question, you wouldn't get the deep understanding you need to answer an idiographic question. Knowing, for example, that someone scores 20/35 on a numerical index of depression symptoms does not tell you what depression means to that person. Similarly, qualitative methods are not often used to deductive reasoning because qualitative methods usually seek to understand a participant's perspective, rather than test what existing theory says about a concept.

However, these are not hard-and-fast rules. There are plenty of qualitative studies that attempt to test a theory. There are fewer social constructionist studies with quantitative methods, though studies will sometimes include quantitative information about participants. Researchers in the critical paradigm can fit into either bucket, depending on their research question, as they focus on the liberation of people from oppressive internal (subjective) or external (objective) forces.

We will explore later on in this chapter how researchers can use both buckets simultaneously in mixed methods research. For now, it's important that you understand the logic that connects the ideas in each bucket. Not only is this fundamental to how knowledge is created and tested in social work, it speaks to the very assumptions and foundations upon which all theories of the social world are built!

Key Takeaways

- Idiographic research focuses on subjectivity, context, and meaning.
- Nomothetic research focuses on objectivity, prediction, and generalizing.
- In qualitative studies, the goal is generally to understand the multitude of causes that account for the specific instance the researcher is investigating.
- In quantitative studies, the goal may be to understand the more general causes of some phenomenon rather than the idiosyncrasies of one particular instance.
- For nomothetic causal explanations, an association must be plausible and nonspurious, and the cause must precede the effect in time.
- In a nomothetic causal explanations, the independent variable causes changes in a dependent variable.
- Hypotheses are statements, drawn from theory, which describe a researcher's expectation about an association between two or more variables.
- Qualitative research may create theories that can be tested quantitatively.
- The choice of idiographic or nomothetic causal explanation requires a consideration of methods, paradigm, and reasoning.
- Depending on whether you seek a nomothetic or idiographic causal explanation, you are likely to employ specific research design components.

Glossary

- Causality-the idea that one event, behavior, or belief will result in the occurrence of another, subsequent event, behavior, or belief

- Control variables- potential "third variables" effects are controlled for mathematically in the data analysis process to highlight the relationship between the independent and dependent variable

- Covariation- the degree to which two variables vary together

- Dependent variable- a variable that depends on changes in the independent variable

- Generalize- to make claims about a larger population based on an examination of a smaller sample

- Hypothesis- a statement describing a researcher's expectation regarding what she anticipates finding

- Idiographic research- attempts to explain or describe your phenomenon exhaustively, based on the subjective understandings of your participants

- Independent variable- causes a change in the dependent variable

- Nomothetic research- provides a more general, sweeping explanation that is universally true for all people

- Plausibility- in order to make the claim that one event, behavior, or belief causes another, the claim has to make sense

- Spurious relationship- an association between two variables appears to be causal but can in fact be explained by some third variable

- Statistical significance- confidence researchers have in a mathematical relationship

- Temporality- whatever cause you identify must happen before the effect

- Theory building- the creation of new theories based on inductive reasoning

- Theory testing- when a hypothesis is created from existing theory and tested mathematically

Image attributions

Mikado by 3dman_eu CC-0

Weather TV Forecast by mohamed_hassan CC-0

Figures 4.2 and 4.3 were copied from Blackstone, A. (2012) Principles of sociological inquiry: Qualitative and quantitative methods. Saylor Foundation. Retrieved from: https://saylordotorg.github.io/text_principles-of-sociological-inquiry-qualitative-and-quantitative-methods/ Shared under CC-BY-NC-SA 3.0 License

Beatrice Birra Storytelling at African Art Museum by Anthony Cross public domain

4.3 UNIT OF ANALYSIS AND UNIT OF OBSERVATION

Learning Objectives

- Define units of analysis and units of observation, and describe the two common errors people make when they confuse the two

Another point to consider when designing a research project, and which might differ slightly in qualitative and quantitative studies, has to do with units of analysis and units of observation. These two items concern what you, the researcher, actually observe in the course of your data collection and what you hope to be able to say about those observations. A **unit of analysis** is the entity that you wish to be able to say something about at the end of your study, probably what you'd consider to be the main focus of your study. A **unit of observation** is the item (or items) that you actually observe, measure, or collect in the course of trying to learn something about your unit of analysis.

In a given study, the unit of observation might be the same as the unit of analysis, but that is not always the case. For example, a study on electronic gadget addiction may interview undergraduate students (our unit of observation) for the purpose of saying something about undergraduate students (our unit of analysis) and their gadget addiction. Perhaps, if we were investigating gadget addiction in elementary school children (our unit of analysis), we might collect observations from teachers and parents (our units of observation) because younger children may not report their behavior accurately. In this case and many others, units of analysis are not the same as units of observation. What is required, however, is for researchers to be clear about how they define their units of analysis and observation, both to themselves and to their audiences.

More specifically, your unit of analysis will be determined by your research question. Your unit of observation, on the other hand, is determined largely by the method of data collection that you use to answer that research question. We'll take a closer look at methods of data collection later on in the textbook. For now, let's consider again a study addressing students' addictions to electronic gadgets. We'll consider first how different kinds of research questions about this topic will yield different units of analysis. Then, we'll think about how those questions might be answered and with what kinds of data. This leads us to a variety of units of observation.

If we were to explore which students are most likely to be addicted to their electronic gadgets, our unit of analysis would be individual students. We might mail a survey to students on campus, and our aim would be to classify individuals according to their membership in certain social groups in order to see how membership in those classes correlated with gadget addiction. For example, we might find that majors in new media, men, and students with high socioeconomic status are all more likely than other students to become addicted to their electronic gadgets. Another possibility would be to explore how students' gadget addictions differ and how are they similar. In this case, we could conduct observations of addicted students and record when, where, why, and how they use their gadgets. In both cases, one using a survey and the other using observations, data are collected from individual students. Thus, the unit of observation in both examples is the individual.

Another common unit of analysis in social science inquiry is groups. Groups of course vary in size, and almost no group is too small or too large to be of interest to social scientists. Families, friendship groups, and group therapy participants are some common examples of micro-level groups examined by social scientists. Employees in an organization, professionals in a particular domain (e.g., chefs, lawyers, social workers), and members of clubs (e.g., Girl Scouts, Rotary, Red Hat Society) are all meso-level groups that social scientists might study. Finally, at the macro-level, social scientists sometimes examine policies, citizens of entire nations, or residents of different continents or other regions.

A study of student addictions to their electronic gadgets at the group level might consider whether certain types of social clubs have more or fewer gadget-addicted members than other sorts of clubs. Perhaps we would find that clubs that emphasize physical fitness, such as the rugby club and the scuba club, have fewer gadget-addicted members than clubs that emphasize cerebral activity, such as the chess club and the women's studies club. Our unit of analysis in this example is groups because groups are what we hope to say something about. If we had instead asked whether individuals who join cerebral clubs are more likely to be gadget-addicted than those who join social clubs, then our unit of analysis would have been individuals. In either case, however, our unit of observation would be individuals.

Organizations are yet another potential unit of analysis that social scientists might wish to say something about. Organizations include entities like corporations, colleges and universities, and even nightclubs. At the organization level, a study of students' electronic gadget addictions might explore how different colleges address the problem of electronic gadget addiction. In this case, our interest lies not in the experience of individual students but instead in the campus-to-campus differences in confronting gadget addictions. A researcher conducting a study of this type might examine schools' written policies and procedures, so her unit of observation would be documents. However, because she ultimately wishes to describe differences across campuses, the college would be her unit of analysis.

In sum, there are many potential units of analysis that a social worker might examine, but some of the most common units include the following: individuals, groups, and organizations.

Table 4.1 Units of analysis and units of observation: An example using a hypothetical study of students' addictions to electronic gadgets

Research question	Unit of analysis	Data collection	Unit of observation	Statement of findings
Which students are most likely to be addicted to their electronic gadgets?	Individuals	Survey of students on campus	Individuals	New Media majors, men, and students with high socioeconomic status are all more likely than other students to become addicted to their electronic gadgets.
Do certain types of social clubs have more gadget-addicted members than other sorts of clubs?	Groups	Survey of students on campus	Individuals	Clubs with a scholarly focus, such as social work club and the math club, have more gadget-addicted members than clubs with a social focus, such as the 100-bottles-of-beer-on-the-wall club and the knitting club.
How do different colleges address the problem of electronic gadget addiction?	Organizations	Content analysis of policies	Documents	Campuses without strong computer science programs are more likely than those with such programs to expel students who have been found to have addictions to their electronic gadgets.

Note: Please remember that the findings described here are hypothetical. There is no reason to think that any of the hypothetical findings described here would actually bear out if tested with empirical research.

One common error people make when it comes to both causality and units of analysis is something called the **ecological fallacy**. This occurs when claims about one lower-level unit of analysis are made based on data from some higher-level unit of analysis. In many cases, this occurs when claims are made about individuals, but only group-level data have been gathered. For example, we might want to understand whether electronic gadget addictions are more common on certain campuses than on others. Perhaps different campuses around the country have provided us with their campus percentage of gadget-addicted students, and we learn from these data that electronic gadget addictions are more common on campuses that have business programs than on campuses without them. We then conclude that business students are more likely than non-business students to become addicted to their electronic gadgets. However, this would be an inappropriate conclusion to draw. Because we only have addiction rates by campus, we can only draw conclusions about campuses, not about the individual students on those campuses. Perhaps the social work majors on the business campuses are the ones that caused the addiction rates on those campuses to be so high. The point is we simply don't know because we only have campus-level data. By drawing conclusions about students when our data are about campuses, we run the risk of committing the ecological fallacy.

On the other hand, another mistake to be aware of is reductionism. **Reductionism** occurs when claims about some higher-level unit of analysis are made based on data from some lower-level unit of analysis. In this case, claims about groups or macro-level phenomena are made based on individual-level data. An example of reductionism can be seen in some descriptions of the civil rights movement. On occasion, people have proclaimed that Rosa Parks started the civil rights movement in the United States by refusing to give up her seat to a white person while on a city bus in Montgomery, Alabama, in December 1955. Although it is true that Parks played an invaluable role in the movement, and that her act of civil disobedience gave others courage to stand up against racist policies, beliefs, and actions, to credit Parks with starting the movement is reductionist. Surely the confluence of many factors, from fights over legalized racial segregation to the Supreme Court's historic decision to desegregate schools in 1954 to the creation of groups such as the Student Nonviolent Coordinating Committee (to name just a few), contributed to the rise and success of the American civil rights movement. In other words, the movement is attributable to many factors—some social, others political and others economic. Did Parks play a role? Of course she did—and a very important one at that. But did she cause the movement? To say yes would be reductionist.

It would be a mistake to conclude from the preceding discussion that researchers should avoid making any claims whatsoever about data or about relationships between levels of analysis. While it is important to be attentive to the possibility for error in causal reasoning about different levels of analysis, this warning should not prevent you from drawing well-reasoned analytic conclusions from your data. The point is to be cautious and conscientious in making conclusions between levels of analysis. Errors in analysis come from a lack of rigor and deviating from the scientific method.

Key Takeaways

- A unit of analysis is the item you wish to be able to say something about at the end of your study while a unit of observation is the item that you actually observe.

- When researchers confuse their units of analysis and observation, they may be prone to committing either the ecological fallacy or reductionism.

- Ecological fallacy- claims about one lower-level unit of analysis are made based on data from some higher-level unit of analysis

- Reductionism- when claims about some higher-level unit of analysis are made based on data at some lower-level unit of analysis

- Unit of analysis- entity that a researcher wants to say something about at the end of her study

- Unit of observation- the item that a researcher actually observes, measures, or collects in the course of trying to learn something about her unit of analysis

Image attributions

Binoculars by nightowl CC-0

4.4 MIXED METHODS

Learning Objectives

- Define sequence and emphasis and describe how they work in qualitative research
- List the five reasons why researchers use mixed methods

So far in this textbook, we have talked about quantitative and qualitative methods as an either/or choice—you can choose quantitative methods or qualitative methods. However, researchers often use both methods inside of their research projects. Take for example a recent study of the possibility of having optometrists refer their older patients to group exercise programs (Miyawaki, Mauldin, & Carman, 2019). In this study, a short, written survey was distributed to optometrists across Texas. The survey asked closed-ended questions about their practice, knowledge about fall prevention, and attitudes about prescribing group exercise programs to their patients. While the study could have just surveyed optometrists for a descriptive quantitative analysis, it was designed to capture more rich details about the perspectives of older optometry patients through conducting focus groups with them. In the focus groups, the older adults were asked about their perceptions of being prescribed group exercise classes by their optometrist. The study used both qualitative and quantitative methods, or a mixed methods design.

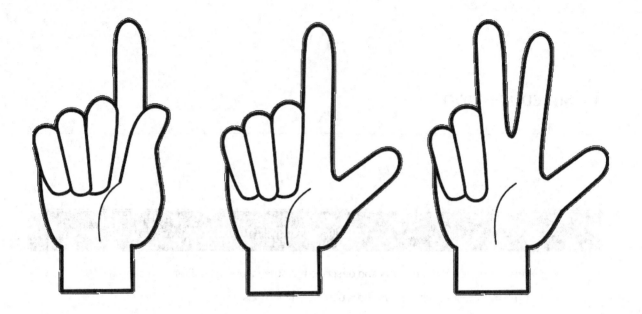

SEQUENCE AND EMPHASIS

There are many different mixed methods designs, each with their own strengths. However, a more simplified synthesis of mixed methods approaches is provided by Engel and Schutt (2016) using two key terms. **Sequence** refers to the order that each method is used. Researchers can use both methods at the same time or *concurrently*. Or, they can use one and then the other, or *sequentially*. The optometry study used a concurrent design in which data were collected and analyzed concurrently. The researchers could have used a sequential design in which one part of the study was conducted first, data analyzed, and then used to inform the researchers about how to conduct the second part of the study.

The other key term in mixed methods research is **emphasis**. In some studies, the qualitative data may be the most important, with the quantitative data providing secondary or background information. In this case qualitative methods are *prioritized*. Other times, however, quantitative methods are emphasized. In these studies, qualitative data are used mainly to provide context for the quantitative findings. For example, demonstrating quantitatively that a particular therapy works is important. By adding a qualitative component, researchers could find out how the participants experienced the intervention, how they understood its effects, and the meaning it had on their lives. These data would add depth and context to the findings of the study and allow researchers to improve the therapeutic technique in the future.

A similar practice is when researchers use qualitative methods to solicit feedback on a quantitative scale or measure. The experiences of individuals allow researchers to refine the measure before they do the quantitative component of their study. Finally, it is possible that researchers are equally interested in qualitative and quantitative information. In studies of *equal emphasis*, researchers consider both methods as the focus of the research project.

WHY RESEARCHERS USE MIXED METHODS

Mixed methods research is more than just sticking an open-ended question at the end of a quantitative survey. Mixed methods researchers use mixed methods for both pragmatic and synergistic reasons. That is, they use both methods because it makes sense with their research questions and because they will get the answers they want by combining the two approaches.

Mixed methods also allows you to use both inductive and deductive reasoning. As we've discussed, qualitative research follows inductive logic, moving from data to empirical generalizations or theory. In a mixed methods study, a researcher could use the results from a qualitative component to inform a subsequent quantitative component. The quantitative component would use deductive logic, using the theory derived from qualitative data to create and test a hypothesis. In this way, mixed methods use the strengths of both research methods, using each method to understand different parts of the same phenomenon. Quantitative allows the researcher to test new ideas. Qualitative allows the researcher to create new ideas.

With these two concepts in mind, we can start to see why researchers use mixed methods in the real world. Mixed methods are often to initiate ideas with one method to study with another. For example, researchers could begin a mixed methods project by using qualitative methods to interview or conduct a focus group with participants. Based on their responses, the researchers could then formulate a quantitative project to follow up on the results.

In addition to providing information for subsequent investigation, using both quantitative and qualitative information provides additional context for the data. For example, in the optometry/group exercise study, most optometrists expressed that they would be willing to prescribe exercise classes to their patients. In the focus groups, the patients were able to describe how they would respond to receiving a prescription from their optometrist and the barriers they faced to going to exercise classes. The context provided by the qualitative focus group data provides important context for practitioners building clinical-community partnerships to help prevent falls among older adults.

Finally, another purpose of mixed methods research is corroborating data from both quantitative and qualitative sources. Ideally, your qualitative and quantitative results should support each other. For example, if interviews with participants showed a relationship between two concepts, that relationship should also be present in the qualitative data you collected. Differences between quantitative and qualitative data require an explanation. Perhaps there are outliers or extreme cases that pushed your data in one direction or another, for example.

In summary, these are a few of the many reasons researchers use mixed methods. They are summarized below:

1. Triangulation or convergence on the same phenomenon to improve validity
2. Complementarity, which aims to get at related but different facets of a phenomenon
3. Development or the use of results from one phase or a study to develop another phase
4. Initiation or the intentional analysis of inconsistent qualitative and quantitative findings to derive new insights
5. Expansion or using multiple components to extend the scope of a study (Burnett, 2012, p. 77).

A WORD OF CAUTION

The use of mixed methods has many advantages. However, researchers should approach mixed methods with caution. Conducting a mixed methods study may mean doubling or even tripling your work. You must conceptualize how to use one method, another method, and how they fit together. This may mean operationalizing and creating a questionnaire, then writing an interview guide, and thinking through how the data on each measure relate to one another—more work than using one quantitative or qualitative method alone. Similarly, in sequential studies, the researcher must collect and analyze data from one component and then conceptualize and conduct the second component. This may also impact how long a project may take. Before beginning a mixed methods project, you should have a clear vision for what the project will entail and how each methodology will contribute to that vision.

Key Takeaways

- Mixed methods studies vary in sequence and emphasis.
- Mixed methods allow the research to corroborate findings, provide context, follow up on ideas, and use the strengths of each method.

Glossary

- Emphasis- in a mixed methods study, refers to the priority that each method is given
- Sequence- in a mixed methods study, refers to the order that each method is used, either concurrently or sequentially

Image attributions

one two three/ un deux trois by Improulx CC-0

caution by geralt CC-0

CHAPTER FIVE: DEFINING AND MEASURING CONCEPTS

This chapter is mainly focused on quantitative research methods, as the level of specificity required to begin quantitative research is far greater than that of qualitative research. In quantitative research, you must specify how you define and plan to measure each concept before you can interact with your participants. In qualitative research, definitions emerge from how participants respond to your questions. Because your participants are the experts, qualitative research does not begin with defining concepts at the level of specificity and clarity required for quantitative research. For this reason, we will focus mostly on quantitative measurement and conceptualization in this chapter, addressing qualitative research later in the textbook.

CHAPTER OUTLINE

- 5.1 Measurement
- 5.2 Conceptualization
- 5.3 Levels of measurement
- 5.4 Operationalization
- 5.5 Measurement quality
- 5.6 Challenges in quantitative measurement

CONTENT ADVISORY

This chapter includes information or discusses measuring depression and loneliness among residents of an assisted living facility.

5.1 MEASUREMENT

Learning Objectives

- Define measurement
- Describe Kaplan's three categories of the things that social scientists measure

Measurement is important. Recognizing that fact, and respecting it, will be of great benefit to you—both in research methods and in other areas of life as well. Measurement is critical to successfully pulling off a social scientific research project. In social science, when we use the term **measurement** we mean the process by which we describe and ascribe meaning to the key facts, concepts, or other phenomena that we are investigating. At its core, measurement is about defining one's terms in as clear and precise a way as possible. Of course, measurement in social science isn't quite as simple as using a measuring cup or spoon, but there are some basic tenants on which most social scientists agree when it comes to measurement. We'll explore those, as well as some of the ways that measurement might vary depending on your unique approach to the study of your topic.

WHAT DO SOCIAL SCIENTISTS MEASURE?

 The question of what social scientists measure can be answered by asking yourself what social scientists study. Think about the topics you've learned about in other social work classes you've taken or the topics you've considered investigating yourself. Let's consider Melissa Milkie and Catharine Warner's study (2011) of first graders' mental health. In order to conduct that study, Milkie and Warner needed to have some idea about how they were going to measure mental health. What does mental health mean, exactly? And how do we know when we're observing someone whose mental health is good and when we see someone whose mental health is compromised? Understanding how measurement works in research methods helps us answer these sorts of questions.

As you might have guessed, social scientists will measure just about anything that they have an interest in investigating. For example, those who are interested in learning something about the correlation between social class and levels of happiness must develop some way to measure both social class and happiness. Those who wish to understand how well immigrants cope in their new locations must measure immigrant status and coping. Those who wish to understand how a person's gender shapes their workplace experiences must measure gender and workplace experiences. You get the idea. Social scientists can and do measure just about anything you can imagine observing or wanting to study. Of course, some things are easier to observe or measure than others.

In 1964, philosopher Abraham Kaplan (1964) wrote *The Conduct of Inquiry,* which has since become a classic work in research methodology (Babbie, 2010). In his text, Kaplan describes different categories of things that behavioral scientists observe. One of those categories, which Kaplan called "observational terms," is probably the simplest to measure in social science. **Observational terms** are the sorts of things that we can see with the naked eye simply by looking at them. They are terms that "lend themselves to easy and confident verification" (Kaplan, 1964, p. 54). If, for example, we wanted to know how the conditions of playgrounds differ across different neighborhoods, we could directly observe the variety, amount, and condition of equipment at various playgrounds.

Indirect observables, on the other hand, are less straightforward to assess. They are "terms whose application calls for relatively more subtle, complex, or indirect observations, in which inferences play an acknowledged part. Such inferences concern presumed connections, usually causal, between what is directly observed and what the term signifies" (Kaplan, 1964, p. 55). If we conducted a study for which we wished to know a person's income, we'd probably have to ask them their income, perhaps in an interview or a survey. Thus, we have observed income, even if it has only been observed indirectly. Birthplace might be another indirect observable. We can ask study participants where they were born, but chances are good we won't have directly observed any of those people being born in the locations they report.

Sometimes the measures that we are interested in are more complex and more abstract than observational terms or indirect observables. Think about some of the concepts you've learned about in other social work classes—for example, ethnocentrism. What is ethnocentrism? Well, from completing an introduction to social work class you might know that it has something to do with the way a person judges another's culture. But how would you *measure* it? Here's another construct: bureaucracy. We know this term has something to do with organizations and how they operate, but measuring such a construct is trickier than measuring, say, a person's income. In both cases, ethnocentrism and bureaucracy, these theoretical notions represent ideas whose meaning we have come to agree on. Though we may not be able to observe these abstractions directly, we can observe the things that they are made up of.

Kaplan referred to these more abstract things that behavioral scientists measure as constructs. **Constructs** are "not observational either directly or indirectly" (Kaplan, 1964, p. 55), but they can be defined based on observables. For example, the construct of bureaucracy could be measured by counting the number of supervisors that need to approve routine spending by public administrators. The greater the number of administrators that must sign off on routine matters, the greater the degree of bureaucracy. Similarly, we might be able to ask a person the degree to which they trust people from different cultures around the world and then assess the ethnocentrism inherent in their answers. We can measure constructs like bureaucracy and ethnocentrism by defining them in terms of what we can observe.

Thus far, we have learned that social scientists measure what Kaplan called observational terms, indirect observables, and constructs. These terms refer to the different sorts of things that social scientists may be interested in measuring. But *how* do social scientists measure these things? That is the next question we'll tackle.

HOW DO SOCIAL SCIENTISTS MEASURE?

Measurement in social science is a process. It occurs at multiple stages of a research project: in the planning stages, in the data collection stage, and sometimes even in the analysis stage. Recall that previously we defined measurement as the process by which we describe and ascribe meaning to the key facts, concepts, or other phenomena that we are investigating. Once we've identified a research question, we begin to think about what some of the key ideas are that we hope to learn from our project. In describing those key ideas, we begin the measurement process.

Let's say that our research question is the following: How do new college students cope with the adjustment to college? In order to answer this question, we'll need some idea about what coping means. We may come up with an idea about what coping means early in the research process, as we begin to think about what to look for (or observe) in our data-collection phase. Once we've collected data on coping, we also have to decide how to report on the topic. Perhaps, for example, there are different types or dimensions of coping, some of which lead to more successful adjustment than others. However we decide to proceed, and whatever we decide to report, the point is that measurement is important at each of these phases.

As the preceding example demonstrates, measurement is a process in part because it occurs at multiple stages of conducting research. We could also think of measurement as a process because it involves multiple stages. From identifying your key terms to defining them to figuring out how to observe them and how to know if your observations are any good, there are multiple steps involved in the measurement process. An additional step in the measurement process involves deciding what elements your measures contain. A measure's elements might be very straightforward and clear, particularly if they are directly observable. Other measures are more complex and might require the researcher to account for different themes or types. These sorts of complexities require paying careful attention to a concept's level of measurement and its dimensions. We'll explore these complexities in greater depth at the end of this chapter, but first let's look more closely at the early steps involved in the measurement process, starting with conceptualization.

Key Takeaways

- Measurement is the process by which we describe and ascribe meaning to the key facts, concepts, or other phenomena that we are investigating.

- Kaplan identified three categories of things that social scientists measure including observational terms, indirect observables, and constructs.

- Measurement occurs at all stages of research.

Glossary

- Constructs- are not observable but can be defined based on observable characteristics
- Indirect observables- things that require indirect observation and inference to measure
- Measurement- the process by which researchers describe and ascribe meaning to the key facts, concepts, or other phenomena they are investigating
- Observational terms- things that we can see with the naked eye simply by looking at them

Image attributions

measuring tape by unknown CC-0

human observer by geralt CC-0

5.2 CONCEPTUALIZATION

Learning Objectives

- Define concept
- Identify why defining our concepts is important
- Describe how conceptualization works in quantitative and qualitative research
- Define dimensions in terms of social scientific measurement
- Apply reification to conceptualization

In this section, we'll take a look at one of the first steps in the measurement process, which is conceptualization. This has to do with defining our terms as clearly as possible and also not taking ourselves too seriously in the process. Our definitions mean only what we say they mean—nothing more and nothing less. Let's talk first about how to define our terms, and then we'll examine not taking ourselves (or our terms, rather) too seriously.

CONCEPTS AND CONCEPTUALIZATION

So far, the word *concept* has come up quite a bit, and it would behoove us to make sure we have a shared understanding of that term. A **concept** is the notion or image that we conjure up when we think of some cluster of related observations or ideas. For example, masculinity is a concept. What do you think of when you hear that word? Presumably, you imagine some set of behaviors and perhaps even a particular style of self-presentation. Of course, we can't necessarily assume that everyone conjures up the same set of ideas or images when they hear the word *masculinity*. In fact, there are many possible ways to define the term. And while some definitions may be more common or have more support than others, there isn't one true, always-correct-in-all-settings definition. What counts as masculine may shift over time, from culture to culture, and even from individual to individual (Kimmel, 2008). This is why defining our concepts is so important.

You might be asking yourself why you should bother defining a term for which there is no single, correct definition. Believe it or not, this is true for any concept you might measure in a research study—there is never a single, always-correct definition. When we conduct empirical research, our terms mean only what we say they mean. There's a *New Yorker* cartoon that aptly represents this idea. It depicts a young George Washington holding an axe and standing near a freshly chopped cherry tree. Young George is looking up at a frowning adult who is standing over him, arms crossed. The caption depicts George explaining, "It all depends on how you define 'chop.'" Young George Washington gets the idea—whether he actually chopped down the cherry tree depends on whether we have a shared understanding of the term *chop*.

Without a shared understanding of this term, our understandings of what George has just done may differ. Likewise, without understanding how a researcher has defined her key concepts, it would be nearly impossible to understand the meaning of that researcher's findings and conclusions. Thus, any decision we make based on findings from empirical research should be made based on full knowledge not only of how the research was designed, but also of how its concepts were defined and measured.

So, how do we define our concepts? This is part of the process of measurement, and this portion of the process is called conceptualization. The answer depends on how we plan to approach our research. We will begin with quantitative conceptualization and then discuss qualitative conceptualization.

In quantitative research, **conceptualization** involves writing out clear, concise definitions for our key concepts. Sticking with the previously mentioned example of masculinity, think about what comes to mind when you read that term. How do you know masculinity when you see it? Does it have something to do with men? With social norms? If so, perhaps we could define masculinity as the social norms that men are expected to follow. That seems like a reasonable start, and at this early stage of conceptualization, brainstorming about the images conjured up by concepts and playing around with possible definitions is appropriate. However, this is just the first step.

It would make sense as well to consult other previous research and theory to understand if other scholars have already defined the concepts we're interested in. This doesn't necessarily mean we must use their definitions, but understanding how concepts have been defined in the past will give us an idea about how our conceptualizations compare with the predominant ones out there. Understanding prior definitions of our key concepts will also help us decide whether we plan to challenge those conceptualizations or rely on them for our own work. Finally, working on conceptualization is likely to help in the process of refining your research question to one that is specific and clear in what it asks.

If we turn to the literature on masculinity, we will surely come across work by Michael Kimmel, one of the preeminent masculinity scholars in the United States. After consulting Kimmel's prior work (2000; 2008), we might tweak our initial definition of masculinity just a bit. Rather than defining masculinity as "the social norms that men are expected to follow," perhaps instead we'll define it as "the social roles, behaviors, and meanings prescribed for men in any given society at any one time" (Kimmel & Aronson, 2004, p. 503). Our revised definition is both more precise and more complex. Rather than simply addressing one aspect of men's lives (norms), our new definition addresses three aspects: roles, behaviors, and meanings. It also implies that roles, behaviors, and meanings may vary across societies and over time. To be clear, we'll also have to specify the particular society and time period we're investigating as we conceptualize masculinity.

As you can see, conceptualization isn't quite as simple as merely applying any random definition that we come up with to a term. Sure, it may involve some initial brainstorming, but conceptualization goes beyond that. Once we've brainstormed a bit about the images a particular word conjures up for us, we should also consult prior work to understand how others define the term in question. And after we've identified a clear definition that we're happy with, we should make sure that every term used in our definition will make sense to others. Are there terms used within our definition that also need to be defined? If so, our conceptualization is not yet complete. And there is yet another aspect of conceptualization to consider—concept dimensions. We'll consider that aspect along with an additional word of caution about conceptualization in the next subsection.

CONCEPTUALIZATION IN QUALITATIVE RESEARCH

Conceptualization in qualitative research proceeds a bit differently than in quantitative research. Because qualitative researchers are interested in the understandings and experiences of their participants, it is less important for the researcher to find one fixed definition for a concept before starting to interview or interact with participants. The researcher's job is to accurately and completely represent how their participants understand a concept, not to test their own definition of that concept.

If you were conducting qualitative research on masculinity, you would likely consult previous literature like Kimmel's work mentioned above. From your literature review, you may come up with a *working definition* for the terms you plan to use in your study, which can change over the course of the investigation. However, the definition that matters is the definition that your participants share during data collection. A working definition is merely a place to start, and researchers should take care not to think it is the only or best definition out there.

In qualitative inquiry, your participants are the experts (sound familiar, social workers?) on the concepts that arise during the research study. Your job as the researcher is to accurately and reliably collect and interpret their understanding of the concepts they describe while answering your questions. Conceptualization of qualitative concepts is likely to change over the course of qualitative inquiry, as you learn more information from your participants. Indeed, getting participants to comment on, extend, or challenge the definitions and understandings of other participants is a hallmark of qualitative research. This is the opposite of quantitative research, in which definitions must be completely set in stone before the inquiry can begin.

A WORD OF CAUTION ABOUT CONCEPTUALIZATION

Whether you have chosen qualitative or quantitative methods, you should have a clear definition for the term *masculinity* and make sure that the terms we use in our definition are equally clear—and then we're done, right? Not so fast. If you've ever met more than one man in your life, you've probably noticed that they are not all exactly the same, even if they live in the same society and at the same historical time period. This could mean there are dimensions of masculinity. In terms of social scientific measurement, concepts can be said to have **multiple dimensions** when there are multiple elements that make up a single concept. With respect to the term *masculinity*, dimensions could be regional (is masculinity defined differently in different regions of the same country?), age-based (is masculinity defined differently for men of different ages?), or perhaps power-based (does masculinity differ based on membership to privileged groups?). In any of these cases, the concept of masculinity would be considered to have multiple dimensions. While it isn't necessarily required to spell out every possible dimension of the concepts you wish to measure, it may be important to do so depending on the goals of your research. The point here is to be aware that some concepts have dimensions and to think about whether and when dimensions may be relevant to the concepts you intend to investigate.

Before we move on to the additional steps involved in the measurement process, it would be wise to remind ourselves not to take our definitions too seriously. Conceptualization must be open to revisions, even radical revisions, as scientific knowledge progresses. Although that we should consult prior scholarly definitions of our concepts, it would be wrong to assume that just because prior definitions exist that they are more real than the definitions we create (or, likewise, that our own made-up definitions are any more real than any other definition). It would also be wrong to assume that just because definitions exist for some concept that the concept itself exists beyond some abstract idea in our heads. This idea, assuming that our abstract concepts exist in some concrete, tangible way, is known as **reification**.

To better understand reification, take a moment to think about the concept of social structure. This concept is central to critical thinking. When social scientists talk about social structure, they are talking about an abstract concept. Social structures shape our ways of being in the world and of interacting with one another, but they do not exist in any concrete or tangible way. A social structure isn't the same thing as other sorts of structures, such as buildings or bridges. Sure, both types of structures are important to how we live our everyday lives, but one we can touch, and the other is just an idea that shapes our way of living.

Here's another way of thinking about reification: Think about the term *family*. If you were interested in studying this concept, we've learned that it would be good to consult prior theory and research to understand how the term has been conceptualized by others. But we should also question past conceptualizations. Think, for example, about how different the definition of family was 50 years ago. Because researchers from that time period conceptualized family using now outdated social norms, social scientists from 50 years ago created research projects based on what we consider now to be a very limited and problematic notion of what family means. Their definitions of family were as real to them as our definitions are to us today. If researchers never challenged the definitions of terms like family, our scientific knowledge would be filled with the prejudices and blind spots from years ago. It makes sense to come to some social agreement about what various concepts mean. Without that agreement, it would be difficult to navigate through everyday living. But at the same time, we should not forget that we have assigned those definitions, they are imperfect and subject to change as a result of critical inquiry.

Key Takeaways

- Conceptualization is a process that involves coming up with clear, concise definitions.
- Conceptualization in quantitative research comes from the researcher's ideas or the literature.
- Qualitative researchers conceptualize by creating working definitions which will be revised based on what participants say.
- Some concepts have multiple elements or dimensions.
- Researchers should acknowledge the limitations of their definitions for concepts.

Glossary

- Concept- notion or image that we conjure up when we think of some cluster of related observations or ideas
- Conceptualization- writing out clear, concise definitions for our key concepts, particularly in quantitative research
- Multi-dimensional concepts- concepts that are comprised of multiple elements

- Reification- assuming that abstract concepts exist in some concrete, tangible way

Image attributions

thought by TeroVesalainen CC-0

mindmap by TeroVesalainen CC-0

5.3 LEVELS OF MEASUREMENT

Learning Objectives

- Define and provide examples for the four levels of measurement

Now that we have figured out how to define, or conceptualize, our terms we'll need to think about operationalizing them. **Operationalization** is the process by which researchers *conducting quantitative research* spell out precisely how a concept will be measured. It involves identifying the specific research procedures we will use to gather data about our concepts. This of course requires that we know what research method(s) we will employ to learn about our concepts, and we'll examine specific research methods later on in the text. For now, let's take a broad look at how operationalization works. We can then revisit how this process works when we examine specific methods of data collection in later chapters. Remember, operationalization is only a process in quantitative research. Measurement in qualitative research will be discussed at the end of this section.

LEVELS OF MEASUREMENT

When social scientists measure concepts, they sometimes use the language of variables and attributes (also called *values*). A **variable** refers to a phenomenon that can vary. It can be thought of as a grouping of several characteristics. For example, hair color could be a variable because it has varying characteristics. **Attributes** are the characteristics that make up a variable. For example, the variable hair color would contain attributes like blonde, brown, black, red, gray, etc.

A variable's attributes determine its **level of measurement**. There are four possible levels of measurement: *nominal, ordinal, interval,* and *ratio*. The first two levels of measurement are **categorical**, meaning their attributes are categories rather than numbers. The latter two levels of measurement are **continuous**, meaning their attributes are numbers, not categories.

NOMINAL LEVEL OF MEASUREMENT

Hair color is an example of a nominal level of measurement. **Nominal** measures are categorical, and those categories cannot be mathematically ranked. There is no ranking order between hair colors. They are simply different. That is what constitutes a nominal level of measurement. Gender and race are also measured at the nominal level.

When using nominal level of measurement in research, it is very important to assign the attributes of potential answers very precisely. The attributes need to be *exhaustive* and *mutually exclusive*. Let's think about the attributes contained in the variable *hair color*. Black, brown, blonde, and red are common colors. But, if we listed only these attributes, people with gray hair wouldn't fit anywhere. That means our attributes were not exhaustive. **Exhaustiveness** means that all possible attributes are listed. We may have to list a lot of colors before we can meet the criteria of exhaustiveness. Clearly, there is a point at which trying to achieve exhaustiveness can get to be too much. If a person insists that their hair color is *light burnt sienna*, it is not your responsibility to list that as an option. Rather, that person could reasonably be described as brown-haired. Perhaps listing a category for *other color* would suffice to make our list of colors exhaustive.

What about a person who has multiple hair colors at the same time, such as red and black? They would fall into multiple attributes. This violates the rule of **mutual exclusivity**, in which a person cannot fall into two different attributes. Instead of listing all of the possible combinations of colors, perhaps you might include a list of attributes like *all black, all brown, all blonde, all red, multi-color, other* to include people with more than one hair color, but keep everyone in only one category.

The discussion of hair color elides an important point with measurement—reification. You should remember reification from our previous discussion in this chapter. For many years, the attributes for gender were male and female. Now, our understanding of gender has evolved to encompass more attributes including transgender, non-binary, or genderqueer. We shouldn't confuse our labeling of attributes or measuring of a variable with the objective truth "out there." Another example could be children of parents from different races were often classified as one race or another in the past, even if they identified with both cultures equally. The option for bi-racial or multi-racial on a survey not only more accurately reflects the racial diversity in the real world but validates and acknowledges people who identify in that manner.

ORDINAL LEVEL OF MEASUREMENT

Unlike nominal-level measures, attributes at the **ordinal** level can be rank ordered. For example, someone's degree of satisfaction in their romantic relationship can be ordered by rank. That is, you could say you are not at all satisfied, a little satisfied, moderately satisfied, or highly satisfied. Note that even though these have a rank order to them (not at all satisfied is certainly worse than highly satisfied), we cannot calculate a mathematical distance between those attributes. We can simply say that one attribute of an ordinal-level variable is more or less than another attribute.

This can get a little confusing when using **Likert scales**. If you have ever taken a customer satisfaction survey or completed a course evaluation for school, you are familiar with Likert scales. "On a scale of 1-5, with one being the lowest and 5 being the highest, how likely are you to recommend our company to other people?" Sound familiar? Likert scales use numbers but only as a shorthand to indicate what attribute (highly likely, somewhat likely, etc.) the person feels describes them best. You wouldn't say you are "2" more likely to recommend the company. But you could say you are not very likely to recommend the company.

Ordinal-level attributes must also be exhaustive and mutually exclusive, as with nominal-level variables.

INTERVAL LEVEL OF MEASUREMENT

At the **interval** level, the distance between attributes is known to be equal. Interval measures are also continuous, meaning their attributes are numbers, rather than categories. IQ scores are interval level, as are temperatures. Interval-level variables are not particularly common in social science research, but their defining characteristic is that we can say how much more or less one attribute differs from another. We cannot, however, say with certainty what the ratio of one attribute is in comparison to another. For example, it would not make sense to say that 50 degrees is half as hot as 100 degrees. But we can say it is 50 degrees cooler than 100. At the interval level, attributes must also be exhaustive and mutually exclusive.

RATIO LEVEL OF MEASUREMENT

Finally, at the **ratio** level, attributes can be rank ordered, the distance between attributes is equal, and attributes have a true zero point. Thus, with these variables, we *can* say what the ratio of one attribute is in comparison to another. Examples of ratio-level variables include age and years of education. We know, for example, that a person who is 12 years old is twice as old as someone who is 6 years old. Just like all other levels of measurement, at the ratio level, attributes must be mutually exclusive and exhaustive.

The differences between each level of measurement are visualized in Table 5.1.

Table 5.1 Criteria for Different Levels of Measurement

	Nominal	Ordinal	Interval	Ratio
Exhaustive	X	X	X	X
Mutually exclusive	X	X	X	X
Rank-ordered		X	X	X
Equal distance between attributes			X	X
Can compare ratios of the values (e.g., twice as large)				X
True zero point				X

Key Takeaways

- In social science, our variables can be one of four different levels of measurement: nominal, ordinal, interval, or ratio.

Glossary

- Categorical measures- a measure with attributes that are categories
- Continuous measures- a measures with attributes that are numbers
- Exhaustiveness- all possible attributes are listed
- Interval level- a level of measurement that is continuous, can be rank ordered, is exhaustive and mutually exclusive, and for which the distance between attributes is known to be equal
- Likert scales- ordinal measures that use numbers as a shorthand (e.g., 1=highly likely,

2=somewhat likely, etc.) to indicate what attribute the person feels describes them best

- Mutual exclusivity- a person cannot identify with two different attributes simultaneously
- Nominal- level of measurement that is categorical and those categories cannot be mathematically ranked, though they are exhaustive and mutually exclusive
- Ordinal- level of measurement that is categorical, those categories can be rank ordered, and they are exhaustive and mutually exclusive
- Ratio level- level of measurement in which attributes are mutually exclusive and exhaustive, attributes can be rank ordered, the distance between attributes is equal, and attributes have a true zero point
- Variable- refers to a grouping of several characteristics

5.4 OPERATIONALIZATION

Learning Objectives

- Define and give an example of indicators for a variable
- Identify the three components of an operational definition
- Describe the purpose of multi-dimensional measures such as indexes, scales, and typologies and why they are used

Now that we have figured out how to define, or conceptualize, our terms we'll need to think about operationalizing them. **Operationalization** is the process by which researchers *conducting quantitative research* spell out precisely how a concept will be measured. It involves identifying the specific research procedures we will use to gather data about our concepts. This of course requires that we know what research method(s) we will employ to learn about our concepts, and we'll examine specific research methods later on in the text. For now, let's take a broad look at how operationalization works. We can then revisit how this process works when we examine specific methods of data collection in later chapters. Remember, operationalization is only a process in quantitative research. Measurement in qualitative research will be discussed at the end of this section.

Operationalization works by identifying specific **indicators** that will be taken to represent the ideas we are interested in studying. If, for example, we are interested in studying masculinity, indicators for that concept might include some of the social roles prescribed to men in society such as breadwinning or fatherhood. Being a breadwinner or a father might therefore be considered *indicators* of a person's masculinity. The extent to which a man fulfills either, or both, of these roles might be understood as clues (or indicators) about the extent to which he is viewed as masculine.

Let's look at another example of indicators. Each day, Gallup researchers poll 1,000 randomly selected Americans to ask them about their well-being. To measure well-being, Gallup asks these people to respond to questions covering six broad areas: physical health, emotional health, work environment, life evaluation, healthy behaviors, and access to basic necessities. Gallup uses these six factors as indicators of the concept that they are really interested in, which is well-being.

Identifying indicators can be even simpler than the examples described thus far. What are the possible indicators of the concept of gender? Most of us would probably agree that "man" and "woman" are both reasonable indicators of gender, but you may want to include other options for people who identify as non-binary or other genders. Political party is another relatively easy concept for which to identify indicators. In the United States, likely indicators include Democrat and Republican and, depending on your research interest, you may include additional indicators such as Independent, Green, or Libertarian as well. Age and birthplace are additional examples of concepts for which identifying indicators is a relatively simple process. What concepts are of interest to you, and what are the possible indicators of those concepts?

We have now considered a few examples of concepts and their indicators, but it is important we don't make the process of coming up with indicators *too* arbitrary or casual. One way to avoid taking an overly casual approach in identifying indicators, as described previously, is to turn to prior theoretical and empirical work in your area. Theories will point you in the direction of relevant concepts and possible indicators; empirical work will give you some very specific examples of how the important concepts in an area have been measured in the past and what sorts of indicators have been used. Often, it makes sense to use the same indicators as researchers who have come before you. On the other hand, perhaps you notice some possible weaknesses in measures that have been used in the past that your own methodological approach will enable you to overcome.

Speaking of your methodological approach, another very important thing to think about when deciding on indicators and how you will measure your key concepts is the strategy you will use for data collection. A survey implies one way of measuring concepts, while focus groups imply a quite different way of measuring concepts. Your design choices will play an important role in shaping how you measure your concepts.

OPERATIONALIZING YOUR VARIABLES

Moving from identifying concepts to conceptualizing them and then to operationalizing them is a matter of increasing specificity. You begin the research process with a general interest, identify a few concepts that are essential for studying that interest you, work to define those concepts, and then spell out precisely how you will measure those concepts. In quantitative research, that final stage is called operationalization.

An **operational definition** consists of the following components: (1) the variable being measured, (2) the measure you will use, (3) how you plan to interpret the results of that measure.

The first component, the variable, should be the easiest part. In much quantitative research, there is a research question that has at least one independent and at least one dependent variable. Remember that variables have to be able to vary. For example, the United States is not a variable. Country of birth is a variable, as is patriotism. Similarly, if your sample only includes men, gender is a *constant* in your study...not a variable.

Let's pick a social work research question and walk through the process of operationalizing variables. Suppose we hypothesize that individuals on a residential psychiatric unit who are more depressed are less likely to be satisfied with care than those who are less depressed. Remember, this would be a negative relationship—as depression increases, satisfaction decreases. In this question, depression is the independent variable (the cause) and satisfaction with care is the dependent variable (the effect). We have our two variables—depression and satisfaction with care—so the first component is done. Now, we move onto the second component–the measure.

How do you measure depression or satisfaction? Many students begin by thinking that they could look at body language to see if a person were depressed. Maybe they would also verbally express feelings of sadness or hopelessness more often. A satisfied person might be happy around service providers and express gratitude more often. These may indicate depression, but they lack coherence. Unfortunately, what this "measure" is actually saying is that "I know depression and satisfaction when I see them." While you are likely a decent judge of depression and satisfaction, you need to provide more information in a research study for how you plan to measure your variables. Your judgment is subjective, based on your own idiosyncratic experiences with depression and satisfaction. They couldn't be replicated by another researcher. They also can't be done consistently for a large group of people. Operationalization requires that you come up with a specific and rigorous measure for seeing who is depressed or satisfied.

Finding a good measure for your variable can take less than a minute. To measure a variable like age, you would probably put a question on a survey that asked, "How old are you?" To evaluate someone's length of stay in a hospital, you might ask for access to their medical records and count the days from when they were admitted to when they were discharged. Measuring a variable like income might require some more thought, though. Are you interested in this person's individual income or the income of their family unit? This might matter if your participant does not work or is dependent on other family members for income. Do you count income from social welfare programs? Are you interested in their income per month or per year? Measures must be specific and clear.

Depending on your research design, your measure may be something you put on a survey or pre/post-test that you give to your participants. For a variable like age or income, one well-worded question may suffice. Unfortunately, most variables in the social world are not so simple. Depression and satisfaction are multi-dimensional variables, as they each contain multiple elements. Asking someone "Are you depressed?" does not do justice to the complexity of depression, which includes issues with mood, sleeping, eating, relationships, and happiness. Asking someone "Are you satisfied with the services you received?" similarly omits multiple dimensions of satisfaction, such as timeliness, respect, meeting needs, and likelihood of recommending to a friend, among many others.

INDICES, SCALES, AND TYPOLOGIES

To account for a variable's dimensions, a researcher might rely on an index, scale, or typology. An **index** is a type of measure that contains several indicators and is used to summarize some more general concept. An index of depression might ask if the person has experienced any of the following indicators in the past month: pervasive feelings of hopelessness, thoughts of suicide, over- or under-eating, and a lack of enjoyment in normal activities. On their own, some of these indicators like over- or under-eating might not be considered depression, but collectively, the answers to each of these indicators add up to an overall experience of depression. The index allows the researcher in this case to better understand what shape a respondent's depression experience takes. If the researcher had only asked whether a respondent had ever experienced depression, she wouldn't know what sorts of behaviors actually made up that respondent's experience of depression.

Taking things one step further, if the researcher decides to rank order the various behaviors that make up depression, perhaps weighting suicidal thoughts more heavily than eating disturbances, then she will have created a **scale** rather than an index. Like an index, a scale is also a measure composed of multiple items or questions. But unlike indexes, scales are designed in a way that accounts for the possibility that different items may vary in intensity.

If creating your own scale sounds complicated, don't worry! For most variables, this work has already been done by other researchers. You do not need to create a scale for depression because scales such as the Patient Health Questionnaire (PHQ-9) and the Center for Epidemiologic Studies Depression Scale (CES-D) and Beck's Depression Inventory (BDI) have been developed and refined over dozens of years to measure variables like depression. Similarly, scales such as the Patient Satisfaction Questionnaire (PSQ-18) have been developed to measure satisfaction with medical care. As we will discuss in the next section, these scales have been shown to be reliable and valid. While you could create a new scale to measure depression or satisfaction, a study with rigor would pilot test and refine that scale over time to make sure it measures the concept accurately and consistently. This high level of rigor is often unachievable in student research projects, so using existing scales is recommended.

Another reason existing scales are preferable is that they can save time and effort. The Mental Measurements Yearbook provides a searchable database of measures for different variables. You can access this database from your library's list of databases. At the University of Texas at Arlington, the Mental Measurements Yearbook can be searched directly or viewed online. If you can't find anything in there, your next stop should be the methods section of the articles in your literature review. The methods section of each article will detail how the researchers measured their variables. In a quantitative study, researchers likely used a scale to measure key variables and will provide a brief description of that scale. A Google Scholar search such as "depression scale" or "satisfaction scale" should also provide some relevant results. As a last resort, a general web search may bring you to a scale for your variable.

Unfortunately, all of these approaches do not guarantee that you will be able to actually see the scale itself or get information on how it is interpreted. Many scales cost money to use and may require training to properly administer. You may also find scales that are related to your variable but would need to be slightly modified to match your study's needs. Adapting a scale to fit your study is a possibility; however, you should remember that changing even small parts of a scale can influence its accuracy and consistency. Pilot testing is always recommended for adapted scales.

A final way of measuring multidimensional variables is a **typology**. A typology is a way of categorizing concepts according to particular themes. Probably the most familiar version of a typology is the micro, meso, macro framework. Students classify specific elements of the social world by their ecological relationship with the person. Let's take the example of depression again. The lack of sleep associated with depression would be classified as a micro-level element while a severe economic recession would be classified as a macro-level element. Typologies require clearly stated rules on what data will get assigned to what categories, so carefully following the rules of the typology is important.

Once you have (1) your variable and (2) your measure, you will need to (3) describe how you plan to interpret your measure. Sometimes, interpreting a measure is incredibly easy. If you ask someone their age, you'll probably interpret the results by noting the raw number (e.g., 22) someone provides. However, you could also re-code age into categories (e.g., under 25, 20-29-years-old, etc.). An index may also be simple to interpret. If there is a checklist of problem behaviors, one might simply add up the number of behaviors checked off–with a higher total indicating worse behavior. Sometimes an index will assign people to categories (e.g., normal, borderline, moderate, significant, severe) based on their total number of checkmarks. As long as the rules are clearly spelled out, you are welcome to interpret measures in a way that makes sense to you. Theory might guide you to use some categories or you might be influenced by the types of statistical tests you plan to run later on in data analysis.

For more complicated measures like scales, you should look at the information provided by the scale's authors for how to interpret the scale. If you can't find enough information from the scale's creator, look at how the results of that scale are reported in the results section of research articles. For example, Beck's Depression Inventory (BDI-II) uses 21 questions to measure depression. A person indicates on a scale of 0-3 how much they agree with a statement. The results for each question are added up, and the respondent is put into one of three categories: low levels of depression (1-16), moderate levels of depression (17-30), or severe levels of depression (31 and over).

In sum, operationalization specifies what measure you will be using to measure your variable and how you plan to interpret that measure. Operationalization is probably the trickiest component of basic research methods. Don't get frustrated if it takes a few drafts and a lot of feedback to get to a workable definition.

QUALITATIVE RESEARCH AND OPERATIONALIZATION

As we discussed in the previous section, qualitative research takes a more open approach towards defining the concepts in your research question. The questions you choose to ask in your interview, focus group, or content analysis will determine what data you end up getting from your participants. For example, if you are researching depression qualitatively, you would not use a scale like the Beck's Depression Inventory, which is a quantitative measure we described above. Instead, you would start off with a tentative definition of what depression means based on your literature review and use that definition to come up with questions for your participants. We will cover how those questions fit into qualitative research designs later on in the textbook. For now, remember that qualitative researchers use the questions they ask participants to measure their variables and that qualitative researchers can change their questions as they gather more information from participants. Ultimately, the concepts in a qualitative study will be defined by the researcher's interpretation of what her participants say. Unlike in quantitative research in which definitions must be explicitly spelled out in advance, qualitative research allows the definitions of concepts to emerge during data analysis.

SPOTLIGHT ON UTA SCHOOL OF SOCIAL WORK

ARE INTERACTIONS WITH A SOCIAL ROBOT ASSOCIATED WITH CHANGES IN DEPRESSION AND LONELINESS?

Robust measurement is very important in research. Furthermore, providing a clear explanation of the measures used in a study helps others to understand the concepts being studied and interpret the findings as well as and helps other researchers to accurately replicate the study in different settings.

Dr. Noelle Fields and Ling Xu from the University of Texas at Arlington's School of Social Work collaborated with Dr. Julienne Greer from the College of Liberal Arts on a pilot study that incorporated a participatory arts intervention with the social robot, NAO. The intervention took place with older adults living in an assisted living facility. The overall aim of this study was to help older adults improve their psychological well-being through participation in a theatre arts activity led by NAO.

The key outcome variables for this pilot study were *psychological well-being* measured by *depression, loneliness,* and *engagement with the robot*. Depression and loneliness were measured by two standardized scales: the 15-item Geriatric Depression Scale (Sheikh & Yesavage, 1986) and the revised 3-item UCLA loneliness scale (Hughes, Waite, Hawkley, & Cacioppo, 2004). However, engagement with the robot did not have a standardized measure. Thus, the research team utilized a measure to capture engagement with the robot based on previous research.

In this study, engagement with robot was defined as the degree of interaction or involvement with a robot. One way to measure engagement is for members of the research team (i.e., observers) to rate the level of participant engagement (see Table 1).

Table 1. Please circle 0-5 to indicate the participant's engagement levels (definitions for each levels can be found in the example column).

Rating	Meaning	Example
0	Intense noncompliance	Participant stood and walked away from the table on which the robot interaction took place
1	Noncompliance	Participant hung head and refused to comply with interviewer's request to speak to the robot
2	Neutral	Participant complied with instructions to speak with the robot after several prompts from the confederate
3	Slight interest	Participant required two or three prompts from the confederate before responding to the robot
4	Engagement	Participant complied immediately following the confederate's request to speak with the robot
5	Intense engagement	Participant spontaneously engaged with the robot

This measurement was easy to apply in this study; however, it may lack the sensitivity to capture more detailed information about engagement, especially among older adult populations. Therefore, the researchers in this pilot study designed additional indicators to describe the participants' reactions when interacting with a robot. More specifically, after watching a video of each participant interacting with NAO, each researcher gave an engagement score based on the following concepts: (1) attentiveness including focus on face of robot or gesture of robot, (2) smiling and/or laughter, (3) head nodding, and (4) facial/vocal expression that included eyes widening, eyebrows arching, and tonal changes in voice. Through video analysis, each of the concepts were counted and tabulated by independent researchers, and mean score among researchers on each concept was then calculated. Sum scores on total engagement were also adapted for analysis. See Table 2 for detailed information of this measurement.

Table 2: Each researcher should provide a score on each item below based on your observation of participants' interaction with the robot.

	1.Strongly disagree	2. Disagree	3. Neither agree or disagree	4. Agree	5.Strongly agree
Attentive					
a. focus on face of robot					
b. focus on gesture of robot					
Smiling and/or laughter					
Head nodding					
Facial/ Vocal expression					
a. Eyes widen					
b. Eyebrow arch					
c. Tonal changes in voice					

The study found that participants reported improvements in mood, loneliness, and depression. The degree of difference/change was slightly greater in participants without dementia, perhaps suggesting social engagement and connection was a more profound attribute in cognitively intact older adults. Further research would be needed to confirm this hypothesis. Although the study is limited by its small scale and non-intervention control group, this exploratory pilot study supports the continuing development of participatory arts interventions with older adults using a social robotic platform. The benefits of performative participatory art between social robots and older adults is an emerging research area for human-robot social interactions and communications.

Key Takeaways

- Operationalization involves spelling out precisely how a concept will be measured.

- Operational definitions must include the variable, the measure, and how you plan to interpret the measure.

- Multi-dimensional concepts can be measured by an index, a scale, or a typology.

- It's a good idea to look at how researchers have measured the concept in previous studies.

Glossary

- Index- measure that contains several indicators and is used to summarize a more general concept

- Indicators- represent the concepts that we are interested in studying

- Operationalization- process by which researchers conducting quantitative research spell out precisely how a concept will be measured and how to interpret that measure

- Scale- composite measure designed in a way that accounts for the possibility that different items on an index may vary in intensity

- Typology- measure that categorizes concepts according to particular themes

Image attributions

Business charts by Pixabay CC-0

Checklist by TeroVesalainen CC-0

5.5 MEASUREMENT QUALITY

Learning Objectives

- Define reliability and describe the types of reliability
- Define validity and describe the types of validity

In quantitative research, once we've defined our terms and specified the operations for measuring them, how do we know that our measures are any good? Without some assurance of the quality of our measures, we cannot be certain that our findings have any meaning or, at the least, that our findings mean what we think they mean. When social scientists measure concepts, they aim to achieve *reliability* and *validity* in their measures. These two aspects of measurement quality are the focus of this section. We'll consider reliability first and then take a look at validity. For both aspects of measurement quality, let's say our interest is in measuring the concepts of alcoholism and alcohol intake. What are some potential problems that could arise when attempting to measure this concept, and how might we work to overcome those problems?

QUALITY ✓

RELIABILITY

First, let's say we've decided to measure alcoholism by asking people to respond to the following question: Have you ever had a problem with alcohol? If we measure alcoholism in this way, it seems likely that anyone who identifies as an alcoholic would respond with a yes to the question. So, this must be a good way to identify our group of interest, right? Well, maybe. Think about how you or others you know would respond to this question. Would responses differ after a wild night out from what they would have been the day before? Might an infrequent drinker's current headache from the single glass of wine she had last night influence how she answers the question this morning? How would that same person respond to the question before consuming the wine? In each of these cases, if the same person would respond differently to the same question at different points, it is possible that our measure of alcoholism has a reliability problem. **Reliability** in measurement is about consistency.

One common problem of reliability with social scientific measures is memory. If we ask research participants to recall some aspect of their own past behavior, we should try to make the recollection process as simple and straightforward for them as possible. Sticking with the topic of alcohol intake, if we ask respondents how much wine, beer, and liquor they've consumed each day over the course of the past 3 months, how likely are we to get accurate responses? Unless a person keeps a journal documenting their intake, there will very likely be some inaccuracies in their responses. If, on the other hand, we ask a person how many drinks of any kind they have consumed in the past week, we might get a more accurate set of responses.

Reliability can be an issue even when we're not reliant on others to accurately report their behaviors. Perhaps a researcher is interested in observing how alcohol intake influences interactions in public locations. She may decide to conduct observations at a local pub, noting how many drinks patrons consume and how their behavior changes as their intake changes. But what if the researcher has to use the restroom and misses the three shots of tequila that the person next to her downs during the brief period she is away? The reliability of this researcher's measure of alcohol intake, counting numbers of drinks she observes patrons consume, depends on her ability to actually observe every instance of patrons consuming drinks. If she is unlikely to be able to observe every such instance, then perhaps her mechanism for measuring this concept is not reliable.

If a measure is reliable, it means that if the measure is given multiple times, the results will be consistent each time. For example, if you took the SATs on multiple occasions before coming to school, your scores should be relatively the same from test to test. This is what is known as **test-retest reliability**. In the same way, if a person is clinically depressed, a depression scale should give similar (though not necessarily identical) results today that it does two days from now.

If your study involves observing people's behaviors, for example watching sessions of mothers playing with infants, you may also need to assess **inter-rater reliability**. Inter-rater reliability is the degree to which different observers agree on what happened. Did you miss when the infant offered an object to the mother and the mother dismissed it? Did the other person rating miss that event? Do you both similarly rate the parent's engagement with the child? Again, scores of multiple observers should be consistent, though perhaps not perfectly identical.

Finally, for scales, **internal consistency reliability** is an important concept. The scores on each question of a scale should be correlated with each other, as they all measure parts of the same concept. Think about a scale of depression, like Beck's Depression Inventory. A person who is depressed would score highly on most of the measures, but there would be some variation. If we gave a group of people that scale, we would imagine there should be a correlation between scores on, for example, mood disturbance and lack of enjoyment. They aren't the same concept, but are related. So, there should be a mathematical relationship between them. A specific statistic known as Cronbach's Alpha provides a way to measure how well each question of a scale is related to the others. Cronbach's alpha (sometimes shown as α) can range from 0 to 1.0. As a general rule, Cronbach's alpha should be at least .7 to reflect acceptable internal consistency with scores of .8 or higher considered an indicator of good internal consistency.

Test-retest, inter-rater, and internal consistency are three important subtypes of reliability. Researchers use these types of reliability to make sure their measures are consistently measuring the concepts in their research questions.

VALIDITY

While reliability is about consistency, validity is about accuracy. What image comes to mind for you when you hear the word *alcoholic*? Are you certain that the image you conjure up is similar to the image others have in mind? If not, then we may be facing a problem of validity.

For a measure to have **validity**, we must be certain that our measures accurately get at the meaning of our concepts. Think back to the first possible measure of alcoholism we considered in the previous few paragraphs. There, we initially considered measuring alcoholism by asking research participants the following question: Have you ever had a problem with alcohol? We realized that this might not be the most reliable way of measuring alcoholism because the same person's response might vary dramatically depending on how they are feeling that day. Likewise, this measure of alcoholism is not particularly valid. What is "a problem" with alcohol? For some, it might be having had a single regrettable or embarrassing moment that resulted from consuming too much. For others, the threshold for "problem" might be different; perhaps a person has had numerous embarrassing drunken moments but still gets out of bed for work every day, so they don't perceive themselves as having a problem. Because what each respondent considers to be problematic could vary so dramatically, our measure of alcoholism isn't likely to yield any useful or meaningful results if our aim is to objectively understand, say, how many of our research participants have alcoholism. [1]

TYPES OF VALIDITY

Below are some basic subtypes of validity, though there are certainly others you can read more about. One way to think of validity is to think of it as you would a portrait. Some portraits of people look just like the actual person they are intended to represent. But other representations of people's images, such as caricatures and stick drawings, are not nearly as accurate. While a portrait may not be an exact representation of how a person looks, what's important is the extent to which it approximates the look of the person it is intended to represent. The same goes for validity in measures. No measure is exact, but some measures are more accurate than others.

Face validity

In the last paragraph, critical engagement with our measure for alcoholism "Do you have a problem with alcohol?" was shown to be flawed. We assessed its **face validity** or whether it is plausible that the question measures what it intends to measure. Face validity is a subjective

1. Of course, if our interest is in how many research participants perceive themselves to have a problem, then our measure may be just fine.

process. Sometimes face validity is easy, as a question about height wouldn't have anything to do with alcoholism. Other times, face validity can be more difficult to assess. Let's consider another example.

Perhaps we're interested in learning about a person's dedication to healthy living. Most of us would probably agree that engaging in regular exercise is a sign of healthy living, so we could measure healthy living by counting the number of times per week that a person visits their local gym. But perhaps they visit the gym to use their tanning beds or to flirt with potential dates or sit in the sauna. These activities, while potentially relaxing, are probably not the best indicators of healthy living. Therefore, recording the number of times a person visits the gym may not be the most valid way to measure their dedication to healthy living.

Content validity

Another problem with this measure of healthy living is that it is incomplete. **Content validity** assesses for whether the measure includes all of the possible meanings of the concept. Think back to the previous section on multidimensional variables. Healthy living seems like a multidimensional concept that might need an index, scale, or typology to measure it completely. Our one question on gym attendance doesn't cover all aspects of healthy living. Once you have created one, or found one in the existing literature, you need to assess for content validity. Are there other aspects of healthy living that aren't included in your measure?

Criterion validity

Let's say you have created (or found) a good scale, index, or typology for your measure of healthy living. A valid measure of healthy living would have scores that are similar to other measures of healthy living. **Criterion validity** occurs when the results from the measure are similar to those from an external criterion (that, ideally, has already been validated or is a more direct measure of the variable).

There are two types of criterion validity — *predictive validity* and *concurrent validity*. They are distinguished by timing — whether or not the measure is similar to something that is measured in the future or at the same time. **Predictive validity** means that your measure predicts things it should be able to predict. A valid measure of healthy living would be able to predict, for example, scores of a blood panel test during a patient's annual physical. In this case, the assumption is that if you have a healthy lifestyle, a standard blood test done a few months later during an annual checkup would show healthy results. On the other hand, if we were to administer the blood panel measure at the same time as the scale of healthy living, we would be assessing concurrent validity. **Concurrent validity** is the same as predictive validity—the scores on your measure should be similar to an established measure—except that both measures are given at the same time.

Construct validity

Another closely related concept is construct validity. The logic behind construct validity is that sometimes there is no established criterion to use for comparison. However, there may be a construct that is theoretically related to the variable being measured. The measure could then be compared to that construct, even though it isn't exactly the same concept as what's being measured. In other words, **construct validity** exists when the measure is related to other measures that are hypothesized to be related to it.

It might be helpful to look at two types of construct validity – *convergent validity* and *discriminant validity*. **Convergent validity** takes an existing measure of the same concept and compares your measure to it. If their scores are similar, then it's probably likely that they are both measuring the same concept.In assessing for convergent validity, one should look for different methods of measuring the same concept. If someone filled out a scale about their substance use and the results from the self-reported scale consistently matched the results of a lab test, then the scale about substance use would demonstrate convergent validity. **Discriminant validity** is a similar concept, except you would be comparing your measure to one that is expected to be unrelated. A participant's scores on a healthy lifestyle measure shouldn't be too closely correlated with a scale that measures self-esteem because you want the measure to discriminate between the two constructs.

RELIABILITY VERSUS VALIDITY

If you are still confused about validity and reliability, Figure 5.2 shows an example of what validity and reliability look like. On the first target, our shooter's aim is all over the place. It is neither reliable (consistent) nor valid (accurate). The second (middle) target demonstrates consistency…but it is reliably off-target, or invalid. The third and final target (bottom right) represents a reliable and valid result. The person is able to hit the target accurately and consistently. This is what you should aim for in your research. An instrument can be reliable without being valid (target 2), but it cannot be valid without also being reliable (target 3).

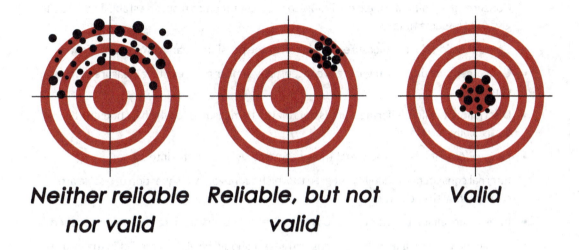

Neither reliable nor valid   **Reliable, but not valid**   **Valid**

Figure 5.2 Reliability and Validity

Key Takeaways

- Reliability is a matter of consistency.
- Validity is a matter of accuracy.
- There are many types of validity and reliability.

Glossary

- Concurrent validity- if a measure is able to predict outcomes from an established measure given at the same time
- Content validity- if the measure includes all of the possible meanings of the concept
- Convergent validity- if a measure is conceptually similar to an existing measure of the same concept
- Discriminant validity- if a measure is not related to measures to which it shouldn't be statistically correlated
- Face validity- if it is plausible that the measure measures what it intends to
- Internal consistency reliability- degree to which scores on each question of a scale are correlated with each other
- Inter-rater reliability- the degree to which different observers agree on what happened
- Predictive validity- if a measure predicts things it should be able to predict in the future
- Reliability- a measure's consistency.
- Test-retest reliability- if a measure is given multiple times, the results will be consistent each time
- Validity- a measure's accuracy

Image attributions

Quality by geralt CC-0

Figure 5.2 was adapted from Nevit Dilmen's "Reliability and validity" (2012) Shared under a CC-BY-SA 3.0 license

5.6 CHALLENGES IN QUANTITATIVE MEASUREMENT

Learning Objectives

- Identify potential sources of error
- Differentiate between systematic and random error

For quantitative methods, you should now have some idea about how conceptualization and operationalization work, and you should also know how to assess the quality of your measures. But measurement is sometimes a complex process, and some concepts are more complex than others. Measuring a person's political party affiliation, for example, is less complex than measuring their sense of alienation. In this section, we'll consider some of these complexities in measurement.

SYSTEMATIC ERROR

Unfortunately, measures never perfectly describe what exists in the real world. Good measures demonstrate reliability and validity but will always have some degree of error. **Systematic error** causes our measures to consistently output incorrect data, usually due to an identifiable process. Imagine you created a measure of height, but you didn't put an option for anyone over six feet tall. If you gave that measure to your local college or university, some of the taller members of the basketball team might not be measured accurately. In fact, you would be under the mistaken impression that the tallest person at your school was six feet tall, when in actuality there are likely plenty of people taller than six feet at your school. This error seems innocent, but if you were using that measure to help you build a new building, those people might hit their heads!

A less innocent form of error arises when researchers using question wording that might cause participants to think one answer choice is preferable to another. For example, someone were to ask you, "Do you think global warming is caused by human activity?" you would probably feel comfortable answering honestly. But what if someone asked you, "Do you agree with 99% of scientists that global warming is caused by human activity?" Would you feel comfortable saying no, if that's what you honestly felt? Possibly not. That is an example of a **leading question**, a question with wording that influences how a participant responds. We'll discuss leading questions and other problems in question wording in greater detail in Chapter 7.

In addition to error created by the researcher, *participants* can cause error in measurement. Some people will respond without fully understanding a question, particularly if the question is worded in a confusing way. That's one source of error. Let's consider another. If we asked people if they always washed their hands after using the bathroom, would we expect people to be perfectly honest? Polling people about whether they wash their hands after using the bathroom might only elicit what people would like others to think they do, rather than what they actually do. This is an example of **social desirability bias**, in which participants in a research study want to present themselves in a positive, socially desirable way to the researcher. People in your study will want to seem tolerant, open-minded, and intelligent, but their true feelings may be closed-minded, simple, and biased. So, they lie. This occurs often in political polling, which may show greater support for a candidate from a minority race, gender, or political party than actually exists in the electorate.

A related form of bias is called **acquiescence bias**, also known as "yea-saying." It occurs when people say yes to whatever the researcher asks, even when doing so contradicts previous answers. For example, a person might say yes to both "I am a confident leader in group discussions" and "I feel anxious interacting in group discussions." Those two responses are unlikely to both be true for the same person. Why would someone do this? Similar to social desirability, people want to be agreeable and nice to the researcher asking them questions or they might ignore contradictory feelings when responding to each question. Respondents may also act on cultural reasons, trying to "save face" for themselves or the person asking the questions. Regardless of the reason, the results of your measure don't match what the person truly feels.

RANDOM ERROR

So far, we have discussed sources of error that come from choices made by respondents or researchers. Usually, systematic errors will result in responses that are incorrect in one direction or another. For example, social desirability bias usually means more people will *say* they will vote for a third party in an election than actually do. Systematic errors such as these can be reduced, but there is another source of error in measurement that can never be eliminated, and that is random error. Unlike systematic error, which biases responses consistently in one direction or another, **random error** is unpredictable and does not consistently result in scores that are consistently higher or lower on a given measure. Instead, random error is more like statistical noise, which will likely average out across participants.

Random error is present in any measurement. If you've ever stepped on a bathroom scale twice and gotten two slightly different results, then you've experienced random error. Maybe you were standing slightly differently or had a fraction of your foot off of the scale the first time. If you were to take enough measures of your weight on the same scale, you'd be able to figure out your true weight. In social science, if you gave someone a scale measuring depression on a day after they lost their job, they would likely score differently than if they had just gotten a promotion and a raise. Even if the person were clinically depressed, our measure is subject to influence by the random occurrences of life. Thus, social scientists speak with humility about our measures. We are reasonably confident that what we found is true, but we must always acknowledge that our measures are only an approximation of reality.

Humility is important in scientific measurement, as errors can have real consequences. When Matthew DeCarlo was writing the source material for this book, he and his wife were expecting their first child. Like most people, they used a pregnancy test from the pharmacy. If the test said his wife was pregnant when she was not, that would be a **false positive**. On the other hand, if the test indicated that she was not pregnant when she was in fact pregnant, that would be a **false negative**. Even if the test is 99% accurate, that means that one in a hundred women will get an erroneous result when they use a home pregnancy test. For them, a false positive would have been initially exciting, then devastating when they found out they were not having a child. A false negative would have been disappointing at first and then quite shocking when they found out they were indeed having a child. While both false positives and false negatives are not very likely for home pregnancy tests (when taken correctly), measurement error can have consequences for the people being measured.

Key Takeaways

- Systematic error may arise from the researcher, participant, or measurement instrument.
- Systematic error biases results in a particular direction, whereas random error can be in any direction.
- All measures are prone to error and should interpreted with humility.

Glossary

- Acquiescence bias- when respondents say yes to whatever the researcher asks
- False negative- when a measure does not indicate the presence of a phenomenon, when in reality it is present
- False positive- when a measure indicates the presence of a phenomenon, when in reality it is not present
- Leading question- a question with wording that influences how a participant responds
- Random error- unpredictable error that does not consistently result in scores that are consistently higher or lower on a given measure
- Social desirability bias- when respondents answer based on what they think other people would like, rather than what is true
- Systematic error- measures consistently output incorrect data, usually in one direction and due to an identifiable process

Image attributions

question by jambulboy CC-0

mistake by stevepb CC-0

CHAPTER SIX: SAMPLING

Sampling involves selecting a subset of a population and drawing conclusions from that subset. How you sample and who you sample shapes what conclusions you are able to draw. Ultimately, this chapter focuses on questions about the who or the what that you want to be able to make claims about in your research. In the following sections, we'll define sampling, discuss different types of sampling strategies, and consider how to judge the quality of samples as consumers and creators of social scientific research.

CHAPTER OUTLINE

- 6.1 Basic concepts of sampling
- 6.2 Nonprobability sampling
- 6.3 Probability sampling
- 6.4 Critical thinking about sampling

CONTENT ADVISORY

This chapter discusses or mentions the following topics: cancer, substance abuse, homelessness, anti-LGBTQ discrimination, mental health, sexually transmitted infections, and intimate partner violence.

6.1 BASIC CONCEPTS OF SAMPLING

Learning Objectives

- Differentiate between populations, sampling frames, and samples
- Describe inclusion and exclusion criteria
- Explain recruitment of participants in a research project

POPULATION

In social scientific research, a **population** is the cluster of people you are most interested in; it is often the "who" that you want to be able to say something about at the end of your study. Populations in research may be rather large, such as "the American people," but they are usually less vague than that. For example, a large study for which the population of interest is more generally "the American people" will likely specify *which* American people, such as adults over the age of 18 or citizens or legal permanent residents it is examining.

It is quite rare for researchers to gather data from their entire population of interest. This might sound surprising or disappointing until you think about the kinds of research questions that social workers typically ask. For example, let's say we wish to answer the following research question: "How does gender impact success in a batterer intervention program?" Would you expect to be able to collect data from all people in batterer intervention programs across all nations from all historical time periods? Unless you plan to make answering this research question your entire life's work (and then some), your answer is probably a resounding no. So, what to do? Do you have to give up your research interest because you don't have the time or resources to gather data from every single person of interest?

Absolutely not. Instead, researchers use a smaller sample that is intended to represent the population in their studies.

SAMPLING FRAMES

An intermediate point between the overall population and the sample that is drawn for the research is called a *sampling frame*. A **sampling frame** is a list of people from which researchers draw a sample. But where do you find a sampling frame? Answering this question is one of the first steps in conducting human subjects research. Social work researchers must think about locations or groups in which their target population gathers or interacts. For example, a study on quality of care in nursing homes may choose a local nursing home because it's easy to access. The sampling frame could be all of the patients at the nursing home. You would select your participants for your study from the list of patients at the nursing home. An administrator at the nursing home would give you a list with every resident's name on it from which you would select your participants. If you decided to include more nursing homes in your study, then your sampling frame could be all of the patients at all of the nursing homes you included.

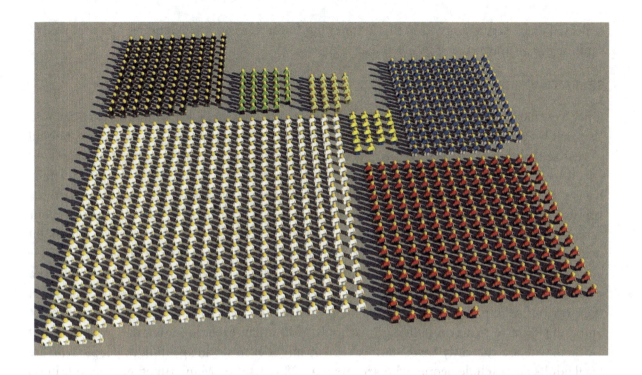

The nursing home example is perhaps an easy one. Let's consider some more examples. Unlike nursing home patients, cancer survivors do not live in an enclosed location and may no longer receive treatment at a hospital or clinic. For social work researchers to reach participants, they may consider partnering with a support group that serves this population. Perhaps there is a support group at a local church in which survivors may cycle in and out based on need. Without a set list of people, your sampling frame would simply be the people who showed up to the support group on the nights you were there. In this case, you don't start with an actual list; you have a hypothetical one. The sampling frame only comes into existence after you go to the support group and collect names.

More challenging still is recruiting people who are homeless, those with very low income, or people who belong to stigmatized groups. For example, a research study by Johnson and Johnson (2014) attempted to learn usage patterns of "bath salts," or synthetic stimulants that are marketed as "legal highs." Users of "bath salts" don't often gather for meetings, and reaching out to individual treatment centers is unlikely to produce enough participants for a study as use of bath salts is rare. To reach participants, these researchers ingeniously used online discussion boards in which users of these drugs share information. Their sampling frame included everyone who participated in the online discussion boards during the time they collected data. Regardless of whether a sampling frame is easy or challenging, the first rule of sampling is: *go where your participants are.*

SELECTING STUDY PARTICIPANTS

Once you have a sampling frame, you need to identify a strategy for sampling participants. You will learn more about sampling strategies later in this chapter. At this point, it is helpful to realize that there may be some people in your sampling frame that you do not ultimately to enroll in your study. You may have certain characteristics or attributes that individuals must have if they participate in your study. These are known as inclusion and exclusion criteria. **Inclusion criteria** are the characteristics a person must possess in order to be included in your sample. If you were conducting a survey on LGBTQ discrimination at your agency, you might want to sample only clients who identify as LGBTQ. In that case, your inclusion criteria for your sample would be that individuals have to identify as LGBTQ. Comparably, **exclusion criteria** are characteristics that disqualify a person from being included in your sample. In the previous example, perhaps you are mainly interested in discrimination in the workplace and don't want to focus on bullying in schools. You might exclude individuals who have not worked, who are currently enrolled in school, or might even set an age limit to people who are legal adults and exclude people who are less than 18 years old. Many times, exclusion criteria are often the mirror image of inclusion criteria. This would be the case if the inclusion criteria included being age 18 or older and the exclusion criteria included being less than 18 years old.

At this stage, you are ready to recruit your participants into your study. **Recruitment** refers to the process by which the researcher informs potential participants about the study and attempts to get them to participate. Recruitment comes in many different forms. If you have ever received a phone call asking for you to participate in a survey, someone has attempted to recruit you for their study. Perhaps you've seen print advertisements on buses, in student centers, or in a periodical. As you learn more about specific types of sampling, you can make sure your recruitment strategy makes sense with your sampling approach.

SAMPLE

Once you recruit and enroll participants, you end up with a sample. A **sample** is the group of people you successfully recruit from your sampling frame to participate in your study. If you are a participant in a research project—answering survey questions, participating in interviews, etc.—you are part of the sample of that research project. Some social work research doesn't use people at all. Instead of people, the elements selected for inclusion into a sample are documents, including client records, blog entries, or television shows. A researcher conducting this kind of analysis, described in detail in Chapter 10, still goes through the stages of sampling—identifying a sampling frame, applying inclusion criteria, and gathering the sample.

APPLYING SAMPLING TERMS

Sampling terms can be a bit daunting at first. However, with some practice, they will become second nature. The process flows sequentially from figuring out your target population to thinking about where to find people from your target population to finding a sampling frame of people in your population to recruiting people from that list to be a part of your sample. Through the sampling process, you must consider where people in your target population are likely to be and how best to get their attention for your study. Sampling can be an easy process, like calling every 100th name from the phone book one afternoon, or challenging, like standing every day for a few weeks in an area in which people who are homeless gather for shelter. In either case, your goal is to recruit enough people who will participate in your study so you can learn about your population.

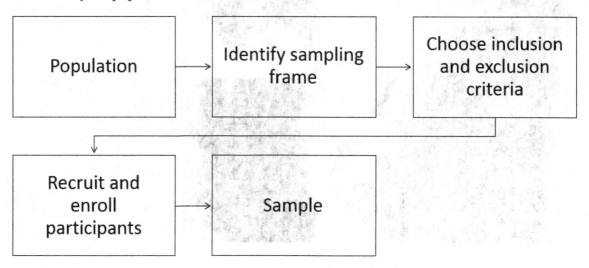

Figure 6.1 Sampling terms in order of the sampling process

In the next two sections of this chapter, we will discuss sampling approaches, also known as sampling techniques or types of samples. Sampling approach determines how a researcher selects people from the sampling frame to recruit into her sample. Because the goals of qualitative and quantitative research differ, so too does the sampling approach. Quantitative approaches often allow researchers to make claims about populations that are much larger than their actual sample with a fair amount of confidence. Qualitative approaches are designed to allow researchers to make conclusions that are specific to one time, place, context, and group of people. We will review both of these approaches to sampling in the coming sections of this chapter. First, we examine sampling types and techniques used in qualitative research. After that, we'll look at how sampling typically works in quantitative research.

Key Takeaways

- A population is the group who is the main focus of a researcher's interest; a sample is the group from whom the researcher actually collects data.
- Sampling involves selecting the observations that you will analyze.
- To conduct sampling, a researcher starts by going where your participants are.
- Sampling frames can be real or hypothetical.
- Recruitment involves informing potential participants about your study and seeking their participation.

Glossary

- Exclusion criteria- characteristics that disqualify a person from being included in a sample
- Inclusion criteria- the characteristics a person must possess in order to be included in a sample
- Population- the cluster of people about whom a researcher is most interested
- Recruitment- the process by which the researcher informs potential participants about the study and attempts to get them to participate
- Sample- the group of people you successfully recruit from your sampling frame to participate in your study
- Sampling frame- a real or hypothetical list of people from which a researcher will draw her sample

Image attributions

crowd by mwewering CC-0

job interview by styles66 CC-0

6.2 NONPROBABILITY SAMPLING

Learning Objectives

- Define nonprobability sampling, and describe instances in which a researcher might choose a nonprobability sampling technique
- Describe the different types of nonprobability samples

Qualitative researchers typically make sampling choices that enable them to achieve a deep understanding of whatever phenomenon it is that they are studying. Sometimes quantitative researchers work with targeted or small samples. Qualitative research often employs a theoretical sampling strategy, where study sites, respondents, or cases are selected based on theoretical considerations such as whether they fit the phenomenon being studied (e.g., sustainable practices can only be studied in organizations that have implemented sustainable practices), whether they possess certain characteristics that make them uniquely suited for the study (e.g., a study of the drivers of firm innovations should include some firms that are high innovators and some that are low innovators, in order to draw contrast between these firms), and so forth. In this section, we'll examine the techniques that these researchers typically employ when sampling as well as the various types of samples that they are most likely to use in their work.

NONPROBABILITY SAMPLING

Nonprobability sampling refers to sampling techniques for which a person's likelihood of being selected for membership in the sample is unknown. Because we don't know the likelihood of selection, with nonprobability samples we don't know whether a sample is likely to represent a larger population. But that's okay. Generalizing to a larger population is not the goal with nonprobability samples or qualitative research. That said, the fact that nonprobability samples do not represent a larger population does not mean that they are drawn arbitrarily or without any specific purpose in mind (that would mean committing one of the errors of informal inquiry discussed in Chapter 1). We'll take a closer look at the process of selecting research elements when drawing a nonprobability sample. But first, let's consider why a researcher might choose to use a nonprobability sample.

When are nonprobability samples ideal? One instance might be when we're starting a big research project. For example, if we're conducting survey research, we may want to administer a draft of our survey to a few people who seem to resemble the folks we're interested in studying in order to help work out kinks in the survey. We might also use a nonprobability sample if we're conducting a pilot study or some exploratory research. This can be a quick way to gather some initial data and help get some idea of the lay of the land before conducting a more extensive study. From these examples, we can see that nonprobability samples can be useful for setting up, framing, or beginning research, even quantitative research. But it isn't just early stage research that relies on and benefits from nonprobability sampling techniques. Researchers also use nonprobability samples in advanced stage research projects. In this case, these projects are usually qualitative in nature, where the researcher's goal is in-depth, idiographic understanding rather than more generalizable, nomothetic understanding.

TYPES OF NONPROBABILITY SAMPLES

There are several types of nonprobability samples that researchers use. These include *purposive samples*, *snowball samples*, *quota samples*, and *convenience samples*.

To draw a **purposive sample**, a researcher selects participants from a sampling frame because they have characteristics that the researcher desires. A researcher begins with specific characteristics in mind that she wishes to examine and then seeks out research participants who cover that full range of characteristics. For example, if you are studying mental health supports on your campus, you may want to be sure to include not only students, but mental health practitioners and student affairs administrators. You might also select students who currently use mental health supports, those who dropped out of supports, and those who are waiting to receive supports. The purposive part of purposive sampling comes from selecting specific participants *on purpose* because you already know they have characteristics—being an administrator, dropping out of mental health supports—that you need in your sample.

Note that these are different than inclusion criteria, which are more general requirements a person must possess to be a part of your sample. For example, one of the inclusion criteria for a study of your campus' mental health supports might be that participants had to have visited the mental health center in the past year. That is different than purposive sampling. In purposive sampling, you know characteristics of individuals and recruit them because of those characteristics. For example, you might recruit Jane because she stopped seeking supports this month, JD because he has worked at the center for many years, and so forth.

Also, it's important to recognize that purposive sampling requires you to have prior information about your participants before recruiting them because you need to know their perspectives or experiences before you know whether you want them in your sample. This is a common mistake that many students make. They may think they're using purposive sampling because they're recruiting people from the health center or something like that. That's not purposive sampling. Purposive sampling is recruiting *specific people* because of the various characteristics and perspectives they bring to your sample. Imagine we were creating a focus group. A purposive sample might gather clinicians, patients, administrators, staff, and former patients together so they can talk as a group. Purposive sampling would seek out people that have each of those attributes.

Quota sampling is another nonprobability sampling strategy that takes purposive sampling one step further. When conducting quota sampling, a researcher identifies categories that are important to the study and for which there is likely to be some variation. Subgroups are created based on each category, and the researcher decides how many people to include from each subgroup and collects data from that number for each subgroup. Let's consider a study of student satisfaction with on-campus housing. Perhaps there are two types of housing on your campus: apartments that include full kitchens and dorm rooms where residents do not cook for themselves and instead eat in a dorm cafeteria. As a researcher, you might wish to understand how satisfaction varies across these two types of housing arrangements. Perhaps you have the time and resources to interview 20 campus residents, so you decide to interview 10 from each housing type. It is possible as well that your review of literature on the topic suggests that campus housing experiences vary by gender. If that is that case, perhaps you'll decide on four important subgroups: men who live in apartments, women who live in apartments, men who live in dorm rooms, and women who live in dorm rooms. Your quota sample would include five people from each of the four subgroups.

In 1936, up-and-coming pollster George Gallup made history when he successfully predicted the outcome of the presidential election using quota sampling methods. The leading polling entity at the time, *The Literary Digest*, predicted that Alfred Landon would beat Franklin Roosevelt in the presidential election by a landslide, but Gallup's polling disagreed. Gallup successfully predicted Roosevelt's win and subsequent elections based on quota samples, but in 1948, Gallup incorrectly predicted that Dewey would beat Truman in the US presidential election.[1] Among other problems, the fact that Gallup's quota categories did not represent those who actually voted (Neuman, 2007) underscores the point that one should avoid attempting to make statistical generalizations from data collected using quota sampling methods. While quota sampling offers the strength of helping the researcher account for potentially relevant variation across study elements, it would be a mistake to think of this strategy as yielding statistically representative findings. For that, you need probability sampling, which we will discuss in the next section.

Researchers can also use snowball sampling techniques to identify study participants. In **snowball sampling**, a researcher identifies one or two people she'd like to include in her

1. For more information about the 1948 election and other historically significant dates related to measurement, see the PBS timeline of "The first measured century"

study and then relies on those initial participants to help identify additional study participants. Thus, the researcher's sample builds and becomes larger as the study continues, much as a snowball builds and becomes larger as it rolls through the snow. Snowball sampling is an especially useful strategy when a researcher wishes to study a stigmatized group or behavior. For example, a researcher who wanted to study how people with genital herpes cope with their medical condition would be unlikely to find many participants by posting a call for interviewees in the newspaper or making an announcement about the study at some large social gathering. Instead, the researcher might know someone with the condition, interview that person, and ask the person to refer others they may know with the genital herpes to contact you to participate in the study. Having a previous participant vouch for the researcher may help new potential participants feel more comfortable about being included in the study.

Snowball sampling is sometimes referred to as chain referral sampling. One research participant refers another, and that person refers another, and that person refers another—thus a chain of potential participants is identified. In addition to using this sampling strategy for potentially stigmatized populations, it is also a useful strategy to use when the researcher's group of interest is likely to be difficult to find, not only because of some stigma associated with the group, but also because the group may be relatively rare.

Steven Kogan and colleagues (2011) used a type sampling similar to snowball sampling called *respondent-driven sampling* (Heckathorn, 2012). They wished to study the sexual behaviors of non-college-bound African American young adults who lived in high-poverty rural areas. The researchers first relied on their own networks to identify study participants, but because members of the study's target population were not easy to find, access to the networks of initial study participants was very important for identifying additional participants. Initial participants were given coupons to pass on to others they knew who qualified for the study. Participants were given an added incentive for referring eligible study participants; they received $50 for participating in the study and an additional $20 for each person they recruited who also participated in the study. Using this strategy, Kogan and colleagues succeeded in recruiting 292 study participants.

Finally, **convenience sampling** is another nonprobability sampling strategy that is employed by both qualitative and quantitative researchers. To draw a convenience sample, a researcher simply collects data from those people or other relevant elements to which she has most convenient access. This method, also sometimes referred to as availability sampling, is most useful in exploratory research or in student projects in which probability sampling is too costly or difficult. If you've ever been interviewed by a fellow student for a class project, you have likely been a part of a convenience sample. While convenience samples offer one major benefit—convenience—they do not offer the rigor needed to make conclusions about larger populations. That is the subject of our next section on probability sampling.

Table 10.1 Types of nonprobability samples

Sample type	Description
Purposive	Researcher seeks out participants with specific characteristics.
Snowball	Researcher relies on participant referrals to recruit new participants.
Quota	Researcher selects cases from within several different subgroups.
Convenience	Researcher gathers data from whatever cases happen to be convenient.

Key Takeaways

- Nonprobability samples might be used when researchers are conducting qualitative (or idiographic) research, exploratory research, student projects, or pilot studies.
- There are several types of nonprobability samples including purposive samples, snowball

samples, quota samples, and convenience samples.

Glossary

- Convenience sample- researcher gathers data from whatever cases happen to be convenient
- Nonprobability sampling- sampling techniques for which a person's likelihood of being selected for membership in the sample is unknown
- Purposive sample- when a researcher seeks out participants with specific characteristics
- Quota sample- when a researcher selects cases from within several different subgroups
- Snowball sample- when a researcher relies on participant referrals to recruit new participants

Image attributions

business by helpsg CC-0

network by geralt CC-0

6.3 PROBABILITY SAMPLING

Learning Objectives

- Describe how probability sampling differs from nonprobability sampling
- Define generalizability, and describe how it is achieved in probability samples
- Identify the various types of probability samples, and describe why a researcher may use one type over another

---

Quantitative researchers are often interested in making generalizations about groups larger than their study samples — that is, they are seeking nomothetic causal explanations. While there are certainly instances when quantitative researchers rely on nonprobability samples (e.g., when doing exploratory research), quantitative researchers tend to rely on probability sampling techniques. The goals and techniques associated with probability samples differ from those of nonprobability samples. We'll explore those unique goals and techniques in this section.

PROBABILITY SAMPLING

Unlike nonprobability sampling, **probability sampling** refers to sampling techniques for which a person's likelihood of being selected from the sampling frame is known. You might ask yourself why we should care about a potential participant's likelihood of being selected for the researcher's sample. The reason is that, in most cases, researchers who use probability sampling techniques are aiming to identify a representative sample from which to collect data. A **representative sample** is one that resembles the population from which it was drawn in all the ways that are important for the research being conducted. If, for example, you wish to be able to say something about differences between men and women at the end of your study, you better make sure that your sample doesn't contain only women. That's a bit of an oversimplification, but the point with representativeness is that if your population contains variations that are important to your study, your sample should contain the same sorts of variation.

Obtaining a representative sample is important in probability sampling because of generalizability. In fact, generalizability is perhaps the key feature that distinguishes probability samples from nonprobability samples. **Generalizability** refers to the idea that a study's results will tell us something about a group larger than the sample from which the findings were generated. In order to achieve generalizability, a core principle of probability sampling is that all elements in the researcher's sampling frame have an equal chance of being selected for inclusion in the study. In research, this is the principle of **random selection**. Researchers often use a computer's random number generator to determine which elements from the sampling frame get recruited into the sample.

Using random selection does not mean that the sample will be perfect. No sample is perfect.

The only way to come with a sample that perfectly reflects the population would be to include everyone in the population in your sample, which defeats the whole point of sampling! Generalizing from a sample to a population always contains some degree of error. This is referred to as **sampling error,** the difference between results from a sample and the actual values in the population.

Generalizability is a pretty easy concept to grasp. Imagine a professor who takes a sample of individuals in your class to see if the material is too hard or too easy. The professor, however, only sampled individuals whose grades were over 90% in the class. Would that be a representative sample of all students in the class? That would be a case of sampling error—a mismatch between the results of the sample and the true feelings of the overall class. In other words, the results of the professor's study don't generalize to the overall population of the class.

Taking this one step further, imagine your professor is conducting a study on binge drinking among college students. The professor uses undergraduates at your school as her sampling frame. Even if that professor were to use probability sampling, perhaps your school differs from other schools in important ways. There are schools that are "party schools" where binge drinking may be more socially accepted, "commuter schools" at which there is little nightlife, and so on. If your professor plans to generalize her results to *all* college students, she will have to make an argument that her sampling frame (undergraduates at your school) is representative of the population (all undergraduate college students).

TYPES OF PROBABILITY SAMPLES

There are a variety of types of probability samples that researchers may use. These include *simple random samples, systematic random samples, stratified random samples*, and *cluster samples*. Let's build on the previous example. Imagine we were concerned with binge drinking and chose the target population of fraternity members. How might you go about getting a probability sample of fraternity members that is representative of the overall population?

SIMPLE RANDOM SAMPLING

Simple random samples are the most basic type of probability sample. A simple random sample requires a sampling frame than contains a list of each person in the sampling frame. Your school likely has a list of all of the fraternity members on campus, as Greek life is subject to university oversight. You could use this as your sampling frame. Using the university's list, you would number each fraternity member, or *element*, sequentially and then randomly select the elements from which you will collect data.

True randomness is difficult to achieve, and it takes complex computational calculations to do so. Although you think you can select things at random, human-generated randomness is actually quite predictable. To truly randomly select elements, researchers must rely on computer-generated help. Many free websites have good pseudo-random number generators. A good example is the website Random.org, which contains a random number generator that can also randomize lists of participants. Sometimes, researchers use a table of numbers that have been generated randomly. There are several possible sources for obtaining a random number table. Some statistics and research methods textbooks offer such tables as appendices to the text.

SYSTEMATIC RANDOM SAMPLING

As you might have guessed, drawing a simple random sample can be quite tedious. **Systematic random sampling** techniques are somewhat less tedious but offer the benefits of a random sample. As with simple random samples, you must possess a list of everyone in your sampling frame. Once you've done that, to draw a systematic sample you'd simply select every k^{th} element on your list. But what is k, and where on the list of population elements does one begin the selection process? k is your **selection interval** or the distance between the elements you select for inclusion in your study. To begin the selection process, you'll need to figure out how many elements you wish to include in your sample. Let's say you want to interview 25 fraternity members on your campus, and there are 100 men on campus who are members of fraternities. In this case, your selection interval, or k, is 4. To arrive at 4, simply divide the total number of population elements by your desired sample size. This process is represented in Figure 6.2.

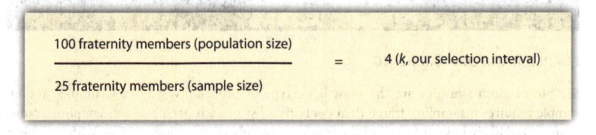

$$\frac{100 \text{ fraternity members (population size)}}{25 \text{ fraternity members (sample size)}} = 4 \ (k, \text{our selection interval})$$

Figure 6.2 Formula for determining selection interval for systematic sample

To determine where on your list of population elements to begin selecting the names of the 25 men you will interview, randomly select a number between 1 and k, and begin there. If we randomly select 3 as our starting point, we'd begin by selecting the third fraternity member on the list and then select every fourth member from there. This might be easier to understand if you can see it visually. Table 6.2 lists the names of our hypothetical 100 fraternity members on campus. You'll see that the third name on the list has been selected for inclusion in our hypothetical study, as has every fourth name after that. A total of 25 names have been selected.

Table 6.2 Systematic sample of 25 fraternity members

Number	Name	Include in study?	Number	Name	Include in study?
1	Jacob		51	Blake	Yes
2	Ethan		52	Oliver	
3	Michael	Yes	53	Cole	
4	Jayden		54	Carlos	
5	William		55	Jaden	Yes
6	Alexander		56	Jesus	
7	Noah	Yes	57	Alex	
8	Daniel		58	Aiden	
9	Aiden		59	Eric	Yes
10	Anthony		60	Hayden	
11	Joshua	Yes	61	Brian	
12	Mason		62	Max	
13	Christopher		63	Jaxon	Yes
14	Andrew		64	Brian	
15	David	Yes	65	Mathew	
16	Logan		66	Elijah	
17	James		67	Joseph	Yes
18	Gabriel		68	Benjamin	
19	Ryan	Yes	69	Samuel	
20	Jackson		70	John	
21	Nathan		71	Jonathan	Yes
22	Christian		72	Liam	
23	Dylan	Yes	73	Landon	
24	Caleb		74	Tyler	
25	Lucas		75	Evan	Yes
26	Gavin		76	Nicholas	
27	Isaac	Yes	77	Braden	
28	Luke		78	Angel	
29	Brandon		79	Jack	
30	Isaiah		80	Jordan	
31	Owen	Yes	81	Carter	

32	Conner			82	Justin	
33	Jose			83	Jeremiah	Yes
34	Julian			84	Robert	
35	Aaron	Yes		85	Adrian	
36	Wyatt			86	Kevin	
37	Hunter			87	Cameron	Yes
38	Zachary			88	Thomas	
39	Charles	Yes		89	Austin	
40	Eli			90	Chase	
41	Henry			91	Sebastian	Yes
42	Jason			92	Levi	
43	Xavier	Yes		93	Ian	
44	Colton			94	Dominic	
45	Juan			95	Cooper	Yes
46	Josiah			96	Luis	
47	Ayden	Yes		97	Carson	
48	Adam			98	Nathaniel	
49	Brody			99	Tristan	Yes
50	Diego			100	Parker	

There is one clear instance in which systematic sampling should not be employed. If your sampling frame has any pattern to it, you could inadvertently introduce bias into your sample by using a systemic sampling strategy. (Bias will be discussed in more depth in the next section.) This is sometimes referred to as the problem of periodicity. **Periodicity** refers to the tendency for a pattern to occur at regular intervals. Let's say, for example, that you wanted to observe binge drinking on campus each day of the week. Perhaps you need to have your observations completed within 28 days and you wish to conduct four observations on randomly chosen days. Table 6.3 shows a list of the population elements for this example. To determine which days we'll conduct our observations, we'll need to determine our selection interval. As you'll recall from the preceding paragraphs, to do so we must divide our population size, in this case 28 days, by our desired sample size, in this case 4 days. This formula leads us to a selection interval of 7. If we randomly select 2 as our starting point and select every seventh day after that, we'll wind up with a total of 4 days on which to conduct our observations. You'll see how that works out in the following table.

Table 6.3 Systematic sample of observation days

Day #	Day	Drinking	Observe?	Day #	Day	Drinking	Observe?
1	Monday	Low		15	Monday	Low	
2	Tuesday	Low	Yes	16	Tuesday	Low	Yes
3	Wednesday	Low		17	Wednesday	Low	
4	Thursday	High		18	Thursday	High	
5	Friday	High		19	Friday	High	
6	Saturday	High		20	Saturday	High	
7	Sunday	Low		21	Sunday	Low	
8	Monday	Low		22	Monday	Low	
9	Tuesday	Low	Yes	23	Tuesday	Low	Yes
10	Wednesday	Low		24	Wednesday	Low	
11	Thursday	High		25	Thursday	High	
12	Friday	High		26	Friday	High	
13	Saturday	High		27	Saturday	High	
14	Sunday	Low		28	Sunday	Low	

Do you notice any problems with our selection of observation days in Table 6.3? Apparently, we'll only be observing on Tuesdays. Moreover, Tuesdays may not be an ideal day to observe binge drinking behavior because binge drinking may be more likely to happen over the weekend.

STRATIFIED RANDOM SAMPLING

Another type of random sampling that could be helpful in cases such as this is stratified random sampling. In **stratified random sampling**, a researcher divides the sampling frame into relevant subgroups and then draw a sample from each subgroup. In this example, we might wish to first divide our sampling frame into two lists: weekend and weekdays. Once we have our two lists, we can then apply either simple random or systematic sampling techniques to each subgroup.

Stratified sampling is a good technique to use when, as in our example, a subgroup of interest makes up a relatively small proportion of the overall sample. In our example of a study of binge drinking, we want to include weekdays and weekends in our sample, but because weekends make up less than a third of an entire week, there's a chance that a simple random or systematic strategy would not yield sufficient weekend observation days. As you might imagine, stratified sampling is even more useful in cases where a subgroup makes up an even smaller proportion of the sampling frame—for example, if we want to be sure to include in our study students who are in year five of their undergraduate program but this subgroup makes up only a small percentage of the population of undergraduates. There's a chance simple random or systematic sampling strategy might not yield any fifth-year students, but by using stratified sampling, we could ensure that our sample contained the proportion of fifth-year students that is reflective of the larger population.

In this case, class year (e.g., freshman, sophomore, junior, senior, and fifth-year and higher) is our **strata**, or the characteristic by which the sample is divided. In using stratified sampling, we are often concerned with how well our sample reflects the population. A sample with too many freshmen may skew our results in one direction because perhaps they binge drink more (or less) than students in other class years. **Proportionate stratified random sampling** allows us to make sure our sample has the same proportion of people from each class year as the overall population of the school. **Disproportionate stratified random sampling** allows us to over-sample smaller groups to ensure we have enough elements from the smaller group(s) for statistical analyses.

CLUSTER SAMPLING

Up to this point in our discussion of probability samples, we've assumed that researchers will be able to access a list of population elements in order to create a sampling frame. This, as you might imagine, is not always the case. Let's say, for example, that you wish to conduct a study of binge drinking across fraternity members at each undergraduate program in your state. Just imagine trying to create a list of every single fraternity member in the state. Even if you could find a way to generate such a list, attempting to do so might not be the most practical use of your time or resources. When this is the case, researchers turn to cluster sampling. **Cluster sampling** occurs when a researcher begins by randomly sampling groups (or clusters) of population elements and then selects elements from within those groups.

Let's work through how we might use cluster sampling in our study of binge drinking. While creating a list of all fraternity members in your state would be next to impossible, you could easily create a list of all undergraduate colleges in your state. Thus, you could draw a random sample of undergraduate colleges (your cluster) and then draw another random sample of elements (in this case, fraternity members) from within the undergraduate college you initially selected. Cluster sampling works in stages. In this example, we sampled in two stages— (1) undergraduate colleges and (2) fraternity members at the undergraduate colleges we selected. However, we could add another stage if it made sense to do so. We could randomly select (1) undergraduate colleges (2) specific fraternities at each school and (3) individual fraternity members. As you might have guessed, sampling in multiple stages does introduce the possibility of greater error (each stage is subject to its own sampling error), but it is nevertheless highly efficien.

Jessica Holt and Wayne Gillespie (2008) used cluster sampling in their study of students' experiences with violence in intimate relationships. Specifically, the researchers randomly selected 14 classes on their campus and then drew a random subsample of students from those classes. But you probably know from your experience with college classes that not all classes are the same size. So, if Holt and Gillespie had simply randomly selected 14 classes and then selected the same number of students from each class to complete their survey, then students in the smaller of those classes would have had a greater chance of being selected for the study than students in the larger classes. Keep in mind, with random sampling the goal is to make sure that each element has the same chance of being selected. When clusters are of different sizes, as in the example of sampling college classes, researchers often use a method called **probability proportionate to size** (PPS). This means that they take into account that their clusters are of different sizes. They do this by giving clusters different chances of being selected based on their size so that each element within those clusters winds up having an equal chance of being selected.

COMPARING RANDOM SAMPLING TECHNIQUES

To summarize, probability samples are used to help a researcher make conclusions about larger groups. Probability samples require a sampling frame from which elements, usually human beings, can be selected at random from a list. The use of random selection reduces the error and bias present in the nonprobability sample types reviewed in the previous section, though some error will always remain. This strength is common to all probability sampling approaches summarized in Table 6.4.

Table 6.4 Types of probability samples

Sample type	Description
Simple random	Researcher randomly selects elements from sampling frame.
Systematic random	Researcher selects every kth element from sampling frame.
Stratified random	Researcher creates subgroups then randomly selects elements from each subgroup.
Cluster	Researcher randomly selects clusters then randomly selects elements from selected clusters.

In determining which probability sampling approach makes the most sense for your project, it helps to know more about your population. A simple random sample and systematic random sample are relatively similar to carry out. They both require a list of all elements in your sampling frame. Systematic random sampling is slightly easier in that it does not require you to use a random number generator for each element; instead it uses a sampling interval that is easy to calculate by hand.

The relative simplicity of both approaches is counter-weighted by their lack of sensitivity to characteristics in of your population. Stratified random samples help ensure that smaller subgroups are included in your sample, thus making the sample more representative of the overall population or allowing statistical analyses on subgroup differences possible. While these benefits are important, creating strata for this purpose requires knowing information about your population before beginning the sampling process. In our binge drinking example, we would need to know how many students are in each class year to make sure our sample contained the same proportions. We would need to know that, for example, fifth-year students make up 5% of the student population to make sure 5% of our sample is comprised of fifth-year students. If the true population parameters are unknown, stratified sampling becomes significantly more challenging.

Common to each of the previous probability sampling approaches is the necessity of using a real list of all elements in your sampling frame. Cluster sampling is different. It allows a researcher to perform probability sampling in cases for which a list of elements is not available or pragmatic to create. Cluster sampling is also useful for making claims about a larger population, in our example, all fraternity members within a state. However, because sampling occurs at multiple stages in the process, in our example at the university and student level, sampling error increases. For many researchers, this weakness is outweighed by the benefits of cluster sampling.

Key Takeaways

- In probability sampling, the aim is to identify a sample that resembles the population from which it was drawn.
- There are several types of probability samples including simple random samples, systematic samples, stratified samples, and cluster samples.
- Probability samples usually require a real list of elements in your sampling frame, though cluster sampling can be conducted without one.

Glossary

- Cluster sampling- a sampling approach that begins by sampling groups (or clusters) of population elements and then selects elements from within those groups
- Disproportionate stratified random sampling-stratified random sampling where the proportion of elements from each group is not proportionate to that in the population (usually used to oversample small groups).
- Generalizability – the idea that a study's results will tell us something about a group larger than the sample from which the findings were generated
- Periodicity- the tendency for a pattern to occur at regular intervals
- Probability proportionate to size- in cluster sampling, giving clusters different chances of being selected based on their size so that each element within those clusters has an equal chance of being selected
- Probability sampling- sampling approaches for which a person's (or element's) likelihood of being selected from the sampling frame is known
- Proportionate stratified random sampling-stratified random sampling where the proportion of elements from each group is proportionate to that in the population
- Random selection- using a randomly generated numbers to determine who from the sampling frame gets recruited into the sample
- Representative sample- a sample that resembles the population from which it was drawn in all the ways that are important for the research being conducted
- Sampling error- a statistical calculation of the difference between results from a sample and the actual parameters of a population
- Simple random sampling- selecting elements from a list using randomly generated numbers
- Strata- the characteristic by which the sample is divided
- Stratified random sampling- dividing the study population into relevant subgroups and then draw a sample from each subgroup
- Systematic random sampling- selecting every *k*th element from a list

Image attributions

crowd men women by DasWortgewand CC-0

roll the dice by 955169 CC-0

Figure 10.2 copied from Blackstone, A. (2012) Principles of sociological inquiry: Qualitative and quantitative methods. Saylor Foundation. Retrieved from: https://saylordotorg.github.io/text_principles-of-sociological-inquiry-qualitative-and-quantitative-methods/ Shared under CC-BY-NC-SA 3.0 License

6.4 CRITICAL THINKING ABOUT SAMPLES

Learning Objectives

- Identify three questions you should ask about samples when reading research results
- Describe how bias impacts sampling

We read and hear about research results so often that we might sometimes overlook the need to ask important questions about where the research participants came from and how they are identified for inclusion. It is easy to focus only on findings when we're busy and when the really interesting stuff is in a study's conclusions, not its procedures. But now that you have some familiarity with the variety of procedures for selecting study participants, you are equipped to ask some very important questions about the findings you read and to be a more responsible consumer of research.

WHO WAS SAMPLED, HOW, AND FOR WHAT PURPOSE?

Have you ever been a participant in someone's research? If you have ever taken an introductory psychology or sociology class at a large university, that's probably a silly question to ask. Social science researchers on college campuses have a luxury that researchers elsewhere may not share—they have access to a whole bunch of (presumably) willing and able human guinea pigs. But that luxury comes at a cost—sample representativeness. One study of top academic journals in psychology found that over two-thirds (68%) of participants in studies published by those journals were based on samples drawn in the United States (Arnett, 2008). Further, the study found that two-thirds of the work that derived from U.S. samples published in the

Journal of Personality and Social Psychology was based on samples made up entirely of American undergraduates taking psychology courses.

These findings certainly raise the question: What do we actually learn from social scientific studies and about whom do we learn it? That is exactly the concern raised by Joseph Henrich and colleagues (Henrich, Heine, & Norenzayan, 2010), authors of the article "The Weirdest People in the World?" In their piece, Henrich and colleagues point out that behavioral scientists very commonly make sweeping claims about human nature based on samples drawn only from WEIRD (Western, Educated, Industrialized, Rich, and Democratic) societies, and often based on even narrower samples, as is the case with many studies relying on samples drawn from college classrooms. As it turns out, many robust findings about the nature of human behavior when it comes to fairness, cooperation, visual perception, trust, and other behaviors are based on studies that excluded participants from outside the United States and sometimes excluded anyone outside the college classroom (Begley, 2010). This certainly raises questions about what we really know about human behavior as opposed to U.S. resident or U.S. undergraduate behavior. Of course, not all research findings are based on samples of WEIRD folks. But even then, it would behoove us to pay attention to the population on which studies are based and the claims that are being made about to whom those studies apply.

In the preceding discussion, the concern is with researchers making claims about populations other than those from which their samples were drawn. A related, but slightly different, potential concern is selection bias. **Selection bias** occurs when the elements selected for inclusion in a study do not represent the larger population from which they were drawn. For example, if you were to sample people walking into the social work building on campus during each weekday, your sample would include too many social work majors and not enough non-social work majors. Furthermore, you would completely exclude students whose classes are at night. Bias may be introduced by the sampling method used or due to conscious or unconscious bias introduced by the researcher (Rubin & Babbie, 2017). A researcher might select people who "look like good research participants," in the process transferring their unconscious biases to their sample.

Another thing to keep in mind is that just because a sample may be representative in all respects that a researcher thinks are relevant, there may be aspects that are relevant that didn't occur to the researcher when she was drawing her sample. You might not think that a person's phone would have much to do with their voting preferences, for example. But had pollsters making predictions about the results of the 2008 presidential election not been careful to include both cell phone-only and landline households in their surveys, it is possible that their predictions would have underestimated Barack Obama's lead over John McCain because Obama was much more popular among cell-only users than McCain (Keeter, Dimock, & Christian, 2008).

So how do we know when we can count on results that are being reported to us? While there might not be any magic or always-true rules we can apply, there are a couple of things we can keep in mind as we read the claims researchers make about their findings.

First, remember that sample quality is determined by the sample actually obtained, not by the sampling method itself. A researcher may set out to administer a survey to a representative sample by correctly employing a random selection technique, but if only a handful of the people sampled actually respond to the survey, the researcher will have to be very careful about the claims she can make about her survey findings.

Another thing to keep in mind, as demonstrated by the preceding discussion, is that researchers may be drawn to talking about implications of their findings as though they apply to some group other than the population actually sampled. Though this tendency is usually quite innocent and does not come from a place of malice, it is all too tempting a way to talk about findings; as consumers of those findings, it is our responsibility to be attentive to this sort of (likely unintentional) bait and switch.

Finally, keep in mind that a sample that allows for comparisons of theoretically important concepts or variables is certainly better than one that does not allow for such comparisons. In a study based on a nonrepresentative sample, for example, we can learn about the strength of our social theories by comparing relevant aspects of social processes. We talked about this as theory-testing in Chapter 4.

At their core, questions about sample quality should address who has been sampled, how they were sampled, and for what purpose they were sampled. Being able to answer those questions will help you better understand, and more responsibly read, research results.

Key Takeaways

- Sometimes researchers may make claims about populations other than those from whom their samples were drawn; other times they may make claims about a population based on a sample that is not representative. As consumers of research, we should be attentive to both possibilities.

- A researcher's findings need not be generalizable to be valuable; samples that allow for comparisons of theoretically important concepts or variables may yield findings that contribute to our social theories and our understandings of social processes.

Glossary

- Selection bias- when the elements selected for inclusion in a study do not represent the larger population from which they were drawn due to sampling method or thought processes of the researcher

Image attributions

men women apparel couple by 5688709 CC-0

ignorance by Rilsonav CC-0

CHAPTER SEVEN: SURVEY RESEARCH

In 2008, the voters of the United States elected our first African American president, Barack Obama. It may not surprise you to learn that when President Obama was coming of age in the 1970s, one-quarter of Americans reported they would not vote for a qualified African American presidential nominee. Three decades later, when President Obama ran for the presidency, fewer than 8% of Americans still held that position, and President Obama won the election (Smith, 2009). We know about these trends in voter opinion because the General Social Survey, a nationally representative survey of American adults, included questions about race and voting over the years described here. Without survey research, we may not know how Americans' perspectives on race and the presidency shifted over these years.

CHAPTER OUTLINE

- 7.1 Survey research: What is it and when should it be used?
- 7.2 Assessing survey research
- 7.3 Types of surveys
- 7.4 Designing effective questions and questionnaires

CONTENT ADVISORY

This chapter discusses or mentions the following topics: physical and psychological abusive behaviors in dating and romantic relationships, racism, mental health, terrorism and 9/11, substance use, and sexism and ageism in the workplace.

Image attributions

All figures in this chapter were copied from Blackstone, A. (2012) *Principles of sociological inquiry: Qualitative and quantitative methods.* Saylor Foundation. Retrieved from: https://saylordotorg.github.io/text_principles-of-sociological-inquiry-qualitative-and-quantitative-methods/ Shared under CC-BY-NC-SA 3.0 License

7.1 SURVEY RESEARCH: WHAT IS IT AND WHEN SHOULD IT BE USED?

<table>
<tr><td colspan="2" align="center">Learning Objectives</td></tr>
<tr><td>•</td><td>Define survey research</td></tr>
<tr><td>•</td><td>Identify when it is appropriate to employ survey research as a data-collection strategy</td></tr>
</table>

Most of you have probably taken a survey at one time or another, so you probably have a pretty good idea of what a survey is. However, there is more to constructing a good survey than meets the eye. Survey design takes a great deal of thoughtful planning and often a great many rounds of revision. But it is worth the effort. As we'll learn in this chapter, there are many benefits to choosing survey research as a method of data collection. We'll take a look at what a survey is exactly, what some of the benefits and drawbacks of this method are, how to construct a survey, and what to do with survey data once it is collected.

Survey research is a quantitative method in which a researcher poses a set of predetermined questions to a sample of individuals. Survey research is an especially useful approach when a researcher aims to describe or explain features of a very large group or groups. This method may also be used as a way of quickly gaining some general details about a population of interest. In this case, a survey may help a researcher identify specific individuals or locations from which to collect additional data.

As is true of all methods of data collection, survey research is better suited to answering some kinds of research questions more than others. In addition, as you'll recall from Chapter 5, operationalization works differently with different research methods. If your interest is in political activism, for example, you might operationalize that concept differently in a survey than you would for an experimental study of the same topic.

SPOTLIGHT ON UTA SCHOOL OF SOCIAL WORK

DIANA PADILLA-MEDINA CONDUCTS SURVEY RESEARCH

Dr. Diana Padilla-Medina, an assistant professor at the University of Texas at Arlington's School of Social Work, and a team of researchers (Padilla-Medina, Rodríguez, & Vega, 2019; Padilla-Medina, Rodríguez, Vega & Williams, 2019) are conducting a cross-sectional survey with a sample of urban Puerto Rican adolescents living in Puerto Rico to study the behavioral factors that influence adolescents' intention to use physical and psychological abusive behaviors in dating and romantic relationships. The study also explores how gender, development stage, and exposure to family violence influence both behavioral factors and intentions. A sample of 2000 adolescents between the ages of 13 and 17 years are being recruited from communities across five towns in Puerto Rico using area sampling techniques. Area sampling is a technique often used in survey research conducted in large geographical settings, such as towns and communities. When using this technique, the target population is divided into clusters, or geographic areas, and a random sample of the clusters are selected. Communities served as the geographic area from which adolescents were recruited. As with any research study involving human subjects, consent and assent was obtained from participants and their parents or caregivers.

An in-person survey in which an interviewer administers the survey is being administered to the adolescents in their homes. For this survey research, an interview schedule (i.e., survey instrument or questionnaire) was developed. When developing a survey instrument or questionnaire, it is important to consider the audience in order to choose the appropriate form to administer the survey. In this case, Dr. Padilla-Medina and her team, based on previous pilot qualitative and quantitative studies, determined that Puerto Ricans prefer to be interviewed in person, particularly when the study topic and questions are personal and sensitive. Additionally, when developing and/or administering a survey instrument it is important to pilot test the instrument to evaluate adequacy, psychometric properties, time, cost, adverse events, and improve upon the instrument prior to using it in a larger sample. For example, in their previous studies, the researchers used focus groups to learn about the adolescents' perceptions about the readability and understandability of the instrument. In addition, the instrument was pilot tested to assess its psychometric properties and ensure it was ready for use in the larger survey research.

Finally, in any type of survey research, there is the potential for social desirability effects. This means that participants' report an answer that he or she thinks would be desirable or acceptable by the interviewer, rather than their "true" answer. These behaviors could bias the study results. There are several social desirability measures that are used to reduce the possibility of these types of biases. Considering the sensitive nature of the current study topic and questions, the researchers used a social desirability measure to assess if the adolescents were or not concerned with social approval.

Key Takeaways

- Survey research is often used by researchers who wish to explain trends or features of large groups. It may also be used to assist those planning some more focused, in-depth study.

Glossary

- Survey research- a quantitative method whereby a researcher poses some set of predetermined questions to a sample

Image attributions

survey by andibreit CC-0

DianaPadilla by William Cordero Photography (c) All rights reserved

7.2 ASSESSING SURVEY RESEARCH

Learning Objectives

- Identify and explain the strengths of survey research
- Identify and explain the weaknesses of survey research
- Define response rate, and discuss some of the current thinking about response rates

Survey research, as with all methods of data collection, comes with both strengths and weaknesses. We'll examine both in this section.

STRENGTHS OF SURVEY METHODS

Researchers employing survey methods to collect data enjoy a number of benefits. First, surveys are an excellent way to gather lots of information from many people. Some methods of administering surveys can be cost effective. In a study of older people's experiences in the workplace, researchers were able to mail a written questionnaire to around 500 people who lived throughout the state of Maine at a cost of just over $1,000. This cost included printing copies of a seven-page survey, printing a cover letter, addressing and stuffing envelopes, mailing the survey, and buying return postage for the survey. In some contexts, $,1,000 is a lot of money, but just imagine what it might have cost to visit each of those people individually to interview them in person. You would have to dedicate a few weeks of your life at least, drive around the state, and pay for meals and lodging to interview each person individually. We could double, triple, or even quadruple our costs pretty quickly by opting for an in-person method of data collection over a mailed survey.

Related to the benefit of cost-effectiveness is a survey's potential for generalizability. Because surveys allow researchers to collect data from very large samples for a relatively low cost, survey methods lend themselves to probability sampling techniques, which we discussed in Chapter 6. Of all the data collection methods described in this textbook, survey research is probably the best method to use when one hopes to gain a representative picture of the attitudes and characteristics of a large group.

Survey research also tends to be a *reliable* method of inquiry. This is because surveys are standardized in that the same questions, phrased in exactly the same way, are posed to participants. Other methods, such as qualitative interviewing, which we'll learn about in Chapter 9, do not offer the same consistency that a quantitative survey offers. This is not to say that all surveys are always reliable. A poorly phrased question can cause respondents to interpret its meaning differently, which can reduce that question's reliability. Assuming well-constructed questions and survey design, one strength of this methodology is its potential to produce reliable results.

The *versatility* of survey research is also an asset. Surveys are used by all kinds of people in all kinds of professions. The versatility offered by survey research means that understanding how to construct and administer surveys is a useful skill to have for all kinds of jobs. Lawyers might use surveys in their efforts to select juries, social service and other organizations (e.g., churches, clubs, fundraising groups, activist groups) use them to evaluate the effectiveness of their efforts, businesses use them to learn how to market their products, governments use them to understand community opinions and needs, and politicians and media outlets use surveys to understand their constituencies.

In sum, the following are benefits of survey research:

- Cost-effectiveness
- Generalizability
- Reliability
- Versatility

WEAKNESSES OF SURVEY METHODS

As with all methods of data collection, survey research also comes with a few drawbacks. First, while one might argue that surveys are flexible in the sense that we can ask any number of questions on any number of topics in them, the fact that the survey researcher is generally stuck with a single instrument for collecting data, the questionnaire. Surveys are in many ways rather *inflexible*. Let's say you mail a survey out to 1,000 people and then discover, as responses start coming in, that your phrasing on a particular question seems to be confusing a number of respondents. At this stage, it's too late for a do-over or to change the question for the respondents who haven't yet returned their surveys. When conducting in-depth interviews, on the other hand, a researcher can provide respondents further explanation if they're confused by a question and can tweak their questions as they learn more about how respondents seem to understand them.

Depth can also be a problem with surveys. Survey questions are usually standardized; thus, it can be difficult to ask anything other than very general questions that a broad range of people will understand. Because of this, survey results may not be as valid as results obtained using methods of data collection that allow a researcher to more comprehensively examine whatever topic is being studied. Let's say, for example, that you want to learn something about voters' willingness to elect an African American president, as in our opening example in this chapter. General Social Survey respondents were asked, "If your party nominated an African American for president, would you vote for him if he were qualified for the job?" Respondents were then asked to respond either yes or no to the question. But what if someone's opinion was more complex than could be answered with a simple yes or no? What if, for example, a person was willing to vote for a qualified African American but not if he chose a vice president the respondent didn't like?

In sum, potential drawbacks to survey research include the following:

- Inflexibility
- Lack of depth

RESPONSE RATES

The relative strength or weakness of an individual survey is strongly affected by the **response rate**, the percent of people invited to take the survey who actually complete it. Let's say researcher sends a survey to 100 people. It would be wonderful if all 100 returned completed the questionnaire, but the chances of that happening are about zero. If the researcher is incredibly lucky, perhaps 75 or so will return completed questionnaires. In this case, the **response rate** would be 75%. The response rate is calculated by dividing the number of surveys returned by the number of surveys distributed.

Though response rates vary, and researchers don't always agree about what makes a good response rate; having 75% of your surveys returned would be considered good—even excellent—by most survey researchers. There has been a lot of research done on how to improve a survey's response rate. Suggestions include personalizing questionnaires by, for example, addressing them to specific respondents rather than to some generic recipient, such as "madam" or "sir"; enhancing the questionnaire's credibility by providing details about the study, contact information for the researcher, and perhaps partnering with agencies likely to be respected by respondents such as universities, hospitals, or other relevant organizations; sending out pre-questionnaire notices and post-questionnaire reminders; and including some token of appreciation with mailed questionnaires even if small, such as a $1 bill.

The major concern with response rates is that a low rate of response may introduce **nonresponse bias** into a study's findings. What if only those who have strong opinions about your study topic return their questionnaires? If that is the case, we may well find that our findings don't at all represent how things really are or, at the very least, we are limited in the claims we can make about patterns found in our data. While high return rates are certainly ideal, a recent body of research shows that concern over response rates may be overblown (Langer, 2003). Several studies have shown that low response rates did not make much difference in findings or in sample representativeness (Curtin, Presser, & Singer, 2000; Keeter, Kennedy, Dimock, Best, & Craighill, 2006; Merkle & Edelman, 2002). For now, the jury may still be out on what makes an ideal response rate and on whether, or to what extent, researchers should be concerned about response rates. Nevertheless, certainly no harm can come from aiming for as high a response rate as possible.

Key Takeaways

- Strengths of survey research include its cost effectiveness, generalizability, reliability, and versatility.
- Weaknesses of survey research include inflexibility and issues with depth.
- While survey researchers should always aim to obtain the highest response rate possible, some recent research argues that high return rates on surveys may be less important than we once thought.

Glossary

- Nonresponse bias- bias reflected differences between people who respond to your survey and those who do not respond
- Response rate- the number of people who respond to your survey divided by the number of people to whom the survey was distributed

Image attributions

experience by mohamed_hassan CC-0

7.3 TYPES OF SURVEYS

Learning Objectives

- Define cross-sectional surveys, provide an example of a cross-sectional survey, and outline some of the drawbacks of cross-sectional research
- Describe the three types of longitudinal surveys
- Describe retrospective surveys and identify their strengths and weaknesses
- Discuss the benefits and drawbacks of the various methods of administering surveys

There is immense variety when it comes to surveys. This variety comes both in terms of *time*—when or with what frequency a survey is administered—and in terms of *administration*—how a survey is delivered to respondents. In this section, we'll look at what types of surveys exist when it comes to both time and administration.

TIME

In terms of time, there are two main types of surveys: cross-sectional and longitudinal. **Cross-sectional surveys** are those that are administered at just one point in time. These surveys offer researchers a snapshot in time and offer an idea about how things are for the respondents at the particular point in time that the survey is administered.

An example of a cross-sectional survey comes from Aniko Kezdy and colleagues' study (Kezdy, Martos, Boland, & Horvath-Szabo, 2011) of the association between religious attitudes, religious beliefs, and mental health among students in Hungary. These researchers administered a single, one-time-only, cross-sectional survey to a convenience sample of 403 high school and college students. The survey focused on how religious attitudes impact various aspects of one's life and health. The researchers found from analysis of their cross-sectional data that anxiety and depression were highest among those who had both strong religious beliefs and some doubts about religion.

Yet another example of cross-sectional survey research can be seen in Bateman and colleagues' study (Bateman, Pike, & Butler, 2011) of how the perceived publicness of social networking sites influences users' self-disclosures. These researchers administered an online survey to undergraduate and graduate business students. They found that even though revealing information about oneself is viewed as key to realizing many of the benefits of social networking sites, respondents were less willing to disclose information about themselves as their perceptions of a social networking site's publicness rose. That is, there was a negative relationship between perceived publicness of a social networking site and plans to self-disclose on the site.

One problem with cross-sectional surveys is that the events, opinions, behaviors, and other phenomena that such surveys are designed to assess don't generally remain stagnant. They change over time. Thus, generalizing from a cross-sectional survey about the way things are can be tricky; perhaps you can say something about the way things were in the moment that you administered your survey, but it is difficult to know whether things remained that way for long after you administered your survey. For example, think about how Americans might have responded to a survey asking their opinions on terrorism on September 10, 2001. Now imagine how responses to the same set of questions might differ were they administered on September 12, 2001. The point is not that cross-sectional surveys are useless; they have many important uses. But researchers must remember what they have captured by administering a cross-sectional survey—a snapshot of life as it was at the time that the survey was administered.

One way to overcome this sometimes problematic aspect of cross-sectional surveys is to administer a longitudinal survey. **Longitudinal surveys** are those that enable a researcher to make observations over some extended period of time. There are several types of longitudinal surveys, including trend, panel, and cohort surveys. We'll discuss all three types here, along with retrospective surveys. Retrospective surveys fall somewhere in between cross-sectional and longitudinal surveys.

The first type of longitudinal survey is called a **trend survey**. The main focus of a trend survey is, perhaps not surprisingly, trends. Researchers conducting trend surveys are interested in how people in a specific group change over time. Each time the researchers gather data, they ask different people from the group they are describing because their concern is the group, not the individual people they survey. Let's look at an example.

The Monitoring the Future Study is a trend study that described the substance use of high school children in the United States. It's conducted annually by the National Institute on Drug Abuse (NIDA). Each year, NIDA distributes surveys to students in high schools around the country to understand how substance use and abuse in that population changes over time. Recently, fewer high school students have reported using alcohol in the past month than at any point over the last 20 years. Recent data also reflect an increased use of e-cigarettes and the popularity of e-cigarettes with no nicotine over those with nicotine. The data points provide insight into targeting substance abuse prevention programs towards the current issues facing the high school population.

Unlike in a trend survey, in a **panel survey** the *same people* participate in the survey each time it is administered. As you might imagine, panel studies can be difficult and costly. Imagine trying to administer a survey to the same 100 people every year for, say, 5 years in a row.

Keeping track of where people live, when they move, and when they die takes resources that researchers often don't have. When they do, however, the results can be quite powerful. The Youth Development Study (YDS), administered from the University of Minnesota, offers an excellent example of a panel study.

Since 1988, YDS researchers have administered an annual survey to the same 1,000 people. Study participants were in ninth grade when the study began, and they are now in their thirties. Several hundred papers, articles, and books have been written using data from the YDS. One of the major lessons learned from this panel study is that work has a largely positive impact on young people (Mortimer, 2003). Contrary to popular beliefs about the impact of work on adolescents' performance in school and transition to adulthood, work in fact increases confidence, enhances academic success, and prepares students for success in their future careers. Without this panel study, we may not be aware of the positive impact that working can have on young people.

Another type of longitudinal survey is a cohort survey. In a **cohort survey**, the participants have a defining age- or time-based characteristic that the researcher is interested in studying. Common cohorts that may be of interest to researchers include people of particular generations or those who were born around the same time period, graduating classes, people who began work in a given industry at the same time, or perhaps people who have some specific historical experience in common. In a cohort study, the same people don't necessarily participate from year to year. But each year, participants must belong to the cohort of interest.

An example of this sort of research can be seen in Christine Percheski's work (2008) on cohort differences in women's employment. Percheski compared women's employment rates across seven different generational cohorts, from Progressives born between 1906 and 1915 to Generation Xers born between 1966 and 1975. She found, among other patterns, that professional women's labor force participation had increased across all cohorts. She also found that professional women with young children from Generation X had higher labor force participation rates than similar women from previous generations, concluding that mothers do not appear to be opting out of the workforce as some journalists have speculated (Belkin, 2003).

All three types of longitudinal surveys share the strength that they permit a researcher to make observations over time. This means that if whatever behavior or other phenomenon the researcher is interested in changes, either because of some world event or because people age, the researcher will be able to capture those changes. Table 7.1 summarizes these three types of longitudinal surveys.

Table 7.1 Types of longitudinal surveys

Sample type	Description
Trend	Researcher examines changes in trends over time; the same people do not necessarily participate in the survey more than once.
Panel	Researcher surveys the exact same sample several times over a period of time.
Cohort	Researcher identifies a defining cohort based on an age- or time-related characteristic and then regularly surveys people in the cohort

Finally, **retrospective surveys** are similar to other longitudinal studies in that they deal with changes over time, but like a cross-sectional study, they are administered only once. In a retrospective survey, participants are asked to report events from the past. By having respondents report past behaviors, beliefs, or experiences, researchers are able to gather longitudinal-*like* data without actually incurring the time or expense of a longitudinal survey. Of course, this benefit must be weighed against the possibility that people's recollections of their pasts may be faulty. Imagine, for example, that you're asked in a survey to respond to questions about where, how, and with whom you spent last Valentine's Day. As last Valentine's Day can't have been more than 12 months ago, chances are good that you might be able to respond accurately to any survey questions about it. But now let's say the researcher wants to know how last Valentine's Day compares to previous Valentine's Days, so she asks you to report on where, how, and with whom you spent the preceding six Valentine's Days. How likely is it that you will remember? Will your responses be as accurate as they might have been had you been asked the question each year over the past 6 years, rather than asked to report on all years today?

In summary, when or with what frequency a survey is administered will determine whether your survey is cross-sectional or longitudinal. While longitudinal surveys are certainly preferable in terms of their ability to track changes over time, the time and cost required to administer a longitudinal survey can be prohibitive. As you may have guessed, the issues of time described here are not necessarily unique to survey research. Other methods of data collection can be cross-sectional or longitudinal—these are really matters of all research design. But we've placed our discussion of these terms here because they are most commonly used by survey researchers to describe the type of survey administered. Another aspect of survey administration deals with how surveys are administered. We'll examine that next.

ADMINISTRATION

Surveys vary not just in terms of when they are administered but also in terms of how they are administered.

SELF-ADMINISTERED QUESTIONNAIRES

One common way to administer surveys is in the form of **self-administered questionnaires.** This means that a research participant is given a set of questions, in writing, to which they are asked to respond. Self-administered questionnaires can be delivered in hard copy format, typically via mail, or increasingly more commonly, online. We'll consider both modes of delivery here.

Hard copy self-administered questionnaires may be delivered to participants in person or via snail mail. Perhaps you've taken a survey that was given to you in person; on many college campuses, it is not uncommon for researchers to administer surveys in large social science classes (as you might recall from the discussion in our chapter on sampling). If you are ever asked to complete a survey in a **large group setting**, it might be interesting to note how your perspective on the survey and its questions could be shaped by the new knowledge you're gaining about survey research in this chapter.

Researchers may also deliver surveys **in person** by going door-to-door and either asking people to fill them out right away or making arrangements for the researcher to return to pick up completed surveys. Though the advent of online survey tools has made door-to-door delivery of surveys less common, it still happens on occasion. This mode of gathering data is apparently still used by political campaign workers, at least in some areas of the country.

If you are not able to visit each member of your sample personally to deliver a survey, you might consider sending your survey **through the mail**. While this mode of delivery may not be ideal (imagine how much *less* likely you'd probably be to return a survey that didn't come with the researcher standing on your doorstep waiting to take it from you), sometimes it is the only available or the most practical option. As mentioned, though, this may not be the most ideal way of administering a survey because it can be difficult to convince people to take the time to complete and return your survey.

Often survey researchers who deliver their surveys through the mail may provide some advance notice to respondents about the survey to get people thinking about and preparing to complete it. They may also follow up with their sample a few weeks after their survey has been sent out. This can be done not only to remind those who have not yet completed the survey to please do so but also to thank those who have already returned the survey. Most survey researchers agree that this sort of follow-up is essential for improving mailed surveys' return rates (Babbie, 2010). Other helpful tools to increase response rate are to create an attractive and professional survey, offer monetary incentives, and provide a pre-addressed, stamped return envelope.

Online surveys are becoming increasingly common, no doubt because it is easy to use, relatively cheap, and may be quicker than knocking on doors or waiting for mailed surveys to be returned. To deliver a survey online, a researcher may subscribe to a service that offers online delivery or use some delivery mechanism that is available for free. Both SurveyMonkey and Qualtrics offer free and paid online survey services. One advantage to using services like these, aside from the advantages of online delivery already mentioned, is that results can be provided to you in formats that are readable by data analysis programs such as SPSS. This saves you, the researcher, the step of having to manually enter data into your analysis program, as you would if you administered your survey in hard copy format.

Many of the suggestions provided for improving the response rate on a hard copy questionnaire apply to online questionnaires as well. One difference of course is that the sort of incentives one can provide in an online format differ from those that can be given in person or sent through the mail. But this doesn't mean that online survey researchers cannot offer completion incentives to their respondents. Sometimes they provide coupon codes for online retailers or the opportunity to provide contact information to participate in a raffle for a gift card or merchandise.

Online surveys, however, may not be accessible to individuals with limited, unreliable, or no access to the internet or less skill at using a computer. If those issues are common in your target population, online surveys may not work as well for your research study. While online surveys may be faster and cheaper than mailed surveys, mailed surveys are more likely to reach your entire sample but also more likely to be lost and not returned. The choice of which delivery mechanism is best depends on a number of factors, including your resources, the resources of your study participants, and the time you have available to distribute surveys and wait for responses. Understanding the characteristics of your study's population is key to identifying the appropriate mechanism for delivering your survey.

INTERVIEWS

Sometimes surveys are administered by having a researcher poses questions verbally to respondents rather than having respondents read the questions on their own. Researchers using phone or in-person surveys use an **interview schedule** which contains the list of questions and answer options that the researcher will read to respondents. Consistency in the way that questions and answer options are presented is very important with an interview schedule. The aim is to pose every question-and-answer option in the very same way to every respondent. This is done to minimize interviewer effect, or possible changes in the way an interviewee responds based on how or when questions and answer options are presented by the interviewer. Survey interviews may be recorded, but because questions tend to be closed ended, taking notes during the interview is less disruptive than it can be during a qualitative interview.

Interview schedules are used in phone or in-person surveys and are also called quantitative interviews. In both cases, researchers pose questions verbally to participants. Phone surveys make it difficult to control the environment in which a person answers your survey. Another challenge comes from the increasing number of people who only have cell phones and do not use landlines (Pew Research, n.d.). Unlike landlines, cell phone numbers are portable across carriers, associated with individuals, not households, and do not change their first three numbers when people move to a new geographical area. However, computer-assisted telephone interviewing (CATI) programs have also been developed to assist quantitative survey researchers. These programs allow an interviewer to enter responses directly into a computer as they are provided, thus saving hours of time that would otherwise have to be spent entering data into an analysis program by hand.

Quantitative interviews must also be administered in such a way that the researcher asks the same question the same way each time. While questions on hard copy questionnaires may create an impression based on the way they are presented, having a person administer questions introduces a slew of additional variables that might influence a respondent. Even a slight shift in emphasis on a word may bias the respondent to answer differently. Consistency is key with quantitative data collection—and human beings are not necessarily known for their consistency. Quantitative interviews can also help reduce a respondent's confusion. If a respondent is unsure about the meaning of a question or answer option on a self-administered questionnaire, they probably won't have the opportunity to get clarification from the researcher. An interview, on the other hand, gives the researcher an opportunity to clarify or explain any items that may be confusing. If a participant asks for clarification, the researcher must use pre-determined responses to make sure each quantitative interview is exactly the same as the others.

In-person surveys are conducted in the same way as phone surveys but must also account for non-verbal expressions and behaviors. In-person surveys have one distinct benefit—they are more difficult to say "no" to. Because the participant is already in the room and sitting across from the researcher, they are less likely to decline than if they clicked "delete" for an emailed online survey or pressed "hang up" during a phone survey. In-person surveys are also much more time consuming and expensive than mailing questionnaires. Thus, quantitative researchers may opt for self-administered questionnaires over in-person surveys on the grounds that they will be able to reach a large sample at a much lower cost than were they to interact personally with each and every respondent.

Table 7.2 summarizes the various ways to collect survey data.

Table 7.2

Self-administered	given in a large group setting
	delivered in person
	sent through the mail
	online
Interviews	in-person
	telephone

Key Takeaways

- Time is a factor in determining what type of survey researcher administers; cross-sectional surveys are administered at one time, and longitudinal surveys are administered over time.

- Retrospective surveys offer some of the benefits of longitudinal research but also come with their own drawbacks.

- Self-administered questionnaires may be delivered in hard copy form to participants in person or via mail or online.

- Interview schedules are used in in-person or phone surveys.

- Each method of survey administration comes with benefits and drawbacks.

Glossary

- Cohort survey- describes how people with a defining characteristic change over time

- Cross-sectional surveys- surveys that are administered at just one point in time

- Interview schedules- a researcher poses questions verbally to respondents

- Longitudinal surveys- surveys in which a researcher to make observations over some extended period of time

- Panel survey- describes how people in a specific group change over time, asking the same people each time the survey is administered

- Retrospective surveys- describe changes over time but are administered only once

- Self-administered questionnaires- a research participant is given a set of questions, in writing, to which they are asked to respond

- Trend survey- describes how people in a specific group change over time, asking different people each time the survey is administered

Image attributions

company social networks by Hurca CC-0

posts submit searching by mohamed_hassan CC-0

talk telephone by MelanieSchwolert CC-0

7.4 DESIGNING EFFECTIVE QUESTIONS AND QUESTIONNAIRES

Learning Objectives

- Identify the steps one should take to write effective survey questions
- Describe some of the ways that survey questions might confuse respondents and how to overcome that possibility
- Apply mutual exclusivity and exhaustiveness to writing closed-ended questions
- Define fence-sitting and floating
- Describe the steps involved in constructing a well-designed questionnaire
- Discuss why piloting a questionnaire is important

Up to this point, we've considered several general points about surveys, including when to use them, some of their strengths and weaknesses, and how often and in what ways to administer surveys. In this section, we'll get more specific and take a look at how to pose understandable questions that will yield useable data and how to present those questions on a questionnaire.

ASKING EFFECTIVE QUESTIONS

The first thing you need to do to write effective survey questions is identify what exactly you wish to know. Perhaps surprisingly, it is easy to forget to include important questions when designing a survey. Begin by looking at your research question. Perhaps you wish to identify the factors that contribute to students' ability to transition from high school to college. To understand which factors shaped successful students' transitions to college, you'll need to include questions in your survey about all the possible factors that could contribute. How do you know what to ask? Consulting the literature on the topic will certainly help, but you should also take the time to do some brainstorming on your own and to talk with others about what they think may be important in the transition to college. Time and space limitations won't allow you to include every single item you've come up with, so you'll also need to think about ranking your questions so that you can be sure to include those that you view as most important. In your study, think back to your work on operationalization. How did you plan to measure your variables? If you planned to ask specific questions or use a scale, those should be in your survey.

We've discussed including questions on all topics you view as important to your overall research question, but you don't want to take an everything-but-the-kitchen-sink approach by uncritically including every possible question that occurs to you. Doing so puts an unnecessary burden on your survey respondents. Remember that you have asked your respondents to give you their time and attention and to take care in responding to your questions; show them your respect by only asking questions that you view as important.

Once you've identified all the topics about which you'd like to ask questions, you'll need to actually write those questions. Questions should be as clear and to the point as possible. This is not the time to show off your creative writing skills; a survey is a technical instrument and should be written in a way that is as direct and concise as possible. To reiterate, survey respondents have agreed to give their time and attention to your survey. The best way to show your appreciation for their time is to not waste it. Ensuring that your questions are clear and concise will go a long way toward showing your respondents the gratitude they deserve.

Related to the point about not wasting respondents' time, make sure that every question you pose will be relevant to every person you ask to complete it. This means two things: first, that respondents have knowledge about whatever topic you are asking them about, and second, that respondents have experience with whatever events, behaviors, or feelings you are asking them to report. You probably wouldn't want to ask a sample of 18-year-old respondents, for example, how they would have advised President Reagan to proceed when news of the United States' sale of weapons to Iran broke in the mid-1980s. For one thing, few 18-year-olds are likely to have any clue about how to advise a president. Furthermore, the 18-year-olds of today were not even alive during Reagan's presidency, so they have had no experience with Iran-Contra affair about which they are being questioned. In our example of the transition to college, heeding the criterion of relevance would mean that respondents must understand what exactly you mean by "transition to college" if you are going to use that phrase in your survey and that respondents must have actually experienced the transition to college themselves.

If you decide that you do wish to pose some questions about matters with which only a portion of respondents will have had experience, it may be appropriate to introduce a filter question into your survey. A **filter question** is designed to identify some subset of survey respondents who are asked additional questions that are not relevant to the entire sample. Perhaps in your survey on the transition to college you want to know whether substance use plays any role in students' transitions. You may ask students how often they drank during their first semester of college. But this assumes that all students drank. Certainly, some may have abstained from using alcohol, and it wouldn't make any sense to ask the nondrinkers how often they drank. Nevertheless, it seems reasonable that drinking frequency may have an impact on someone's transition to college, so it is probably worth asking this question even if doing means the question will not be relevant for some respondents. This is just the sort of instance when a filter question would be appropriate. With a filter question such as question # 10 in Figure 7.1, you can filter out respondents who have not had alcohol from answering questions about their alcohol use.

10. Did you drink any alcoholic beverages at any time during your first semester of college?

☐ Yes (If yes, answer Questions 10a and 10b.)

☐ No (If no, skip to Question 11.)

    10a. On average, how many times per week did you consume alcoholic beverages during your first semester of college?

        ☐ less than one time per week

        ☐ 1–2

        ☐ 3–4

        ☐ 5–6

        ☐ 7+

    10b. On average, how many drinks did you consume each time you drank during your first semester of college?

        ☐ less than one drink each time

        ☐ 1–2

        ☐ 3–4

        ☐ 5–6

        ☐ 7+

11. Did any of your friends on campus drink alcoholic beverages at any time during your first semester of college?

☐ Yes

☐ No

Figure 7.1 Filter question

There are some ways of asking questions that are bound to confuse many survey respondents. Survey researchers should take great care to avoid these kinds of questions. These include questions that pose *double negatives*, those that use *confusing or culturally specific terms*, and those that ask *more than one question within a single question*. Any time respondents are forced to decipher questions that use **double negatives**, confusion is bound to ensue. Taking the previous question about drinking as our example, what if we had instead asked, "Did you not abstain from drinking during your first semester of college?" This example is obvious, but hopefully it drives home the point to be careful about question wording so that respondents are not asked to decipher double negatives. In general, avoiding negative terms in your question wording will help to increase respondent understanding.

You should also avoid using **terms or phrases that may be regionally or culturally specific** (unless you are absolutely certain all your respondents come from the region or culture whose terms you are using). A similar issue arises when you use **jargon**, or technical language, that people do not commonly know. For example, if you asked adolescents how they experience imaginary audience, they likely would not be able to link that term to the concepts from David Elkind's theory. Instead, you would need to break down that term into language that is easier to understand and common to adolescents.

Asking multiple questions as though they are a single question can also confuse survey respondents. There's a specific term for this sort of question; it is called a **double-barreled question**. Using our example of the transition to college, Figure 7.2 shows a double-barreled question.

Did you find the classes you took during your first semester of college to be more demanding and interesting than your high school classes?

☐ Yes

☐ No

Figure 7.2 Double-barreled question

Do you see what makes the question double-barreled? How would someone respond if they felt their college classes were more demanding but also less interesting than their high school classes? Or less demanding but more interesting? Because the question combines "demanding" and "interesting," there is no way to respond yes to one criterion but no to the other.

Another thing to avoid when constructing survey questions is the problem of social desirability. We all want to look good, right? And we all probably know the politically correct response to a variety of questions whether we agree with the politically correct response or not. In survey research, **social desirability** refers to the idea that respondents will try to answer questions in a way that will present them in a favorable light. (You may recall we covered social desirability bias in Chapter 5.) Let's go back to our example about transitioning to college to explore this concept further.

Perhaps we decide that to understand the transition to college, we need to know whether respondents ever cheated on an exam in high school or college. Cheating on exams is generally frowned upon. So it may be difficult to get people taking a survey to admit to cheating on an exam. But if you could guarantee respondents' confidentiality, or even better, their anonymity, chances are much better that they will be honest about having engaged in this socially undesirable behavior. Another way to avoid problems of social desirability is to try to phrase difficult questions in the most benign way possible. Earl Babbie (2010) offers a useful suggestion for helping you do this—simply imagine how you would feel responding to your survey questions. If you would be uncomfortable, chances are others would as well.

Finally, it is important to get feedback on your survey questions from as many people as possible, especially people who are like those in your sample. Now is not the time to be shy. Ask your friends for help, ask your mentors for feedback, ask your family to take a look at your survey as well. The more feedback you can get on your survey questions, the better the chances that you will come up with a set of questions that are understandable to a wide variety of people and, most importantly, to those in your sample.

In sum, in order to pose effective survey questions, researchers should do the following:

- Identify what it is they wish to know.
- Keep questions clear and succinct.
- Make questions relevant to respondents.
- Use filter questions when necessary.
- Avoid questions that are likely to confuse respondents—including those that use double negatives, use culturally specific terms or jargon, or pose more than one question at a time.

- Imagine how respondents would feel responding to questions.
- Get feedback, especially from people who resemble those in the researcher's sample.

RESPONSE OPTIONS

While posing clear and understandable questions in your survey is certainly important, so too is providing respondents with unambiguous response options. Response options are the answers that you provide to the people taking your survey. Generally, respondents will be asked to choose a single (or best) response to each question you pose, though certainly it makes sense in some cases to instruct respondents to choose multiple response options. One caution to keep in mind when accepting multiple responses to a single question, however, is that doing so may add complexity when it comes to tallying and analyzing your survey results.

Offering response options assumes that your questions will be **closed-ended questions**. In a quantitative written survey, which is the type of survey we've been discussing here, chances are good that most, if not all, your questions will be closed-ended. This means that you, the researcher, will provide respondents with a limited set of options for their responses. To write an effective closed-ended question, there are a couple of guidelines worth following. First, be sure that your response options are *mutually exclusive*. Look back at Figure 7.1, which contains questions about how often and how many drinks respondents consumed. Do you notice that there are no overlapping categories in the response options for these questions? This is another one of those points about question construction that seems fairly obvious but that can be easily overlooked. Response options should also be *exhaustive*. In other words, every possible response should be covered in the set of response options that you provide. For example, note that in question 10a in Figure 7.1, we have covered all possibilities—those who drank, say, an average of once per month can choose the first response option ("less than one time per week") while those who drank multiple times a day each day of the week can choose the last response option ("7+"). All the possibilities in between these two extremes are covered by the middle three response options.

Surveys need not be limited to closed-ended questions. Sometimes survey researchers include open-ended questions in their survey instruments as a way to gather additional details from respondents. An **open-ended question** does not include response options; instead, respondents are asked to reply to the question in their own way, using their own words. These questions are generally used to find out more about a survey participant's experiences or feelings about whatever they are being asked to report in the survey. If, for example, a survey includes closed-ended questions asking respondents to report on their involvement in extracurricular activities during college, an open-ended question could ask respondents why they participated in those activities or what they gained from their participation. While responses to such questions may also be captured using a closed-ended format, allowing participants to share some of their responses in their own words can make the experience of completing the survey more satisfying to respondents and can also reveal new motivations or explanations that had not occurred to the researcher.

Earlier in this section, we discussed double-barreled questions, but response options can also be double barreled, and this should be avoided. Figure 7.3 provides an example of a question that uses **double-barreled response options**.

How did the classes you took during your first semester of college compare with your high school classes?

☐ More demanding and interesting

☐ Less demanding and interesting

Figure 7.3 Double-barreled response options

Other things to avoid when it comes to response options include fence-sitting and floating. **Fence-sitters** are respondents who choose neutral response options, even if they have an opinion. This can occur if respondents are given, say, five rank-ordered response options, such as strongly agree, agree, no opinion, disagree, and strongly disagree. You'll remember this is called a Likert scale. Some people will be drawn to respond, "no opinion" even if they have an opinion, particularly if their true opinion is the not a socially desirable opinion. **Floaters**, on the other hand, are those that choose a substantive answer to a question when really, they don't understand the question or don't have an opinion. If a respondent is only given four rank-ordered response options, such as strongly agree, agree, disagree, and strongly disagree, those who have no opinion have no choice but to select a response that suggests they have an opinion.

As you can see, floating is the flip side of fence-sitting. Thus, the solution to one problem is often the cause of the other. How you decide which approach to take depends on the goals of your research. Sometimes researchers specifically want to learn something about people who claim to have no opinion. In this case, allowing for fence-sitting would be necessary. Other times researchers feel confident their respondents will all be familiar with every topic in their survey. In this case, perhaps it is okay to force respondents to choose an opinion. Other times, researchers can provide a scale with *anchors* at either end and ask the respondent to indicate where there answer fits between the two anchors. An example would be a question that says, "On a scale from 0 to 10 where 0 is completely disagree and 10 is completely agree, what number would indicate your level of agreement?" There is no always-correct solution to either problem.

Finally, using a matrix is a nice way of streamlining response options. A **matrix** is a question type that that lists a set of questions for which the answer categories are all the same. If you have a set of questions for which the response options are the same, it may make sense to create a matrix rather than posing each question and its response options individually. Not only will this save you some space in your survey but it will also help respondents progress through your survey more easily. A sample matrix can be seen in Figure 7.4.

Instructions: For each statement, please check whether you Strongly Agree, Agree, Disagree, or Strongly Disagree				
My college classes are . . .	Strongly Agree	Agree	Disagree	Strongly Disagree
more demanding than my high school classes.	☐	☐	☐	☐
more interesting than my high school classes.	☐	☐	☐	☐
more interactive than my high school classes.	☐	☐	☐	☐
larger than my high school classes.	☐	☐	☐	☐

Figure 7.4 Survey questions using a matrix format

USING STANDARDIZED INSTRUMENTS

You may be thinking writing good survey questions and clear responses is a complicated task with a lot of pitfalls. In many ways it is! The good news is that for many of the constructs you would like to measure, other researchers have already designed and tested survey questions. You may remember from from Chapter 5 that there are scales, indices, and typologies to measure variables. Many of these instruments have already demonstrated reliability and validity. If there are validated instruments available, it is always advisable to use them rather than to write your own survey questions. Not only do you save time and effort, but you can have a fair amount of confidence that the validated instruments will avoid many of the question-writing pitfalls discussed above.

DESIGNING QUESTIONNAIRES

In addition to constructing quality questions and posing clear response options, you'll also need to think about how to present your written questions and response options to survey respondents. Questions are presented on a questionnaire, which is the document (either hard copy or online) that contains all your survey questions for respondents to read and answer. Designing questionnaires takes some thought.

One of the first things to do once you've come up with a set of survey questions you feel confident about is to group those questions thematically. In our example of the transition to college, perhaps we'd have a few questions asking about study habits, others focused on friendships, and still others on exercise and eating habits. Those may be the themes around which we organize our questions. Or perhaps it would make more sense to present any questions we had about pre-college life and then present a series of questions about life after beginning college. The point here is to be deliberate about how you present your questions to respondents.

Once you have grouped similar questions together, you'll need to think about the order in which to present those question groups. Most survey researchers agree that it is best to begin a survey with questions that will make respondents want to continue (Babbie, 2010; Dillman, 2000; Neuman, 2003). In other words, don't bore respondents, but don't scare them away either. There's some disagreement over where on a survey to place demographic questions, such as those about a person's age, gender, and race. On the one hand, placing them at the beginning of the questionnaire may lead respondents to think the survey is boring, unimportant, and not something they want to bother completing. But these are important pieces of data and you don't want your participant to quit the survey without providing their demographic information. Another thing to consider if the placement of sensitive or difficult topics, such as child sexual abuse or other criminal activity. You don't want to scare respondents away or shock them by beginning with your most intrusive questions.

In truth, the order in which you present questions on a survey is best determined by the unique characteristics of your research—only you, the researcher, hopefully in consultation with people who are willing to provide you with feedback, can determine how best to order your questions. To do so, think about the unique characteristics of your topic, your questions, and most importantly, your sample. Keeping in mind the characteristics and needs of the people you will ask to complete your survey should help guide you as you determine the most appropriate order in which to present your questions.

You'll also need to consider the time it will take respondents to complete your questionnaire. Surveys vary in length, from just a page or two to a dozen or more pages, which means they also vary in the time it takes to complete them. How long to make your survey depends on several factors. First, what is it that you wish to know? Wanting to understand how grades vary by gender and year in school certainly requires fewer questions than wanting to know how people's experiences in college are shaped by demographic characteristics, college attended, housing situation, family background, college major, friendship networks, and extracurricular activities. Keep in mind that even if your research question requires a sizable number of questions be included in your questionnaire, do your best to keep the questionnaire as brief as possible. Any hint that you've thrown in a bunch of useless questions just for the sake of it will turn off respondents and may make them not want to complete your survey.

Second, and perhaps more important, is the length of time respondents are likely to be willing to spend completing the questionnaire. If you are studying college students, asking them to use their precious fun time away from studying to complete your survey may mean they won't want to spend more than a few minutes on it. But if you have the endorsement of a professor who is willing to allow you to administer your survey in class, students may be willing to give you a little more time (though perhaps the professor will not). The time that survey researchers ask respondents to spend on questionnaires varies greatly. Some researchers advise that surveys should not take longer than about 15 minutes to complete (as cited in Babbie 2010), whereas others suggest that up to 20 minutes is acceptable (Hopper, 2012). As with question order, there is no clear-cut, always-correct answer about questionnaire length. The unique characteristics of your study and your sample should be considered to determine how long to make your questionnaire.

A good way to estimate the time it will take respondents to complete your questionnaire is through piloting the questionnaire. Piloting allows you to get feedback on your questionnaire so you can improve it before you actually administer it. Piloting can be quite expensive and time consuming if you wish to test your questionnaire on a large sample of people who very much resemble the sample to whom you will eventually administer the finalized version of your questionnaire. But you can learn a lot and make great improvements to your questionnaire simply by pretesting with a small number of people to whom you have easy access (perhaps you have a few friends who owe you a favor). By piloting your questionnaire, you can find out how understandable your questions are, get feedback on question wording and order, find out whether any of your questions are boring or offensive, and learn whether there are places where you should have included filter questions. You can also time respondents as they take your survey. This will give you a good idea about the estimate to provide when you administer your survey for your study and whether you have some wiggle room to add additional items or need to cut a few items.

Perhaps this goes without saying, but your questionnaire should also have an attractive design. A messy presentation style can confuse respondents or, at the very least, annoy them. Be brief, to the point, and as clear as possible. Avoid cramming too much into a single page. Make your font size readable (at least 12 point or larger, depending on the characteristics of your sample), leave a reasonable amount of space between items, and make sure all instructions are exceptionally clear. Think about books, documents, articles, or web pages that you have read yourself—which were relatively easy to read and easy on the eyes and why? Try to mimic those features in the presentation of your survey questions.

Key Takeaways

- Brainstorming and consulting the literature are two important early steps to take when preparing to write effective survey questions.
- Make sure your survey questions will be relevant to all respondents and that you use filter questions when necessary.
- Getting feedback on your survey questions is a crucial step in the process of designing a survey.
- When it comes to creating response options, the solution to the problem of fence-sitting might cause floating, whereas the solution to the problem of floating might cause fence sitting.
- Piloting is an important step for improving a survey before actually administering it.

Glossary

- Closed-ended questions- questions for which the researcher offers response options
- Double-barreled question- a question that asks two different questions at the same time, making it difficult to respond accurately

- Fence-sitters- respondents who choose neutral response options, even if they have an opinion
- Filter question- question that identifies some subset of survey respondents who are asked additional questions that are not relevant to the entire sample
- Floaters- respondents that choose a substantive answer to a question when really, they don't understand the question or don't have an opinion
- Matrix question- lists a set of questions for which the answer categories are all the same
- Open-ended questions- questions for which the researcher does not include response options

CHAPTER EIGHT: EXPERIMENTAL DESIGN

When you think of the term *experiment*, what comes to mind? Perhaps you thought about trying a new soda or changing your cat's litter to a different brand. We all design informal experiments in our life. We try new things and seek to learn how those things changed us or how they compare to other things we might try. We even create entertainment programs like *Mythbusters* whose hosts use experimental methods to test whether common myths or bits of folk knowledge are actually true. It's likely you've already developed an intuitive sense of how experiments work. The content of this chapter will increase your existing competency about using experiments to learn about the social world.

CHAPTER OUTLINE

- 8.1 Experimental design: What is it and when should it be used?
- 8.2 Quasi-experimental and pre-experimental designs
- 8.3 The logic of experimental design

CONTENT ADVISORY

This chapter discusses or mentions the following topics: substance abuse; eating disorders; prejudice; hurricane Katrina; domestic violence; racism; poverty; trauma; teen pregnancy, sexually transmitted infections and condom use.

8.1 EXPERIMENTAL DESIGN: WHAT IS IT AND WHEN SHOULD IT BE USED?

Learning Objectives

- Define experiment
- Identify the core features of true experimental designs
- Describe the difference between an experimental group and a control group
- Identify and describe the various types of true experimental designs

Experiments are an excellent data collection strategy for social workers wishing to observe the effects of a clinical intervention or social welfare program. Understanding what experiments are and how they are conducted is useful for all social scientists, whether they actually plan to use this methodology or simply aim to understand findings from experimental studies. An **experiment** is a method of data collection designed to test hypotheses under controlled conditions. In social scientific research, the term experiment has a precise meaning and should not be used to describe all research methodologies.

Experiments have a long and important history in social science. Behaviorists such as John Watson, B. F. Skinner, Ivan Pavlov, and Albert Bandura used experimental design to demonstrate the various types of conditioning. Using strictly controlled environments, behaviorists were able to isolate a single stimulus as the cause of measurable differences in behavior or physiological responses. The foundations of social learning theory and behavior modification are found in experimental research projects. Moreover, behaviorist experiments brought psychology and social science away from the abstract world of Freudian analysis and towards empirical inquiry, grounded in real-world observations and objectively-defined variables. Experiments are used at all levels of social work inquiry, including agency-based experiments that test therapeutic interventions and policy experiments that test new programs.

Several kinds of experimental designs exist. In general, designs considered to be **true experiments** contain three basic key features:

1. random assignment of participants into experimental and control groups
2. a "treatment" (or intervention) provided to the experimental group
3. measurement of the effects of the treatment in a post-test administered to both groups

Some true experiments are more complex. Their designs can also include a pre-test and can have more than two groups, but these are the minimum requirements for a design to be a true experiment.

EXPERIMENTAL AND CONTROL GROUPS

In a true experiment, the effect of an intervention is tested by comparing two groups: one that is exposed to the intervention (the **experimental group**, also known as the treatment group) and another that does not receive the intervention (the **control group**). Importantly, participants in a true experiment need to be randomly assigned to either the control or experimental groups. **Random assignment** uses a random number generator or some other random process to assign people into experimental and control groups. Random assignment is important in experimental research because it helps to ensure that the experimental group and control group are comparable and that any differences between the experimental and control groups are due to random chance. We will address more of the logic behind random assignment in the next section.

TREATMENT OR INTERVENTION

In an experiment, the independent variable is receiving the intervention being tested—for example, a therapeutic technique, prevention program, or access to some service or support. It is less common in of social work research, but social science research may also have a stimulus, rather than an intervention as the independent variable. For example, an electric shock or a reading about death might be used as a stimulus to provoke a response.

In some cases, it may be immoral to withhold treatment completely from a control group within an experiment. If you recruited two groups of people with severe addiction and only provided treatment to one group, the other group would likely suffer. For these cases, researchers use a control group that receives "treatment as usual." Experimenters must clearly define what treatment as usual means. For example, a standard treatment in substance abuse recovery is attending Alcoholics Anonymous or Narcotics Anonymous meetings. A substance abuse researcher conducting an experiment may use twelve-step programs in their control group and use their experimental intervention in the experimental group. The results would show whether the experimental intervention worked better than normal treatment, which is useful information.

POST-TEST

The dependent variable is usually the intended effect the researcher wants the intervention to have. If the researcher is testing a new therapy for individuals with binge eating disorder, their dependent variable may be the number of binge eating episodes a participant reports. The researcher likely expects her intervention to decrease the number of binge eating episodes reported by participants. Thus, she must, at a minimum, measure the number of episodes that occur after the intervention, which is the **post-test**. In a classic experimental design, participants are also given a **pretest** to measure the dependent variable before the experimental treatment begins.

TYPES OF EXPERIMENTAL DESIGN

Let's put these concepts in chronological order so we can better understand how an experiment runs from start to finish. Once you've collected your sample, you'll need to randomly assign your participants to the experimental group and control group. In a common type of experimental design, you will then give both groups your pretest, which measures your dependent variable, to see what your participants are like before you start your intervention. Next, you will provide your intervention, or independent variable, to your experimental group, but not to your control group. Many interventions last a few weeks or months to complete, particularly therapeutic treatments. Finally, you will administer your post-test to both groups to observe any changes in your dependent variable. What we've just described is known as the **classical experimental design** and is the simplest type of true experimental design. All of the designs we review in this section are variations on this approach. Figure 8.1 visually represents these steps.

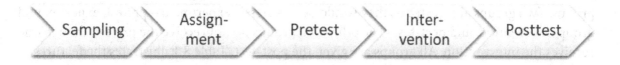

Figure 8.1 Steps in classic experimental design

An interesting example of experimental research can be found in Shannon K. McCoy and Brenda Major's (2003) study of people's perceptions of prejudice. In one portion of this multifaceted study, all participants were given a pretest to assess their levels of depression. No significant differences in depression were found between the experimental and control groups during the pretest. Participants in the experimental group were then asked to read an article suggesting that prejudice against their own racial group is severe and pervasive, while participants in the control group were asked to read an article suggesting that prejudice against a racial group other than their own is severe and pervasive. Clearly, these were not meant to be interventions or treatments to help depression, but were stimuli designed to elicit changes in people's depression levels. Upon measuring depression scores during the post-test period, the researchers discovered that those who had received the experimental stimulus (the article citing prejudice against their same racial group) reported greater depression than those in the control group. This is just one of many examples of social scientific experimental research.

In addition to classic experimental design, there are two other ways of designing experiments that are considered to fall within the purview of "true" experiments (Babbie, 2010; Campbell & Stanley, 1963). The **posttest-only control group design** is almost the same as classic experimental design, except it does not use a pretest. Researchers who use posttest-only designs want to eliminate **testing effects**, in which participants' scores on a measure change because they have already been exposed to it. If you took multiple SAT or ACT practice exams before you took the real one you sent to colleges, you've taken advantage of testing effects to get a better score. Considering the previous example on racism and depression, participants who are given a pretest about depression before being exposed to the stimulus would likely assume that the intervention is designed to address depression. That knowledge could cause them to answer differently on the post-test than they otherwise would. In theory, as long as the control and experimental groups have been determined randomly and are therefore comparable, no pretest is needed. However, most researchers prefer to use pretests in case randomization did not result in equivalent groups and to help assess change over time within both the experimental and control groups.

Researchers wishing to account for testing effects but also gather pretest data can use a

Solomon four-group design. In the **Solomon four-group design**, the researcher uses four groups. Two groups are treated as they would be in a classic experiment—pretest, experimental group intervention, and post-test. The other two groups do not receive the pretest, though one receives the intervention. All groups are given the post-test. Table 8.1 illustrates the features of each of the four groups in the Solomon four-group design. By having one set of experimental and control groups that complete the pretest (Groups 1 and 2) and another set that does not complete the pretest (Groups 3 and 4), researchers using the Solomon four-group design can account for testing effects in their analysis.

Table 8.1 Solomon four-group design

	Pretest	Stimulus	Posttest
Group 1	X	X	X
Group 2	X		X
Group 3		X	X
Group 4			X

Solomon four-group designs are challenging to implement in the real world because they are time- and resource-intensive. Researchers must recruit enough participants to create four groups and implement interventions in two of them.

Overall, true experimental designs are sometimes difficult to implement in a real-world practice environment. It may be impossible to withhold treatment from a control group or randomly assign participants in a study. In these cases, *pre-experimental* and *quasi-experimental* designs—which we will discuss in the next section—can be used. However, the differences in rigor from true experimental designs leave their conclusions more open to critique.

EXPERIMENTAL DESIGN IN MACRO-LEVEL RESEARCH

You can imagine that social work researchers may be limited in their ability to use random assignment when examining the effects of governmental policy on individuals. For example, it is unlikely that a researcher could randomly assign some states to implement decriminalization of recreational marijuana and some states not to in order to assess the effects of the policy change. There are, however, important examples of policy experiments that use random assignment, including the Oregon Medicaid experiment. In the Oregon Medicaid experiment, the wait list for Oregon was so long, state officials conducted a lottery to see who from the wait list would receive Medicaid (Baicker et al., 2013). Researchers used the lottery as a natural experiment that included random assignment. People selected to be a part of Medicaid were the experimental group and those on the wait list were in the control group. There are some practical complications macro-level experiments, just as with other experiments. For example, the ethical concern with using people on a wait list as a control group exists in macro-level research just as it does in micro-level research.

Key Takeaways

- True experimental designs require random assignment.
- Control groups do not receive an intervention, and experimental groups receive an intervention.
- The basic components of a true experiment include a pretest, posttest, control group, and experimental group.
- Testing effects may cause researchers to use variations on the classic experimental design.

Glossary

- Classic experimental design- uses random assignment, an experimental and control group, as well as pre- and posttesting
- Control group- the group in an experiment that does not receive the intervention
- Experiment- a method of data collection designed to test hypotheses under controlled conditions
- Experimental group- the group in an experiment that receives the intervention
- Posttest- a measurement taken after the intervention
- Posttest-only control group design- a type of experimental design that uses random assignment, and an experimental and control group, but does not use a pretest
- Pretest- a measurement taken prior to the intervention
- Random assignment-using a random process to assign people into experimental and control groups
- Solomon four-group design- uses random assignment, two experimental and two control groups, pretests for half of the groups, and posttests for all

- Testing effects- when a participant's scores on a measure change because they have already been exposed to it
- True experiments- a group of experimental designs that contain independent and dependent variables, pretesting and post testing, and experimental and control groups

Image attributions

exam scientific experiment by mohamed_hassan CC-0

8.2 QUASI-EXPERIMENTAL AND PRE-EXPERIMENTAL DESIGNS

Learning Objectives

- Identify and describe the various types of quasi-experimental designs
- Distinguish true experimental designs from quasi-experimental and pre-experimental designs
- Identify and describe the various types of quasi-experimental and pre-experimental designs

As we discussed in the previous section, time, funding, and ethics may limit a researcher's ability to conduct a true experiment. For researchers in the medical sciences and social work, conducting a true experiment could require denying needed treatment to clients, which is a clear ethical violation. Even those whose research may not involve the administration of needed medications or treatments may be limited in their ability to conduct a classic experiment. When true experiments are not possible, researchers often use quasi-experimental designs.

QUASI-EXPERIMENTAL DESIGNS

Quasi-experimental designs are similar to true experiments, but they lack random assignment to experimental and control groups. Quasi-experimental designs have a **comparison group** that is similar to a control group except assignment to the comparison group is not determined by random assignment. The most basic of these quasi-experimental designs is the **nonequivalent comparison groups design** (Rubin & Babbie, 2017). The nonequivalent comparison group design looks a lot like the classic experimental design, except it does not use random assignment. In many cases, these groups may already exist. For example, a researcher might conduct research at two different agency sites, one of which receives the intervention and the other does not. No one was assigned to treatment or comparison groups. Those groupings existed prior to the study. While this method is more convenient for real-world research, it is less likely that that the groups are comparable than if they had been determined by random assignment. Perhaps the treatment group has a characteristic that is unique–for example, higher income or different diagnoses–that make the treatment more effective.

Quasi-experiments are particularly useful in social welfare policy research. Social welfare policy researchers often look for what are termed **natural experiments**, or situations in which comparable groups are created by differences that already occur in the real world. Natural experiments are a feature of the social world that allows researchers to use the logic of experimental design to investigate the connection between variables. For example, Stratmann and Wille (2016) were interested in the effects of a state healthcare policy called Certificate of Need on the quality of hospitals. They clearly could not randomly assign states to adopt one set of policies or another. Instead, researchers used hospital referral regions, or the areas from which hospitals draw their patients, that spanned across state lines. Because the hospitals were in the same referral region, researchers could be pretty sure that the client characteristics were pretty similar. In this way, they could classify patients in experimental and comparison groups without dictating state policy or telling people where to live.

Matching is another approach in quasi-experimental design for assigning people to experimental and comparison groups. It begins with researchers thinking about what variables are important in their study, particularly demographic variables or attributes that might impact their dependent variable. *Individual matching* involves pairing participants with similar attributes. Then, the matched pair is split—with one participant going to the experimental group and the other to the comparison group. An *ex post facto control group*, in contrast, is when a researcher matches individuals after the intervention is administered to some participants. Finally, researchers may engage in *aggregate matching*, in which the comparison group is determined to be similar on important variables.

TIME SERIES DESIGN

There are many different quasi-experimental designs in addition to the nonequivalent comparison group design described earlier. Describing all of them is beyond the scope of this textbook, but one more design is worth mentioning. The **time series design** uses multiple observations before and after an intervention. In some cases, experimental and comparison groups are used. In other cases where that is not feasible, a single experimental group is used.

By using multiple observations before and after the intervention, the researcher can better understand the true value of the dependent variable in each participant before the intervention starts. Additionally, multiple observations afterwards allow the researcher to see whether the intervention had lasting effects on participants. Time series designs are similar to single-subjects designs, which we will discuss in Chapter 15.

PRE-EXPERIMENTAL DESIGN

When true experiments and quasi-experiments are not possible, researchers may turn to a **pre-experimental design** (Campbell & Stanley, 1963). Pre-experimental designs are called such because they often happen as a pre-cursor to conducting a true experiment. Researchers want to see if their interventions will have some effect on a small group of people before they seek funding and dedicate time to conduct a true experiment. Pre-experimental designs, thus, are usually conducted as a first step towards establishing the evidence for or against an intervention. However, this type of design comes with some unique disadvantages, which we'll describe below.

A commonly used type of pre-experiment is the **one-group pretest post-test design**. In this design, pre- and posttests are both administered, but there is no comparison group to which to compare the experimental group. Researchers may be able to make the claim that participants receiving the treatment experienced a change in the dependent variable, but they cannot begin to claim that the change was the result of the treatment without a comparison group. Imagine if the students in your research class completed a questionnaire about their level of stress at the beginning of the semester. Then your professor taught you mindfulness techniques throughout the semester. At the end of the semester, she administers the stress survey again. What if levels of stress went up? Could she conclude that the mindfulness techniques caused stress? Not without a comparison group! If there was a comparison group, she would be able to recognize that all students experienced higher stress at the end of the semester than the beginning of the semester, not just the students in her research class.

In cases where the administration of a pretest is cost prohibitive or otherwise not possible, a **one-shot case study** design might be used. In this instance, no pretest is administered, nor is a comparison group present. If we wished to measure the impact of a natural disaster, such as Hurricane Katrina for example, we might conduct a pre-experiment by identifying a community that was hit by the hurricane and then measuring the levels of stress in the community. Researchers using this design must be extremely cautious about making claims regarding the effect of the treatment or stimulus. They have no idea what the levels of stress in the community were before the hurricane hit nor can they compare the stress levels to a community that was not affected by the hurricane. Nonetheless, this design can be useful for exploratory studies aimed at testing a measures or the feasibility of further study.

In our example of the study of the impact of Hurricane Katrina, a researcher might choose to examine the effects of the hurricane by identifying a group from a community that experienced the hurricane and a comparison group from a similar community that had not been hit by the hurricane. This study design, called a **static group comparison**, has the advantage of including a comparison group that did not experience the stimulus (in this case, the hurricane). Unfortunately, the design only uses for post-tests, so it is not possible to know if the groups were comparable before the stimulus or intervention. As you might have guessed from our example, static group comparisons are useful in cases where a researcher cannot control or predict whether, when, or how the stimulus is administered, as in the case of natural disasters.

As implied by the preceding examples where we considered studying the impact of Hurricane Katrina, experiments, quasi-experiments, and pre-experiments do not necessarily need to take place in the controlled setting of a lab. In fact, many applied researchers rely on experiments to assess the impact and effectiveness of various programs and policies. You might recall our discussion of arresting perpetrators of domestic violence in Chapter 2, which is an excellent example of an applied experiment. Researchers did not subject participants to conditions in a lab setting; instead, they applied their stimulus (in this case, arrest) to some subjects in the field and they also had a control group in the field that did not receive the stimulus (and therefore were not arrested).

Key Takeaways

- Quasi-experimental designs do not use random assignment.
- Comparison groups are used in quasi-experiments.
- Matching is a way of improving the comparability of experimental and comparison groups.
- Quasi-experimental designs and pre-experimental designs are often used when experimental designs are impractical.
- Quasi-experimental and pre-experimental designs may be easier to carry out, but they lack the rigor of true experiments.

Glossary

- Aggregate matching – when the comparison group is determined to be similar to the experimental group along important variables
- Comparison group – a group in quasi-experimental design that does not receive the experimental treatment; it is similar to a control group except assignment to the comparison group is not determined by random assignment
- Ex post facto control group – a control group created when a researcher matches individuals after the intervention is administered
- Individual matching – pairing participants with similar attributes for the purpose of assignment to groups
- Natural experiments – situations in which comparable groups are created by differences that already occur in the real world
- Nonequivalent comparison group design – a quasi-experimental design similar to a classic experimental design but without random assignment
- One-group pretest post-test design – a pre-experimental design that applies an intervention to one group but also includes a pretest
- One-shot case study – a pre-experimental design that applies an intervention to only one group without a pretest
- Pre-experimental designs – a variation of experimental design that lacks the rigor of experiments and is often used before a true experiment is conducted
- Quasi-experimental design – designs lack random assignment to experimental and control groups
- Static group design – uses an experimental group and a comparison group, without random assignment and pretesting
- Time series design – a quasi-experimental design that uses multiple observations before and after an intervention

Image attributions

cat and kitten matching avocado costumes on the couch looking at the camera by Your Best Digs CC-BY-2.0

8.3 THE LOGIC OF EXPERIMENTAL DESIGN

Learning Objectives

- Apply the criterion of causality to experimental design
- Define internal validity and external validity
- Identify and define threats to internal validity

As we discussed at the beginning of this chapter, experimental design is commonly understood and implemented informally in everyday life. Trying out a new restaurant, dating a new person—we often call these things "experiments." As you've learned over the past two sections, in order for something to be a true experiment, or even a quasi- or pre-experiment, you must rigorously apply the various components of experimental design. A true experiment for trying a new restaurant would include recruitment of a large enough sample, random assignment to control and experimental groups, pretesting and posttesting, as well as using clearly and objectively defined measures of satisfaction with the restaurant.

Social scientists use this level of rigor and control because they try to maximize the **internal validity** of their research. Internal validity is the confidence researchers have about whether the independent variable intervention truly produced a change in the dependent variable. In the case of experimental design, the independent variable is the intervention or treatment. Experiments are attempts to establish causality between two variables—the treatment and its intended outcome.

As we talked about in Chapter 4, nomothetic causal explanations must establish four criteria: covariation, plausibility, temporality, and nonspuriousness. The logic and rigor of experimental design allows for causality to be established. Experimenters can assess *covariation* on the dependent variable through pre- and post-tests. The use of experimental and control conditions ensures that some people receive the intervention and others do not, providing variation in the independent variable (i.e., receiving the treatment). Moreover, since the researcher controls when the intervention is administered, she can be assured that changes in the independent variable (the treatment) happened before changes the dependent variable (the outcome). In this way, experiments assure *temporality*. In our restaurant experiment, we would know through assignment to experimental and control groups that people varied in the restaurant they attended. We would also know whether their level of satisfaction changed, as measured by the pre- and posttest. We would also know that changes in our diners' satisfaction occurred after they left the restaurant, not before they walked in because of the pre- and post-tests.

Experimenters also have a *plausible* reason why their intervention would cause changes in the dependent variable. Usually, a theory or previous empirical evidence should indicate the potential for a causal relationship. Perhaps we found a national poll that found the type of food our experimental restaurant served, let's say pizza, is the most popular food in America. Perhaps this restaurant has good reviews on Yelp or Google. This evidence would give us a plausible reason to establish the restaurant as causing satisfaction.

While you may not need a clean suit like these scientists, you need to similarly control for threats to the validity of your experiment.

One of the most important features of experiments is that they allow researchers to *eliminate spurious variables*. True experiments are usually conducted under strictly controlled conditions. The intervention is given in the same way to each person, with a minimal number of other variables that might cause their post-test scores to change. In our restaurant example, this level of control might prove difficult. We cannot control how many people are waiting for a table, whether participants saw someone famous there, or if there is bad weather. Any of these factors might cause a diner to be less satisfied with their meal. These spurious variables may cause changes in satisfaction that have nothing to do with the restaurant itself, an important problem in real-world research. For this reason, experiments try to control as many aspects of the research process as possible: using control groups, having large enough sample sizes, standardizing the treatment, etc. Researchers in large experiments often employ clinicians or other research staff to help them. Researchers train their staff members exhaustively, provide pre-scripted responses to common questions, and control the physical environment of the experiment so each person who participates receives the exact same treatment.

Experimental researchers also document their procedures, so that others can review them and make changes in future research if they think it will improve on the ability to control for spurious variables. An interesting example is Bruce Alexander's (2010) Rat Park experiments. Much of the early research conducted on addictive drugs, like heroin and cocaine, was conducted on animals other than humans, usually mice or rats. The scientific consensus up until Alexander's experiments was that cocaine and heroin were so addictive that rats, if offered the drugs, would consume them repeatedly until they perished. Researchers claimed this behavior explained how addiction worked in humans, but Alexander was not so sure. He knew rats were social animals and the experimental procedure from previous experiments did not allow them to socialize. Instead, rats were kept isolated in small cages with only food, water, and metal walls. To Alexander, social isolation was a spurious variable, causing changes in addictive behavior not due to the drug itself. Alexander created an experiment of his own, in which rats were allowed to run freely in an interesting environment, socialize and mate with other rats, and of course, drink from a solution that contained an addictive drug. In this environment, rats did not become hopelessly addicted to drugs. In fact, they had little interest in the substance. To Alexander, the results of his experiment demonstrated that social isolation was more of a causal factor for addiction than the drug itself.

One challenge with Alexander's findings is that subsequent researchers have had mixed success replicating his findings (e.g., Petrie, 1996; Solinas, Thiriet, El Rawas, Lardeux, & Jaber, 2009). **Replication** involves conducting another researcher's experiment in the same manner and seeing if it produces the same results. If the causal relationship is real, it should occur in all (or at least most) replications of the experiment.

One of the defining features of experiments is that they report their procedures diligently, which allows for easier replication. Recently, researchers at the Reproducibility Project have caused a significant controversy in social science fields like psychology (Open Science Collaboration, 2015). In one study, researchers attempted reproduce the results of 100 experiments published in major psychology journals between 2008 and the present. What they found was shocking. The results of only 36% of the studies were reproducible. Despite coordinating closely with the original researchers, the Reproducibility Project found that nearly two-thirds of psychology experiments published in respected journals were not reproducible. The implications of the Reproducibility Project are staggering, and social scientists are coming up with new ways to ensure researchers do not cherry-pick data or change their hypotheses, simply to get published.

Let's return to Alexander's Rat Park study and consider the implications of his experiment for substance use professionals. The conclusions he drew from his experiments on rats were meant to generalize to the population of people with substance use disorders. If this could be done, the experiment would have high degree of **external validity**, which is the degree to which conclusions generalize to larger populations and different situations. Alexander argues his conclusions about addiction and social isolation help us understand why people living in deprived, isolated environments may become addicted to drugs more often than those in more enriching environments. Similarly, earlier rat researchers argued their results showed these drugs were instantly addictive to humans, often to the point of death.

Neither study's results will match up perfectly with real life. There are clients in social work practice who may fit into Alexander's social isolation model, but social isolation is complex. Clients can live in environments with other sociable humans, work jobs, and have romantic relationships; does this mean they are not socially isolated? On the other hand, clients may face structural racism, poverty, trauma, and other challenges that may contribute their social environment. Alexander's work helps understand clients' experiences, but the explanation is incomplete. Human existence is more complicated than the experimental conditions in Rat Park.

Social workers are especially attentive to how social context shapes social life. So, we are likely to point out a specific disadvantage of experiments. They are rather artificial. How often do real-world social interactions occur in the same way that they do in a controlled experiment? Experiments that are conducted in community settings may not be as subject to artificiality as those in a research lab, but their conditions are less easily controlled. This demonstrates the tension between internal and external validity. Internal validity and external validity are conceptually linked. Internal validity refers to the degree to which the intervention causes its intended outcomes, and external validity refers to how well that relationship applies to different groups and circumstances. However, the more researchers tightly control the environment to ensure internal validity, the less they can claim external validity for generalizing their results to different populations and circumstances. Correspondingly, researchers whose settings are just like the real world will be less able to ensure internal validity, as there are many factors that could pollute the research process. This is not to suggest that experimental research cannot have external validity, but that experimental researchers must always be aware that external validity problems can occur and be forthcoming in their reports of findings about this potential weakness.

THREATS TO INTERNAL VALIDITY

There are a number of factors that may influence a study's internal validity. You might consider these threats to all be spurious variables, as we discussed at the beginning of this section. Each threat proposes something other than the treatment (or intervention) is changing the outcome. The threats introduce error and bias into the experiment.

Throughout this chapter, we reviewed the importance of experimental and control groups. These groups must be comparable in order for experimental design to work. **Comparable groups** are groups that are similar across factors important for the study. Researchers can help establish comparable groups by using probability sampling, random assignment, or matching techniques. Control or comparison groups give researchers an opportunity to explore what happens when similar people who do not receive the intervention. But if the experimental and control groups are not comparable, then the differences in outcome may not be due to the intervention. No groups are ever perfectly comparable. What's important is ensuring groups are as similar as possible along variables relevant to the research project.

In our restaurant example, if one of the groups had far more vegetarians or people with gluten issues, it might influence how satisfied they were with the restaurant. The groups, in that case, would not be comparable. Researchers can account for this by measuring other variables, like dietary preference, and controlling for their effects statistically, after the data are collected. We discussed control variables like these in Chapter 4. When some factor related to selecting research participants prevents the groups from being comparable, then **selection bias** is introduced into the sample. This could happen if a researcher cho0ses clients from one agency to belong to the experimental group and those from another agency to be in the comparison group, when the agencies serve different types of people. Selection bias is a reason experimenters use random assignment, so conscious and unconscious bias do not influence to which group a participant is assigned. Sometimes, the groups are comparable at the start of the experiment, but people drop out of the experiment. **Mortality** is the term we use to describe when a group changes because of people dropping out of the study. In our restaurant example, this could happen if vegetarians dropped out of the experimental group because the restaurant being tested didn't have vegetarian options.

Experiments themselves are often the source of threats to validity. Experiments are different from participants' normal routines. The novelty of a research environment or experimental treatment may cause them to expect to feel differently, independently of the actual intervention. **Reactivity** is a threat to internal validity that occurs because the participants realize they are being observed. In this case, being observed makes the difference in outcome, not the intervention.

What if the people in the control group are aware that they aren't receiving the potential benefits from the experimental treatment? Maybe they respond by increasing their efforts to improve in spite of not receiving the treatment. This introduces a threat to internal validity called **compensatory rivalry**. On the other hand, it might have the opposite effect. **Resentful demoralization** occurs when people in the control group decrease their efforts because they aren't getting the treatment. These threats could be decreased by keeping the experimental and control groups completely separate, so the control group isn't aware of what's happening with the experimental group. An advantage to this is that it can help prevent **diffusion of treatment**, in which members of the control group learn about the experimental treatment from people in the experimental group and start implementing the intervention for themselves. This can occur if participants in the experimental group begin to behave differently or share insights from the intervention with individuals in the control group. Whether through social learning or conversation, participants in the control group may receive parts of the intervention of which they were supposed to be unaware.

Researchers may also introduce error. For example, researchers may expect the experimental group to feel better and may give off conscious or unconscious cues to participants that influence their outcomes. Control groups could be expected to fare worse, and research staff might cue participants that they should feel worse than they otherwise would. It is also possible that research staff administering treatment as usual to the control group might try to equalize treatment or engage in a rivalry with research staff administering the experimental group (Engel & Schutt, 2016). To prevent these threats that are caused by researchers or participants being aware of their role in the experiment, **double-blind** designs prevent both the research staff interacting with participants and the participants themselves from knowing who is assigned to which group.

There are some additional threats to internal validity that using double-blind designs cannot reduce. You have likely heard of the **placebo effect**, in which a participant in the control group feels better because they think they are receiving treatment, despite not having received the experimental treatment at all. Researchers may introduce a threat to internal validity called **instrumentation** when they choose measures that do not accurately measure participants or implement the measure in a way that biases participant responses. **Testing** is a threat to internal validity in which the fact that participants take a pretest–not the intervention–affects their score on the post-test. The Solomon Four Group and Post-test Only designs are used to reduce the testing threat to internal validity. Sometimes, the change in an experiment would have happened even without any intervention because of the natural passage of time. This is called **maturation**. Imagine researchers testing the effects of a parenting class on the beliefs and attitudes of adolescent fathers. Perhaps the changes in their beliefs and attitudes are based on growing older, not on the class. Having a control or comparison group helps with this threat. It also helps reduce the threat of **history**, when something happens outside the experiment but affects its participants.

As you can see, there are several ways in which the internal validity of a study can be threatened. No study can eliminate all threats, but the best ones consider the threats and do their best to reduce them as much as is feasible based on the resources available. When you read and critique research articles, it is important to consider these threats so you can assess the validity of a study's results.

SPOTLIGHT ON UTA SCHOOL OF SOCIAL WORK

ASSESSING A TEEN PREGNANCY AND STI PREVENTION PROGRAM

Dr. Holli Slater and Dr.Diane Mitschke implemented an experimental design to conduct a randomized two-group cohort-based longitudinal study using repeated measures to assess outcomes related to a teen pregnancy prevention program (Slater & Mitschke, 2015). *Crossroads* was a co-ed program targeting academically at risk youth enrolled in local school district. It was administered by trained facilitators in a large-group setting across three consecutive days for a total of 18.75 hours of program instruction. Each day had a separate focus, including building relationships, prevention of pregnancy and sexually transmitted infections (STIs), and identifying resources available within the community.

Potential participants were recruited on an ongoing basis and put into a pool of potential candidates to join the study. Prior to each intervention series, 60 youth were randomly assigned to either treatment or control groups. Youth assigned to the treatment group attended a three day intervention and received ongoing support from assigned facilitators. Youth who were assigned to the control group did not attend the intervention and continued to receive *services as usual*. Services as usual comprised of being assigned a graduation coach who provided dropout prevention services and assisted youth to meet their academic goals. Graduation coach services were available to all at-risk students in the school district, regardless of their enrollment in the study and/or assignment to treatment or control groups.

The primary research aim of the study was to assess the impact of being offered participation in the intervention on condom use. Essentially, the researchers wanted to see if condom use increased more among sexually active youth following the intervention compared to youth who did not attend the intervention. In addition to this primary research aim, Drs. Mitschke and Slater explored whether this effect was sustained over time. They collected data through an online survey at four separate time points (baseline, 3-, 6-, and 12- months post intervention). Due to the longitudinal nature of the study and the highly transient population, the researchers provided incentives of a $20 gift card at each data collection point. They still had a challenge in retaining youth for the duration of the study.

An intent-to-treat framework was used to assess the impact of the program, meaning data analysis included all youth who were randomized regardless of their level of participation in the program. The researchers compared the outcomes between youth in treatment and youth in the control groups. Significant differences between the treatment and control groups ($p<.05$) would support the argument that changes in behavior (e.g., increase in condom use) were attributed to participation in the intervention.

Results of the study did not identify significant findings in condom usage at 3 months and 12 months after the intervention. However, it did find significant results at 6 months, indicating that youth who participated in the intervention were less likely to engage in intercourse without a condom than youth in the control group. While it is disappointing to not find significant results in a large scale study, such as this, negative results can be just as powerful.

Dr. Slater and Dr. Mitschke explored reasons why the intervention may not have been as effective immediately following the intervention by talking with youth and their counselors to gain insight. One possible explanation is that youth enrolled in this study had already established their sexual norms prior to the intervention. The majority of youth in the study were already sexually active. If this was the case, then practitioners developing interventions for pregnancy prevention should take this into consideration when developing program. Perhaps implementing an intervention at an earlier age when youth are not yet sexually active would have a greater impact on behaviors than waiting until they are already engaging in risky sexual behaviors and trying to create a change.

It is interesting that behaviors did seem to change with youth at the six month follow up. It is possible this is a spurious result and should be explored more fully. Interviews with youth indicated that the repeated follow up from the intervention team over time resulted in an increase in trust between the youth and their counselor. Some even suggested they changed their behaviors because a caring adult took time to continually follow up with them. This alternate explanation should also be further explored to better understand what components of the intervention have the greatest impact on the behavior of youth.

Key Takeaways

- Experimental design provides researchers with the ability to best establish causality between their variables.
- Experiments provide strong internal validity but may have trouble achieving external validity.
- Experimental deigns should be reproducible by future researchers.
- Threats to validity come from both experimenter and participant reactivity.

Glossary

- Comparable groups – groups that are similar across factors important for the study
- Compensatory rivalry – a threat to internal validity in which participants in the control group increasing their efforts to improve because they know they are not receiving the experimental

treatment

- Diffusion of treatment – a threat to internal validity in which members of the control group learn about the experimental treatment from people in the experimental group and start implementing the intervention for themselves

- Double-blind – when researchers interact with participants are unaware of who is in the control or experimental group

- External validity – the degree to which experimental conclusions generalize to larger populations and different situations

- Instrumentation – a threat to internal validity when measures do not accurately measure participants or are implemented in a way that biases participant responses

- Internal validity – the confidence researchers have about whether their intervention produced variation in their dependent variable

- Maturation – a threat to internal validity in which the change in an experiment would have happened even without any intervention because of the natural passage of time

- Mortality – a threat to internal validity caused when either the experimental or control group composition changes because of people dropping out of the study

- Placebo effect- when a participant feels better, despite having received no intervention at all

- Reactivity – a threat to internal validity that occurs because the participants realize they are being observed

- Replication – conducting another researcher's experiment in the same manner and seeing if it produces the same results

- Resentful demoralization – a threat to internal validity that occurs when people in the control group decrease their efforts because they aren't getting the experimental treatment

- Selection bias – when the elements selected for inclusion in a study do not represent the larger population from which they were drawn due to sampling method or thought processes of the researcher

Image attributions

One of Juno's solar panels before illumination test by NASA/Jack Pfaller public domain

mistake by Tumisu CC-0

CHAPTER NINE: UNIQUE FEATURES OF QUALITATIVE RESEARCH

What is it like to be a young man entering adulthood? According to sociologist Michael Kimmel, they are "totally confused," "cannot commit to their relationships, work, or lives," and are
"obsessed with never wanting to grow up."[1] If that sounds like a bunch of malarkey to you, hold on a minute. Kimmel (2008) interviewed 400 young men, ages 16 to 26, over the course of four years across the United States to learn how young men made the transition from adolescence into adulthood. Since the results of Kimmel's research were published in 2008, his book *Guyland* made quite a splash. Whatever your take on Kimmel's research, one thing remains true—we surely would not know nearly as much as we now do about the lives of many young American men were it not for qualitative interview research.

CHAPTER OUTLINE

- 9.1 Qualitative research: What is it and when should it be used?
- 9.2 Qualitative interviews
- 9.3 Issues to consider for all interview types
- 9.4 Types of Qualitative Research Designs
- 9.5 Spotlight on UTA School of Social Work
- 9.6 Analyzing qualitative data

1. 1. These quotes come from a summary of reviews on the website dedicated to Kimmel's book, Guyland

CONTENT ADVISORY

This chapter discusses or mentions the following topics: childfree adults, sexual harassment, juvenile delinquency, drunk driving, racist hate groups, ageism, sexism, police interviews, and mental health policy for children and adolescents.

9.1 QUALITATIVE RESEARCH: WHAT IS IT AND WHEN SHOULD IT BE USED?

Learning Objectives

- Define qualitative research
- Explain the differences between qualitative and quantitative research
- Identify the benefits and challenges of qualitative research

Qualitative versus quantitative research methods refers to data-oriented considerations about the type of data to collected and how they are analyzed. **Qualitative research** relies mostly on non-numeric data, such as interviews and observations to understand their meaning, in contrast to quantitative research which employs numeric data such as scores and metrics. Hence, qualitative research is not amenable to statistical procedures, but is coded using techniques like content analysis. Sometimes, coded qualitative data are tabulated quantitatively as frequencies of codes, but this data is not statistically analyzed. Qualitative research has its roots in anthropology, sociology, psychology, linguistics, and semiotics, and has been available since the early 19th century, long before quantitative statistical techniques were employed.

DISTINCTIONS FROM QUANTITATIVE RESEARCH

In qualitative research, the role of the researcher receives critical attention. In some methods such as ethnography, action research, and participant observation, the researcher is considered part of the social phenomenon, and her specific role and involvement in the research process must be made clear during data analysis. In other methods, such as case research, the researcher must take a "neutral" or unbiased stance during the data collection and analysis processes, and ensure that her personal biases or preconceptions does not taint the nature of subjective inferences derived from qualitative research.

Analysis in qualitative research is holistic and contextual, rather than being reductionist and isolationist. Qualitative interpretations tend to focus on language, signs, and meanings from the perspective of the participants involved in the social phenomenon, in contrast to statistical techniques that are employed heavily in positivist research. Rigor in qualitative research is viewed in terms of systematic and transparent approaches for data collection and analysis rather than statistical benchmarks for construct validity or significance testing.

Lastly, data collection and analysis can proceed simultaneously and iteratively in qualitative research. For instance, the researcher may conduct an interview and code it before proceeding to the next interview. Simultaneous analysis helps the researcher correct potential flaws in the interview protocol or adjust it to capture the phenomenon of interest better. The researcher may even change her original research question if she realizes that her original research questions are unlikely to generate new or useful insights. This is a valuable but often understated benefit of qualitative research, and is not available in quantitative research, where the research project cannot be modified or changed once the data collection has started without redoing the entire project from the start.

BENEFITS AND CHALLENGES OF QUALITATIVE RESEARCH

Qualitative research has several unique advantages. First, it is well-suited for exploring hidden reasons behind complex, interrelated, or multifaceted social processes, such as inter-firm relationships or inter-office politics, where quantitative evidence may be biased, inaccurate, or otherwise difficult to obtain. Second, it is often helpful for theory construction in areas with no or insufficient pre-existing theory. Third, qualitative research is also appropriate for studying context-specific, unique, or idiosyncratic events or processes. Fourth, it can help uncover interesting and relevant research questions and issues for follow-up research.

At the same time, qualitative research also has its own set of challenges. First, this type of research tends to be more time and resource intensive than quantitative research in data collection and analytic efforts. Too little data can lead to false or premature assumptions, while too much data may not be effectively processed by the researcher. Second, qualitative research requires well-trained researchers who are capable of seeing and interpreting complex social phenomenon from the perspectives of the embedded participants and reconciling the diverse perspectives of these participants, without injecting their personal biases or preconceptions into their inferences. Third, all participants or data sources may not be equally credible, unbiased, or knowledgeable about the phenomenon of interest, or may have undisclosed political agendas, which may lead to misleading or false impressions. Inadequate trust between participants and researcher may hinder full and honest self-representation by participants, and such trust building takes time. It is the job of the qualitative researcher to "see through the smoke" (hidden or biased agendas) and understand the true nature of the problem. Finally, given the heavily contextualized nature of inferences drawn from qualitative research, such inferences do not lend themselves well to replicability or generalizability.

Key Takeaways

- Qualitative research examines words and other non-numeric media
- Analysis in qualitative research is holistic and contextual
- Qualitative research offers unique benefits, while facing challenges to generalizability and replicability

Glossary

- Qualitative methods – examine words or other media to understand their meaning

9.2 QUALITATIVE INTERVIEWS

Learning Objectives

- Define interviews from the social scientific perspective
- Identify when it is appropriate to employ interviews as a data-collection strategy
- Identify the primary aim of in-depth interviews
- Describe what makes qualitative interview techniques unique
- Define the term interview guide and describe how to construct an interview guide
- Outline the guidelines for constructing good qualitative interview questions
- Describe how writing field notes and journaling function in qualitative research
- Identify the strengths and weaknesses of interviews

Knowing how to create and conduct a good interview is an essential skill. Interviews are used by market researchers to learn how to sell their products, and journalists use interviews to get information from a whole host of people from VIPs to random people on the street. Police use interviews to investigate crimes.

In social science, **interviews** are a method of data collection that involves two or more people exchanging information through a series of questions and answers. The questions are designed by the researcher to elicit information from interview participants on a specific topic or set of topics. These topics are informed by the research questions. Typically, interviews involve an in-person meeting between two people—an interviewer and an interviewee — but interviews need not be limited to two people, nor must they occur in-person.

The question of when to conduct an interview might be on your mind. Interviews are an excellent way to gather detailed information. They also have an advantage over surveys—they can change as you learn more information. In a survey, you cannot change what questions you ask if a participant's response sparks some follow-up question in your mind. All participants must get the same questions. The questions you decided to put on your survey during the design stage determine what data you get. In an interview, however, you can follow up on new and unexpected topics that emerge during the conversation. Trusting in emergence and learning from participants are hallmarks of qualitative research. In this way, interviews are a useful method to use when you want to know the story behind the responses you might receive in a written survey.

Interviews are also useful when the topic you are studying is rather complex, requires lengthy explanation, or needs a dialogue between two people to thoroughly investigate. Also, if people will describe the process by which a phenomenon occurs, like how a person makes a decision, then interviews may be the best method for you. For example, you could use interviews to gather data about how people reach the decision not to have children and how others in their lives have responded to that decision. To understand these "how's" you would need to have some back-and-forth dialogue with respondents. When they begin to tell you their story, inevitably new questions that hadn't occurred to you from prior interviews would come up because each person's story is unique. Also, because the process of choosing not to have children is complex for many people, describing that process by responding to closed-ended questions on a survey wouldn't work particularly well.

Interview research is especially useful when:

- You wish to gather very detailed information
- You anticipate wanting to ask respondents follow-up questions based on their responses
- You plan to ask questions that require lengthy explanation
- You are studying a complex or potentially confusing topic to respondents
- You are studying processes, such as how people make decisions

Qualitative interviews are sometimes called intensive or in-depth interviews. These interviews are **semi-structured**; the researcher has a particular topic about which she would like to hear from the respondent, but questions are open-ended and may not be asked in exactly the same way or in exactly the same order to each and every respondent. For **in-depth interviews**, the primary aim is to hear from respondents about what they think is important about the topic at hand and to hear it in their own words. In this section, we'll take a look at how to conduct qualitative interviews, analyze interview data, and identify some of the strengths and weaknesses of this method.

CONSTRUCTING AN INTERVIEW GUIDE

Qualitative interviews might feel more like a conversation than an interview to respondents, but the researcher is in fact usually guiding the conversation with the goal in mind of gathering specific information from a respondent. Qualitative interviews use open-ended questions, which are questions that a researcher poses but does not provide answer options for. Open-ended questions are more demanding of participants than closed-ended questions because they require participants to come up with their own words, phrases, or sentences to respond.

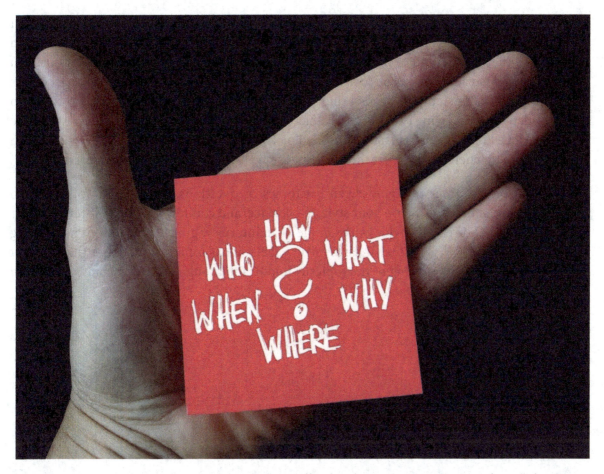

In a qualitative interview, the researcher usually develops an interview guide in advance to refer to during the interview (or memorizes in advance of the interview). An **interview guide** is a list of questions or topics that the interviewer hopes to cover during the course of an interview. It is called a guide because it is simply that—it is used to guide the interviewer, but it is not set in stone. Think of an interview guide like an agenda for the day or a to-do list—both probably contain all the items you hope to check off or accomplish, though it probably won't be the end of the world if you don't accomplish everything on the list or if you don't accomplish it in the exact order that you have it written down. Perhaps new events will come up that cause you to rearrange your schedule just a bit, or perhaps you simply won't get to everything on the list.

Interview guides should outline issues that a researcher feels are likely to be important. Because participants are asked to provide answers in their own words and to raise points they believe are important, each interview is likely to flow a little differently. While the opening question in an in-depth interview may be the same across all interviews, from that point on, what the participant says will shape how the interview proceeds. Sometimes participants answer a question on the interview guide before it is asked. When the interviewer comes to that question later on in the interview, it's a good idea to acknowledge that they already addressed part of this question and ask them if they have anything to add to their response. All of this uncertainty can make in-depth interviewing exciting and rather challenging. It takes a skilled interviewer to be able to ask questions; listen to respondents; and pick up on cues about when to follow up, when to move on, and when to simply let the participant speak without guidance or interruption.

As we've discussed, interview guides can list topics or questions. The specific format of an interview guide might depend on your style, experience, and comfort level as an interviewer or with your topic. Figure 9.1 provides an example of an interview guide for a study of how young people experience workplace sexual harassment. The guide is topic-based, rather than a list of specific questions. The ordering of the topics is important, though how each comes up during the interview may vary.

Workplace Harassment Interview Guide

1 Work history—before and since high school

    a. Jobs held
    b. Gender (coworkers and managers)
    c. Interactions/environment
    d. Interactions outside of work

2. Problems in the workplace

    a. Describe problems experienced
    b. Any problems you define as sexual harassment
    c. Define sexual harassment
    d. Examples of behaviors that qualify
    e. Describe harassment training

3. Feelings today

    a. How do you feel about past experiences?
    b. If happened again, how would you respond?

4. Sexual harassment in general

    a. Why does it occur?
    b. Why some are targeted and others are not?
    c. Why some tell and others do not?

5. Other forms of harassment/discrimination

    a. Housing, education, other work problems
    b. Additional information about workplace interactions

Figure 9.1 Interview guide displaying topics rather than questions.

For interview guides that use questions, there can also be specific words or phrases for follow-up in case the participant does not mention those topics in their responses. These *probes*, as well as the questions are written out in the interview guide, but may not always be used. Figure 9.2 provides an example of an interview guide that uses questions rather than topics.

Self-Directed Supports Interview Guide

1. In general, how would you define self-directed supports?

2. Programmatically, in your state, what are the necessary components for a program to be considered self-direction?

3. What factors lead to your state's decision to use self-directed supports?

4. How have your interactions with stakeholders impacted your implementation of self-directed supports?

5. You provided a list of goods and services covered in self-directed supports. How did you make the determination to include those services?

   a. Did you make the decision to exclude other goods and services?

   b. Have there been any issues in your state around what goods and services are covered in self-direction?

   c. Have you received any feedback from self-directed waiver participants about goods and services?

Figure 9.2 Interview guide displaying questions rather than topics

As you might have guessed, interview guides do not appear out of thin air. They are the result of thoughtful and careful work on the part of a researcher. As you can see in both of the preceding guides, the topics and questions have been organized thematically and in the order in which they are likely to proceed (though keep in mind that the flow of a qualitative interview is in part determined by what a respondent has to say). Sometimes qualitative interviewers may create two versions of the interview guide: one version contains a very brief outline of the interview, perhaps with just topic headings, and another version contains detailed questions underneath each topic heading. In this case, the researcher might use the very detailed guide to prepare and practice in advance of actually conducting interviews and then just bring the brief outline to the interview. Bringing an outline, as opposed to a very long list of detailed questions, to an interview encourages the researcher to actually listen to what a participant is saying. An overly detailed interview guide can be difficult to navigate during an interview and could give respondents the mis-impression the interviewer is more interested in the questions than in the participant's answers.

Constructing an interview guide often begins with brainstorming. There are no rules at the brainstorming stage—simply list all the topics and questions that come to mind when you think about your research question. Once you've got a pretty good list, you can begin to pare it down by cutting questions and topics that seem redundant and group similar questions and topics together. If you haven't done so yet, you may also want to come up with question and topic headings for your grouped categories. You should also consult the scholarly literature to find out what kinds of questions other interviewers have asked in studies of similar topics and what theory indicates might be important. As with quantitative survey research, it is best not to place very sensitive or potentially controversial questions at the very beginning of your qualitative interview guide. You need to give participants the opportunity to warm up to the interview and to feel comfortable talking with you. Finally, get some feedback on your interview guide. Ask your friends, other researchers, and your professors for some guidance and suggestions once you've come up with what you think is a strong guide. Chances are they'll catch a few things you hadn't noticed. Once you begin your interviews, your participants may also suggest revisions or improvements.

In terms of the specific questions you include in your guide, there are a few guidelines worth noting. First, avoid questions that can be answered with a simple yes or no. Try to rephrase your questions in a way that invites longer responses from your interviewees. If you choose to include yes or no questions, be sure to include follow-up questions. Remember, one of the benefits of qualitative interviews is that you can ask participants for more information—be sure to do so. While it is a good idea to ask follow-up questions, try to avoid asking "why" as your follow-up question, as this particular question can come off as confrontational, even if that is not your intent. Often people won't know how to respond to "why," perhaps because they don't even know why themselves. Instead of asking "why," you say something like, "Could you tell me a little more about that?" This allows participants to explain themselves further without feeling that they're being doubted or questioned in a hostile way.

Also, try to avoid phrasing your questions in a leading way. For example, rather than asking,

"Don't you think most people who don't want to have children are selfish?" you could ask, "What comes to mind for you when you hear someone doesn't want to have children?" Finally, remember to keep most, if not all, of your questions open-ended. The key to a successful qualitative interview is giving participants the opportunity to share information in their own words and in their own way. Documenting the decisions made along the way regarding which questions are used, thrown out, or revised can help a researcher remember the thought process behind the interview guide when she is analyzing the data. Additionally, it promotes the rigor of the qualitative project as a whole, ensuring the researcher is proceeding in a reflective and deliberate manner that can be checked by others reviewing her study.

RECORDING QUALITATIVE DATA

Even after the interview guide is constructed, the interviewer is not yet ready to begin conducting interviews. The researcher has to decide how to collect and maintain the information that is provided by participants. Researchers keep **field notes** or written recordings produced by the researcher during the data collection process. Field notes can be taken before, during, or after interviews. Field notes help researchers document what they observe, and in so doing, they form the first step of data analysis. Field notes may contain many things—observations of body language or environment, reflections on whether interview questions are working well, and connections between ideas that participants share.

Unfortunately, even the most diligent researcher cannot write down everything that is seen or heard during an interview. In particular, it is difficult for a researcher to be truly present and observant if she is also writing down everything the participant is saying. For this reason, it is quite common for interviewers to create audio recordings of the interviews they conduct. Recording interviews allows the researcher to focus on the interaction with the interview participant.

Of course, not all participants will feel comfortable being recorded and sometimes even the interviewer may feel that the subject is so sensitive that recording would be inappropriate. If this is the case, it is up to the researcher to balance excellent note-taking with exceptional question-asking and even better listening.

Whether you will be recording your interviews or not (and especially if not), practicing the interview in advance is crucial. Ideally, you'll find a friend or two willing to participate in a couple of trial runs with you. Even better, find a friend or two who are similar in at least some ways to your sample. They can give you the best feedback on your questions and your interview demeanor.

Another issue interviewers face is documenting the decisions made during the data collection process. Qualitative research is open to new ideas that emerge through the data collection process. For example, a participant might suggest a new concept you hadn't thought of before or define a concept in a new way. This may lead you to create new questions or ask questions in a different way to future participants. These processes should be documented in a process called **journaling** or memoing. Journal entries are notes to yourself about reflections or methodological decisions that emerge during the data collection process. Documenting these are important, as you'd be surprised how quickly you can forget what happened. Journaling makes sure that when it comes time to analyze your data, you remember how, when, and why certain changes were made. The discipline of journaling in qualitative research helps to ensure the rigor of the research process—that is its trustworthiness and authenticity which we will discuss later in this chapter.

STRENGTHS AND WEAKNESSES OF QUALITATIVE INTERVIEWS

As we've mentioned in this section, qualitative interviews are an excellent way to gather detailed information. Any topic can be explored in much more depth with interviews than with almost any other method. Not only are participants given the opportunity to elaborate in a way that is not possible with other methods such as survey research, but they also are able share information with researchers in their own words and from their own perspectives. Whereas, quantitative research asks participants to fit their perspectives into the limited response options provided by the researcher. And because qualitative interviews are designed to elicit detailed information, they are especially useful when a researcher's aim is to study social processes or the "how" of various phenomena. Yet another, and sometimes overlooked, benefit of in-person qualitative interviews is that researchers can make observations beyond those that a respondent is orally reporting. A respondent's body language, and even their choice of time and location for the interview, might provide a researcher with useful data.

Of course, all these benefits come with some drawbacks. As with quantitative survey research, qualitative interviews rely on respondents' ability to accurately and honestly recall specific details about their lives, circumstances, thoughts, opinions, or behaviors. Further, as you may have already guessed, qualitative interviewing is time-intensive and can be quite expensive. Creating an interview guide, identifying a sample, and conducting interviews are just the beginning. Writing out what was said in interviews and analyzing the qualitative interview data are time consuming processes. Keep in mind you are also asking for more of participants' time than if you'd simply mailed them a questionnaire containing closed-ended questions. Conducting qualitative interviews is not only labor-intensive but can also be emotionally taxing. Seeing and hearing the impact that social problems have on respondents is difficult.

Researchers embarking on a qualitative interview project should keep in mind their own abilities to receive stories that may be difficult to hear.

Key Takeaways

- Understanding how to design and conduct interview research is a useful skill to have.
- In a social scientific interview, two or more people exchange information through a series of questions and answers.
- Interview research is often used when detailed information is required and when a researcher wishes to examine processes.
- In-depth interviews are semi-structured interviews where the researcher has topics and questions in mind to ask, but questions are open-ended and flow according to how the participant responds to each.
- Interview guides can vary in format but should contain some outline of the topics you hope to cover during the course of an interview.
- Qualitative interviews allow respondents to share information in their own words and are useful for gathering detailed information and understanding social processes.
- Field notes and journaling are ways to document thoughts and decisions about the research process
- Drawbacks of qualitative interviews include reliance on respondents' accuracy and their intensity in terms of time, expense, and possible emotional strain.

Glossary

- Field notes- written notes produced by the researcher during the data collection process
- In-depth interviews- interviews in which researchers hear from respondents about what they think is important about the topic at hand in the respondent's own words
- Interviews- a method of data collection that involves two or more people exchanging information through a series of questions and answers

- Interview guide- a list of questions or topics that the interviewer hopes to cover during the course of an interview

- Journaling- making notes of emerging issues and changes during the research process

- Semi-structured interviews- questions are open ended and may not be asked in exactly the same way or in exactly the same order to each and every respondent

Image attributions

interview restaurant a pair by alda2 CC-0

questions by geralt CC-0

Figure 9.1 is copied from Blackstone, A. (2012) Principles of sociological inquiry: Qualitative and quantitative methods. Saylor Foundation. Retrieved from: https://saylordotorg.github.io/ text_principles-of-sociological-inquiry-qualitative-and-quantitative-methods/ Shared under CC-BY-NC-SA 3.0 License

writing by StockSnap CC-0

9.3 ISSUES TO CONSIDER FOR ALL INTERVIEW TYPES

Learning Objectives

- Identify the three main issues that interviewers should consider
- Describe how interviewers can address power imbalances
- Describe and define rapport
- Define the term probe

Qualitative researchers are attentive to the complexities that arise during the interview process. Interviews are intimate processes. Your participants will share with you how they view the world, how they understand themselves, and how they cope with events that happened to them. Conscientious researchers should keep in mind the following topics to ensure the authenticity and trust necessary for successful interviews.

POWER DIFFERENTIAL

First and foremost, interviewers must be aware of and attentive to the power differential between themselves and interview participants. The interviewer sets the agenda and leads the conversation. Qualitative interviewers aim to allow participants to have some control over which or to what extent various topics are discussed, but at the end of the day, it is the researcher who is in charge of the interview and how the data are reported to the public. The participant loses the ability to shape the narrative after the interview is over because it is the researcher who tells the story to the world. As the researcher, you are also asking someone to reveal things about themselves they may not typically share with others. Researchers do not reciprocate by revealing much or anything about themselves. All these factors shape the power dynamics of an interview.

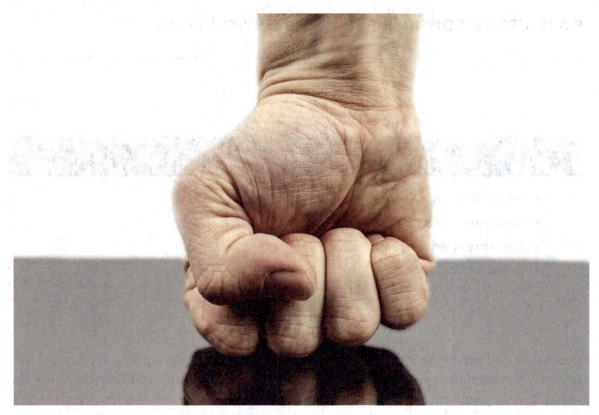

A number of excellent pieces have been written dealing with issues of power in research and data collection. Feminist researchers in particular paved the way in helping researchers think about and address issues of power in their work (Oakley, 1981). Suggestions for overcoming the power imbalance between researcher and respondent include having the researcher reveal some aspects of her own identity and story so that the interview is a more reciprocal experience rather than one-sided, allowing participants to view and edit interview transcripts before the researcher uses them for analysis, and giving participants an opportunity to read and comment on analysis before the researcher shares it with others through publication or presentation (Reinharz, 1992; Hesse-Biber, Nagy, & Leavy, 2007). On the other hand, some researchers suggest that sharing too much with interview participants can give the false impression there is no power differential, when in reality, researchers can analyze and present participants' stories in whatever way they see fit (Stacey, 1988).

However you feel about sharing details about your background with an interview participant, another way to balance the power differential between yourself and your interview participants is to make the intent of your research very clear to the subjects. Share with them your rationale for conducting the research and the research question(s) that frame your work. Be sure that you also share with participants how the data you gather will be used and stored. Also, explain to participants how their confidentiality will be protected including who will have access to the data you gather from them and what procedures, such as using pseudonyms, you will take to protect their identities. Social workers also must disclose the reasons why confidentiality may be violated to prevent danger to self or others. Many of these details will be covered by your IRB's informed consent procedures and requirements. However, even if they are not, as researchers we should be attentive to how informed consent can help balance the power differences between ourselves and those who participate in our research.

There are no easy answers when it comes to handling the power differential between the researcher and researched. Even social scientists do not agree on the best approach. Because qualitative research involves interpersonal interactions and building a relationship with research participants, power is a particularly important issue.

LOCATION, LOCATION, LOCATION

One way to address the power between researcher and respondent is to conduct the interview in a location of the participant's choosing, where they will feel most comfortable answering your questions. Interviews can take place in any number of locations—in respondents' homes or offices, researchers' homes or offices, coffee shops, restaurants, public parks, or hotel lobbies, to name just a few possibilities. Each location comes with its own set of benefits and its own challenges. Allowing the respondent to choose the location that is most convenient and most comfortable for them is important, but identifying a location where there will be few distractions is helpful. For example, some coffee shops and restaurants are so loud that recording the interview can be a challenge. Other locations may present different sorts of distractions. For example, if you conduct interviews with parents in their home, they may out of necessity spend more time attending to their children during an interview than responding to your questions (of course, depending on the topic of your research, the opportunity to observe such interactions could be invaluable). As an interviewer, you may want to suggest a few possible locations, and note the goal of avoiding distractions, when you ask your respondents to choose a location.

The extent to which a respondent has control over choosing a location must also be balanced by accessibility of the location to the interviewer, and by the safety and comfort level with the location. You may not feel comfortable conducting an interview in an area with posters for hate groups on the wall. Not only might you fear for your safety, you may be too distracted to conduct a good interview. While it is important to conduct interviews in a location that is comfortable for respondents, doing so should never come at the expense of your safety.

RESEARCHER-PARTICIPANT RAPPORT

A unique feature of interviews is that they require some social interaction, which means that a relationship is formed between interviewer and interviewee. One essential element in building a productive relationship is respect. You should respect the person's time and their story. Demonstrating respect will help interviewees feel comfortable sharing with you.

There are no big secrets or tricks for how to show respect for research participants. At its core, the interview interaction should not differ from any other social interaction in which you show gratitude for a person's time and respect for a person's humanity. It is crucial that you, as the interviewer, conduct the interview in a way that is culturally sensitive. In some cases, this might mean educating yourself about your study population and even receiving some training to help you learn to effectively communicate with your research participants. Do not judge your research participants; you are there to listen to them, and they have been kind enough to give you their time and attention. Even if you disagree strongly with what a participant shares in an interview, your job as the researcher is to gather the information being shared with you, not to make personal judgments about it. Respect provides a solid foundation for rapport.

Rapport is the sense of connection you establish with a participant. Developing good rapport requires good listening. In fact, listening during an interview is an active, not a passive, practice. Active listening means that you, the researcher, participate with the respondent by showing you understand and follow whatever it is that they are telling you (Devault, 1990). The questions you ask respondents should indicate you've actually heard what they've just said.

Active listening means you will probe the respondent for more information from time to time throughout the interview. A **probe** is a request for more information. Probes are used because qualitative interviewing techniques are designed to go with the flow and take whatever direction the respondent goes during the interview. It is worth your time to come up with helpful probes in advance of an interview. You certainly do not want to find yourself stumped or speechless after a respondent has just said something about which you'd like to hear more. This is another reason why practicing your interview in advance with people who are similar to those in your sample is a good idea.

The responsibilities that a social work clinician has to clients differ significantly from a researcher's responsibilities. Clinicians provide services whereas researchers do not. A research participant is not your client, and your goals for the interaction are different from those of a clinical relationship.

Key Takeaways

- Interviewers should take into consideration the power differential between themselves and their respondents.
- Feminist researchers paved the way for helping interviewers think about how to balance the power differential between themselves and interview participants.
- Attend to the location of an interview and the relationship that forms between the interviewer and interviewee.
- Interviewers should always be respectful of interview participants.

Glossary

- Probe- a request for more information in qualitative research

Image attributions

punch fist by PublicDomainPictures CC-0

action collaborate by rawpixel CC-0

9.4 TYPES OF QUALITATIVE RESEARCH DESIGNS

Learning Objectives

- Define focus groups and outline how they differ from one-on-one interviews
- Describe how to determine the best size for focus groups
- Identify the important considerations in focus group composition
- Discuss how to moderate focus groups
- Identify the strengths and weaknesses of focus group methodology
- Describe case study research, ethnography, and phenomenology.

There are various types of approaches to qualitative research. This chapter presents information about focus groups, which are often used in social work research. It also introduces case studies, ethnography, and phenomenology.

FOCUS GROUPS

Focus groups resemble qualitative interviews in that a researcher may prepare a guide in advance and interact with participants by asking them questions. But anyone who has conducted both one-on-one interviews and focus groups knows that each is unique. In an interview, usually one member (the research participant) is most active while the other (the researcher) plays the role of listener, conversation guider, and question-asker. **Focus groups**, on the other hand, are planned discussions designed to elicit group interaction and "obtain perceptions on a defined area of interest in a permissive, nonthreatening environment" (Krueger & Casey, 2000, p. 5). In focus groups, the researcher play a different role than in a one-on-one interview. The researcher's aim is to get participants talking to each other, to observe interactions among participants, and moderate the discussion.

There are numerous examples of focus group research. In their 2008 study, for example, Amy Slater and Marika Tiggemann (2010) conducted six focus groups with 49 adolescent girls between the ages of 13 and 15 to learn more about girls' attitudes towards' participation in sports. In order to get focus group participants to speak with one another rather than with the group facilitator, the focus group interview guide contained just two questions: "Can you tell me some of the reasons that girls stop playing sports or other physical activities?" and "Why do you think girls don't play as much sport/physical activity as boys?" In another focus group study, Virpi Ylanne and Angie Williams (2009) held nine focus group sessions with adults of different ages to gauge their perceptions of how older characters are represented in television commercials. Among other considerations, the researchers were interested in discovering how focus group participants position themselves and others in terms of age stereotypes and identities during the group discussion. In both examples, the researchers' core interest in group interaction could not have been assessed had interviews been conducted on a one-on-one basis, making the focus group method an ideal choice.

WHO SHOULD BE IN YOUR FOCUS GROUP?

In some ways, focus groups require more planning than other qualitative methods of data collection, such as one-on-one interviews in which a researcher may be better able to the dialogue. Researchers must take care to form focus groups with members who will want to interact with one another and to control the timing of the event so that participants are not asked nor expected to stay for a longer time than they've agreed to participate. The researcher should also be prepared to inform focus group participants of their responsibility to maintain the confidentiality of what is said in the group. But while the researcher can and should encourage all focus group members to maintain confidentiality, she should also clarify to participants that the unique nature of the group setting prevents her from being able to promise that confidentiality will be maintained by other participants. Once focus group members leave the research setting, researchers cannot control what they say to other people.

Group size should be determined in part by the topic of the interview and your sense of the likelihood that participants will have much to say without much prompting. If the topic is one about which you think participants feel passionately and will have much to say, a group of 3–5 could make sense. Groups larger than that, especially for heated topics, can easily become unmanageable. Some researchers say that a group of about 6–10 participants is the ideal size for focus group research (Morgan, 1997); others recommend that groups should include 3–12 participants (Adler & Clark, 2008). The size of the focus group is ultimately the decision of the researcher. When forming groups and deciding how large or small to make them, take into consideration what you know about the topic and participants' potential interest in, passion for, and feelings about the topic. Also consider your comfort level and experience in conducting focus groups. These factors will help you decide which size is right in your particular case.

It may seem counterintuitive, but in general, it is better to form focus groups consisting of participants who do not know one another than to create groups consisting of friends, relatives, or acquaintances (Agar & MacDonald, 1995). The reason is that group members who know each other may not share some taken-for-granted knowledge or assumptions. In research, it is precisely the taken-for-granted knowledge that is often of interest; thus, the focus group researcher should avoid setting up interactions where participants may be discouraged to question or raise issues that they take for granted. However, group members should not be so different from one another that participants will be unlikely to feel comfortable talking with one another.

Focus group researchers must carefully consider the composition of the groups they put together. In his text on conducting focus groups, Morgan (1997) suggests that "homogeneity in background and not homogeneity in attitudes" (p. 36) should be the goal, since participants must feel comfortable speaking up but must also have enough differences to facilitate a productive discussion. Whatever composition a researcher designs for her focus groups, the important point to keep in mind is that focus group dynamics are shaped by multiple social contexts (Hollander, 2004). Participants' silences as well as their speech may be shaped by gender, race, class, sexuality, age, or other background characteristics or social dynamics—all of which might be suppressed or exacerbated depending on the composition of the group. Hollander (2004) suggests that researchers must pay careful attention to group composition, must be attentive to group dynamics during the focus group discussion, and should use multiple methods of data collection in order to "untangle participants' responses and their relationship to the social contexts of the focus group" (p. 632).

THE ROLE OF THE MODERATOR

In addition to the importance of group composition, focus groups also require skillful moderation. A **moderator** is the researcher tasked with facilitating the conversation in the focus group. Participants may ask each other follow-up questions, agree or disagree with one another, display body language that tells us something about their feelings about the conversation, or even come up with questions not previously conceived of by the researcher. It is just these sorts of interactions and displays that are of interest to the researcher. A researcher conducting focus groups collects data on more than people's direct responses to her question, as in interviews.

The moderator's job is not to ask questions to each person individually, but to stimulate conversation between participants. It is important to set ground rules for focus groups at the outset of the discussion. Remind participants you've invited them to participate because you want to hear from all of them. Therefore, the group should aim to let just one person speak at a time and avoid letting just a couple of participants dominate the conversation. One way to do this is to begin the discussion by asking participants to briefly introduce themselves or to provide a brief response to an opening question. This will help set the tone of having all group members participate. Also, ask participants to avoid having side conversations; thoughts or reactions to what is said in the group are important and should be shared with everyone.

As the focus group gets rolling, the moderator will play a less active role as participants talk to one another. There may be times when the conversation stagnates or when you, as moderator, wish to guide the conversation in another direction. In these instances, it is important to demonstrate that you've been paying attention to what participants have said. Being prepared to interject statements or questions such as "I'd really like to hear more about what Sunil and Joe think about what Dominick and Jae have been saying" or "Several of you have mentioned X. What do others think about this?" will be important for keeping the conversation going. It can also help redirect the conversation, shift the focus to participants who have been less active in the group, and serve as a cue to those who may be dominating the conversation that it is time to allow others to speak. Researchers may choose to use multiple moderators to make managing these various tasks easier.

Moderators are often too busy working with participants to take diligent notes during a focus group. It is helpful to have a note-taker who can record participants' responses (Liamputtong, 2011). The note-taker creates, in essence, the first draft of interpretation for the data in the study. They note themes in responses, nonverbal cues, and other information to be included in the analysis later on. Focus groups are analyzed in a similar way as interviews; however, the interactive dimension between participants adds another element to the analytical process. Researchers must attend to the group dynamics of each focus group, as "verbal and nonverbal expressions, the tactical use of humour, interruptions in interaction, and disagreement between participants" are all data that are vital to include in analysis (Liamputtong, 2011, p. 175). Note-takers record these elements in field notes, which allows moderators to focus on the conversation.

STRENGTHS AND WEAKNESSES OF FOCUS GROUPS

Focus groups share many of the strengths and weaknesses of one-on-one qualitative interviews. Both methods can yield very detailed, in-depth information; are excellent for studying social processes; and provide researchers with an opportunity not only to hear what participants say but also to observe what they do in terms of their body language. Focus groups offer the added benefit of giving researchers a chance to collect data on human interaction by observing how group participants respond and react to one another. Like one-on-one qualitative interviews, focus groups can also be quite expensive and time-consuming. However, there may be some savings with focus groups as it takes fewer group events than one-on-one interviews to gather data from the same number of people. Another potential drawback of focus groups, which is not a concern for one-on-one interviews, is that one or two participants might dominate the group, silencing other participants. Careful planning and skillful moderation on the part of the researcher are crucial for avoiding, or at least dealing with, such possibilities. The various strengths and weaknesses of focus group research are summarized in Table 91.

Table 9.1 Strengths and weaknesses of focus group research

Strengths	Weaknesses
Yield detailed, in-depth data	Expensive
Less time-consuming than one-on-one interviews	May be more time-consuming than survey research
Useful for studying social processes	Minority of participants may dominate entire group
Allow researchers to observe body language in addition to self-reports	Some participants may not feel comfortable talking in groups
Allow researchers to observe interaction between multiple participants	Cannot ensure confidentiality

GROUNDED THEORY

Grounded theory has been widely used since its development in the late 1960s (Glaser & Strauss, 1967). Largely derived from schools of sociology, grounded theory involves emersion of the researcher in the field and in the data. Researchers follow a systematic set of procedures and a simultaneous approach to data collection and analysis. Grounded theory is most often used to generate rich explanations of complex actions, processes, and transitions. The primary mode of data collection is one-on-one participant interviews. Sample sizes tend to range from 20 to 30 individuals, sampled purposively (Padgett, 2016). However, sample sizes can be larger or smaller, depending on data saturation. **Data saturation** is the point in the qualitative research data collection process when no new information is being discovered. Researchers use a constant comparative approach in which previously collected data are analyzed during the same time frame as new data are being collected. This allows the researchers to determine when new information is no longer being gleaned from data collection and analysis — that data saturation has been reached — in order to conclude the data collection phase.

Rather than apply or test existing grand theories, or "Big T" theories, grounded theory focuses on "small t" theories (Padgett, 2016). Grand theories, or "Big T" theories, are systems of principles, ideas, and concepts used to predict phenomena. These theories are backed up by facts and tested hypotheses. "Small t" theories are speculative and contingent upon specific contexts. In grounded theory, these "small t" theories are grounded in events and experiences and emerge from the analysis of the data collected.

One notable application of grounded theory produced a "small t" theory of acceptance following cancer diagnoses (Jakobsson, Horvath, & Ahlberg, 2005). Using grounded theory, the researchers interviewed nine patients in western Sweden. Data collection and analysis stopped when saturation was reached. The researchers found that action and knowledge, given with respect and continuity led to confidence which led to acceptance. This "small t" theory continues to be applied and further explored in other contexts.

CASE STUDY RESEARCH

Case study research is an intensive longitudinal study of a phenomenon at one or more research sites for the purpose of deriving detailed, contextualized inferences and understanding the dynamic process underlying a phenomenon of interest. Case research is a unique research design in that it can be used in an interpretive manner to build theories or in a positivist manner to test theories. The previous chapter on case research discusses both techniques in depth and provides illustrative exemplars. Furthermore, the case researcher is a neutral observer (direct observation) in the social setting rather than an active participant (participant observation). As with any other interpretive approach, drawing meaningful inferences from case research depends heavily on the observational skills and integrative abilities of the researcher.

ETHNOGRAPHY

The ethnographic research method, derived largely from the field of anthropology, emphasizes studying a phenomenon within the context of its culture. The researcher must be deeply immersed in the social culture over an extended period of time (usually 8 months to 2 years) and should engage, observe, and record the daily life of the studied culture and its social participants within their natural setting. The primary mode of data collection is participant observation, and data analysis involves a "sense-making" approach. In addition, the researcher must take extensive field notes, and narrate her experience in descriptive detail so that readers may experience the same culture as the researcher. In this method, the researcher has two roles: rely on her unique knowledge and engagement to generate insights (theory), and convince the scientific community of the trans-situational nature of the studied phenomenon.

The classic example of ethnographic research is Jane Goodall's study of primate behaviors, where she lived with chimpanzees in their natural habitat at Gombe National Park in Tanzania, observed their behaviors, interacted with them, and shared their lives. During that process, she learnt and chronicled how chimpanzees seek food and shelter, how they socialize with each other, their communication patterns, their mating behaviors, and so forth. A more contemporary example of ethnographic research is Myra Bluebond-Langer's (1996)14 study of decision making in families with children suffering from life-threatening illnesses, and the physical, psychological, environmental, ethical, legal, and cultural issues that influence such decision-making. The researcher followed the experiences of approximately 80 children with incurable illnesses and their families for a period of over two years. Data collection involved participant observation and formal/informal conversations with children, their parents and relatives, and health care providers to document their lived experience.

PHENOMENOLOGY

Phenomenology is a research method that emphasizes the study of conscious experiences as a way of understanding the reality around us. Phenomenology is concerned with the systematic reflection and analysis of phenomena associated with conscious experiences, such as human judgment, perceptions, and actions, with the goal of (1) appreciating and describing social reality from the diverse subjective perspectives of the participants involved, and (2) understanding the symbolic meanings ("deep structure") underlying these subjective experiences. Phenomenological inquiry requires that researchers eliminate any prior assumptions and personal biases, empathize with the participant's situation, and tune into existential dimensions of that situation, so that they can fully understand the deep structures that drives the conscious thinking, feeling, and behavior of the studied participants.

Some researchers view phenomenology as a philosophy rather than as a research method. In response to this criticism, Giorgi and Giorgi (2003) developed an existential phenomenological research method to guide studies in this area. This method can be grouped into data collection and data analysis phases. In the data collection phase, participants embedded in a social phenomenon are interviewed to capture their subjective experiences and perspectives regarding the phenomenon under investigation. Examples of questions that may be asked include "can you describe a typical day" or "can you describe that particular incident in more detail?" These interviews are recorded and transcribed for further analysis. During data analysis, the researcher reads the transcripts to: (1) get a sense of the whole, and (2) establish "units of significance" that can faithfully represent participants' subjective experiences. Examples of such units of significance are concepts such as "felt space" and "felt time," which are then used to document participants' psychological experiences. For instance, did participants feel safe, free, trapped, or joyous when experiencing a phenomenon ("felt-space")? Did they feel that their experience was pressured, slow, or discontinuous ("felt-time")? Phenomenological analysis should take into account the participants' temporal landscape (i.e., their sense of past, present, and future), and the researcher must transpose herself in an imaginary sense in the participant's situation (i.e., temporarily live the participant's life). The participants' lived experience is described in form of a narrative or using emergent themes. The analysis then delves into these themes to identify multiple layers of meaning while retaining the fragility and ambiguity of subjects' lived experiences.

Key Takeaways

- In terms of focus group composition, homogeneity of background among participants is recommended while diverse attitudes within the group are ideal.
- The goal of a focus group is to get participants to talk with one another rather than the researcher.
- Like one-on-one qualitative interviews, focus groups can yield very detailed information, are excellent for studying social processes, and provide researchers with an opportunity to observe participants' body language; they also allow researchers to observe social interaction.
- Focus groups can be expensive and time-consuming, as are one-on-one interviews; there is also the possibility that a few participants will dominate the group and silence others in the group.
- Other types of qualitative research include case studies, ethnography, and phenomenology.

Glossary

- Data saturation – the point in the qualitative research data collection process when no new information is being discovered
- Focus groups- planned discussions designed to elicit group interaction and "obtain perceptions on a defined area of interest in a permissive, nonthreatening environment" (Krueger & Casey,

2000, p. 5)

- Moderator- the researcher tasked with facilitating the conversation in the focus group

Image attributions

target group by geralt CC-0

workplace team by Free-Photos CC-0

9.5 SPOTLIGHT ON UTA SCHOOL OF SOCIAL WORK

DR. GENEVIEVE GRAAF CONDUCTS RESEARCH USING INTERVIEWS AND FOCUS GROUPS

As a mental health policy researcher, interviews and focus groups are a critical technique that Dr. Genevieve Graaf of the University of Texas at Arlington's School of Social Work uses to understand policy making processes and decisions, as well as the intricacies of mental health policy itself. These research tools enable the collection of information that is not readily or easily available, or can help to provide explanation, context, or clarification for information that is public knowledge.

In her most recent study, Dr. Graaf interviewed and conducted focus groups with children's mental health administrators and policy makers in 32 different states. These interviews focused on understanding how each state organized and funded home and community-based mental health services for children and adolescents with significant emotional or behavioral disorders. Information was also gathered about the historical, political, and financial factors that shaped state approaches to addressing the needs of this population.

In smaller states, interviews were conducted with one policy informant, due to the small scope of the mental health administration. However, in some larger and more complex states, where policy makers collaborated across a variety of departments—child and family services, Medicaid administrations, juvenile justice divisions—focus groups were required to hear the shared perspectives and information available through a variety of stakeholders. Dr. Graaf used semi-structured interviews in which a set of topics and questions included on the interview protocol guided the discussion, but participants were able to change topics, move through topics out of the planned order, and offer information on topics not included in the interview protocol. This allowed for data collection to be comprehensive but also include the depth of nuanced and minor details relevant to aims of the study.

By collecting detailed data directly from knowledgeable informants who are involved in state mental health policy making on a daily basis, these interviews and focus groups provide in-depth illustrations of the variation in mental health policy making, mental health administrations, and the financial and governmental structures that exist across and between states. This type of knowledge can be shared among policy makers across states and nations as inspiration and lessons learned about best practices in the funding and organization of mental health care for children. After completing these interviews and focus groups, and analyzing the data, findings from these interviews and focus groups have been reported in three peer-reviewed journal articles (see for example, Graaf & Snowden, 2019) presented at conferences filled with state mental health policy makers, and shared directly with the state mental health policy makers who participated in the study. Many participants, when interviewed, asked to see the final report because they were very interested to learn about the practices and strategies used in other states.

The in-depth information collected through these interviews and focus groups can also help to advance further research about the accessibility, effectiveness, and quality of mental health services for children and their families by providing detailed contexts in which to examine further questions. For example, Dr. Graaf used interview and focus group findings to shape her approach to analyzing national quantitative data and enhanced her understanding of those quantitative findings. Factors that informants reported as shaping their decision making around their children's mental health policies were used as control variables in her statistical models. Also, findings that were unexpected or surprising could be partially explained by variations across state mental health systems that were reported in interviews and captured through focus groups.

9.6 ANALYZING QUALITATIVE DATA

Learning Objectives

- Describe how to transcribe qualitative data
- Identify and describe the two types of coding in qualitative research
- Assess the rigor of qualitative analysis using the criteria of trustworthiness and authenticity

Analysis of qualitative data typically begins with a set of transcripts of the interviews or focus groups conducted. Obtaining these transcripts requires having either taken exceptionally good notes or, preferably, having recorded the interview or focus group and then transcribed it. Researchers create a complete written copy, or **transcript**, of the recording by playing it back and typing in each word that is spoken, noting who spoke which words. In general, it is best to aim for a verbatim transcript, one that reports word for word exactly what was said in the recording. If possible, it is also best to include nonverbals in a transcript. Gestures made by participants should be noted, as should the tone of voice and notes about when, where, and how spoken words may have been emphasized by participants. Because these are difficult to capture via audio, it is important to have a note-taker in focus groups or to write useful field notes during interviews.

The goal of qualitative data analysis is to reach some inferences, lessons, or conclusions by condensing large amounts of data into relatively smaller, more manageable bits of understandable information. Analysis of qualitative data often works inductively (Glaser & Strauss, 1967; Charmaz, 2006). To move from the specific observations a researcher collects to identifying patterns across those observations, qualitative researchers will often begin by reading through transcripts and trying to identify codes. A **code** is a shorthand representation of some more complex set of issues or ideas.

Qualitative researcher and textbook author Kristin Esterberg (2002) describes coding as a multistage process. To analyze qualitative data, one can begin by **open coding** transcripts. This means that you read through each transcript, line by line, and make a note of whatever categories or themes jump out to you. Open coding will probably require multiple rounds. That is, you will read through all of your transcripts multiple times. Once you have completed a few passes and started noticing commonalities, you might begin focused coding. In **focused coding** a final list of codes is identified from the results of the open coding. Once you come up with a final list of codes, make sure each one has a definition that clearly spells out what the code means. Finally, the dataset is recoded using the final list of codes, making sure to apply the definition of the code consistently throughout each transcript.

Using multiple researchers to code the same dataset can be quite helpful. You may miss something a participant said that another coder catches. Similarly, you may shift your understanding of what a code means and not realize it until another coder asks you about it. If multiple researchers are coding the dataset simultaneously, researchers must come to a consensus about the meaning of each code and ensure that codes are applied consistently by each researcher. We discussed this previously in Chapter 5 as inter-rater reliability. Even if only one person will code the dataset, it is important to work with other researchers. If other researchers have the time, you may be able to have them check your work for trustworthiness and authenticity, which are discussed in detail below.

Table 13.2, presents two codes that emerged from an inductive analysis of transcripts from interviews with child-free adults. It also includes a brief description of each code and a few (of many) interview excerpts from which each code was developed.

Table 9.2 Interview coding example

Code	Code definition	Interview excerpts
Reify Gender	Participants *reinforce* heteronormative ideals in two ways: (a) by calling up stereotypical images of gender and family and (b) by citing their own "failure" to achieve those ideals.	"The woman is more involved with taking care of the child. [As a woman] I'd be the one waking up more often to feed the baby and more involved in the personal care of the child, much more involved. I would have more responsibilities than my partner. I know I would feel that burden more than if I were a man."
		"I don't have that maternal instinct."
		"I look at all my high school friends on Facebook, and I'm the only one who isn't married and doesn't have kids. I question myself, like if there's something wrong with me that I don't have that."
		"I feel badly that I'm not providing my parents with grandchildren."
Resist Gender	Participants *resist* gender norms in two ways: (a) by pushing back against negative social responses and (b) by redefining family for themselves in a way that challenges normative notions of family.	"Am I less of a woman because I don't have kids? I don't think so!"
		"I think if they're gonna put their thoughts on me, I'm putting it back on them. When they tell me, 'Oh, Janet, you won't have lived until you've had children. It's the most fulfilling thing a woman can do!' then I just name off the 10 fulfilling things I did in the past week that they didn't get to do because they have kids."
		"Family is the group of people that you want to be with. That's it."

As you might imagine, wading through all these data is quite a process. Just as quantitative researchers rely on the assistance of special computer programs designed to help with sorting through and analyzing their data, so too do qualitative researchers. There are programs specifically designed to assist qualitative researchers with organizing, managing, sorting, and analyzing large amounts of qualitative data. The programs work by allowing researchers to import transcripts contained in an electronic file and then label or code passages, cut and paste passages, search for various words or phrases, and organize complex interrelationships among passages and codes. They even include advanced features that allow researchers to code multimedia files, visualize relationships between a network of codes, and count the number of times a code was applied.

TRUSTWORTHINESS AND AUTHENTICITY

In qualitative research, the standards for analysis quality differ than quantitative research for an important reason. Analysis in quantitative research can be done objectively or impartially. The researcher chooses a statistical analysis based on the research questions and data, and reads the results. The extent to which the results are accurate and consistent is a problem with the data, not the researcher.

The same cannot be said for qualitative research. Qualitative researchers are deeply involved in the data analysis process. There is no external measurement tool, like a quantitative scale. Rather, the researcher herself is the measurement instrument. Researchers build connections between different ideas that participants discuss and draft an analysis that accurately reflects the depth and complexity of what participants have said. This is a challenging task for a researcher. It involves acknowledging her own biases, either from personal experience or previous knowledge about the topic, and allowing the meaning that participants shared to emerge as the data is analyzed. It's not necessarily about being objective, as there is always some subjectivity in qualitative analysis, but more about the rigor with which the individual researcher engages in data analysis.

For this reason, researchers speak of rigor in more personal terms. **Trustworthiness** refers to the "truth value, applicability, consistency, and neutrality" of the results of a research study (Rodwell, 1998, p. 96). **Authenticity** refers to the degree to which researchers capture the multiple perspectives and values of participants in their study and foster change across participants and systems during their analysis. Both trustworthiness and authenticity contain criteria that help a researcher gauge the rigor with which the results were obtained.

Most analogous to the quantitative concepts of validity and reliability are qualitative research's trustworthiness criteria of *credibility*, *dependability*, and *confirmability*. **Credibility** refers to the degree to which the results are accurate and viewed as important and believable by participants. Qualitative researchers will often check with participants before finalizing and publishing their results to make sure participants agree with them. They may also seek out assistance from another qualitative researcher to review or audit their work. As you might expect, it's difficult to view your own research without bias, so another set of eyes is often helpful. Unlike in quantitative research, the ultimate goal is not to find the Truth (with a capital T) using a predetermined measure, but to create a credible interpretation of the data. Credibility is seen as akin to validity, as it mainly speaks to the accuracy of the research product.

The criterion of dependability, on the other hand, is similar to reliability. As you may recall, reliability is the consistency of a measure (if you give the same measure each time, you should get similar results). However, qualitative research questions, hypotheses, and interview questions may change during the research process. How can one achieve reliability under such conditions? Because qualitative research understands the importance of context, it would be impossible to control all of the things that would make a qualitative measure the same when you give it to each person. The location, timing, or even the weather can and do influence participants to respond differently. Therefore, qualitative researchers assess dependability rather than reliability. **Dependability** ensures that proper qualitative procedures were followed and that any changes that emerged during the research process are accounted for, justified, and described in the final report. Researchers should document changes to their methodology and the justification for them in a journal or log. In addition, researchers may again use another qualitative researcher to examine their logs and results to ensure dependability.

Finally, the criterion of **confirmability** refers to the degree to which the results reported are linked to the data obtained from participants. While it is possible that another researcher could view the same data and come up with a different analysis, confirmability ensures that a researcher's results are actually grounded in what participants said. Another researcher should be able to read the results of your study and trace each point made back to something specific that one or more participants shared. This process is called an audit.

The criteria for trustworthiness were created as a reaction to critiques of qualitative research as unscientific (Guba, 1990). They demonstrate that qualitative research is equally as rigorous as quantitative research. Subsequent scholars conceptualized the dimension of authenticity without referencing the standards of quantitative research at all. Instead, they wanted to understand the rigor of qualitative research on its own terms.

While there are multiple criteria for authenticity, the one that is most important for undergraduate social work researchers to understand is **fairness**. Fairness refers to the degree to which "different constructions, perspectives, and positions are not only allowed to emerge, but are also seriously considered for merit and worth" (Rodwell, 1998, p. 107). Qualitative researchers, depending on their design, may involve participants in the data analysis process, try to equalize power dynamics among participants, and help negotiate consensus on the final interpretation of the data. As you can see from the talk of power dynamics and consensus-building, authenticity attends to the social justice elements of social work research.

Key Takeaways

- Open coding involves allowing codes to emerge from the dataset.

- Codes must be clearly defined before focused coding can begin, so the researcher applies them in the same way to each unit of data.

- The criteria that qualitative researchers use to assess rigor are trustworthiness and authenticity.

Glossary

- Authenticity- the degree to which researchers capture the multiple perspectives and values of participants in their study and foster change across participants and systems during their analysis

- Code- a shorthand representation of some more complex set of issues or ideas
- Coding- identifying themes across qualitative data by reading transcripts
- Confirmability- the degree to which the results reported are linked to the data obtained from participants
- Credibility- the degree to which the results are accurate and viewed as important and believable by participants
- Dependability- ensures that proper qualitative procedures were followed and that any changes that emerged during the research process are accounted for, justified, and described in the final report
- Fairness- the degree to which "different constructions, perspectives, and positions are not only allowed to emerge, but are also seriously considered for merit and worth" (Rodwell, 1998, p. 107)
- Focused coding- collapsing or narrowing down codes, defining codes, and recoding each transcript using a final code list
- Open coding- reading through each transcript, line by line, and make a note of whatever categories or themes seem to jump out to you
- Transcript- a complete, written copy of the recorded interview or focus group containing each word that is spoken on the recording, noting who spoke which words
- Trustworthiness- the "truth value, applicability, consistency, and neutrality" of the results of a research study (Rodwell, 1998, p. 96)

Image attributions

Compact Cassette by Petr Kvashin CC-0

concept of learning by unknown CC-0

Trust by Terry Johnston CC-BY-2.0

CHAPTER TEN: UNOBTRUSIVE RESEARCH

Are female and male athletes at the professional and college levels treated equally? You might think decades after the passage of Title IX (the civil rights law that prohibits sex discrimination in education including athletics) and with growing visibility of women athletes in sports, such as golf, basketball, hockey, and tennis, that the answer would be an easy yes. But in the early 2000s, Professor Michael Messner's (2002) unobtrusive research showed otherwise, as did Professors Jo Ann M. Buysse and Melissa Sheridan Embser-Herbert's (2004) content analysis of college athletics media guide photographs.

In fact, Buysse and Embser-Herbert's unobtrusive research showed that traditional definitions of femininity were fiercely maintained through colleges' visual representations of women athletes as passive and overtly feminine (as opposed to strong and athletic). In addition, Messner and colleagues' (Messner, Duncan, & Jensen, 1993) content analysis of verbal commentary in televised coverage of men's and women's sports showed that announcers' comments varied depending on an athlete's gender identity. Such commentary not only infantilized women athletes but also asserted an ambivalent stance toward their accomplishments. Without this unobtrusive research we might have been inclined to think that more had changed for women athletes in the 30 years since it passed than actually had changed.

CHAPTER OUTLINE

- 10.1 Unobtrusive research: What is it and when should it be used?
- 10.2 Strengths and weaknesses of unobtrusive research
- 10.3 Unobtrusive data collected by the researcher
- 10.4 Secondary data analysis

CONTENT ADVISORY

This chapter discusses or mentions the following topics: sexism, racism, depression, suicide, and cognitive impairment among older adults.

10.1 UNOBTRUSIVE RESEARCH: WHAT IS IT AND WHEN SHOULD IT BE USED?

Learning Objectives

- Define unobtrusive research and describe why it is used

In this chapter, we will explore unobtrusive methods of collecting data. **Unobtrusive research** refers to methods of collecting data that don't interfere with the subjects under study (i.e., these methods are not "obtrusive"). Both qualitative and quantitative researchers use unobtrusive research methods. Unobtrusive methods share the unique quality that they do not require the researcher to interact with the people she is studying. It may seem strange that social work, a discipline dedicated to helping people, would employ a methodology that requires no interaction with human beings. But humans create plenty of evidence of their behaviors—they write letters to the editor of their local paper, they create various sources of entertainment for themselves such as movies and televisions shows, they consume goods, they walk on sidewalks, and they lie on the grass in public parks. All these activities leave something behind—worn paths, trash, recorded shows, and printed papers. These are all potential sources of data for the unobtrusive researcher.

Social workers interested in history are likely to use unobtrusive methods, which are also well suited to comparative research. **Historical comparative research** is "research that focuses either on one or more cases over time (the historical part) or on more than one nation or society at one point in time (the comparative part)" (Esterberg, 2002, p. 129). While not all unobtrusive researchers necessarily conduct historical, comparative, or even some combination of historical and comparative work, unobtrusive methods are well suited to such work. As an example, Melissa Weiner (2010) used a historical comparative approach to study racial barriers historically experienced by Jewish people and African Americans in New York City public schools. Weiner analyzed public records from several years of newspapers, trial transcripts, and several organizations as well as private manuscript collections to understand how parents, children, and other activists responded to inequality and worked to reform schools. Not only did this work inform readers about little-known similarities between Jewish and African American experiences, but it also informs current debates over inequalities experienced in public schools today.

In this chapter, we'll examine content analysis as well as analysis of data collected by others. Both types of analyses have in common their use of data that do not require direct interaction with human subjects, but the particular type and source of data for each type of analysis differs.

We'll explore these similarities and differences in the following sections, after we look at some of the pros and cons of unobtrusive research methods.

<table>
<tr><td>

Key Takeaways

</td></tr>
</table>

- Unobtrusive methods allow researchers to collect data without interfering with the subjects under study.
- Historical comparative methods, which are unobtrusive, focus on changes in multiple cases over time or on more than one nation or society at a single point in time.

Glossary

- Unobtrusive research- methods of collecting data that don't interfere with the subjects under study

Image attributions

office business by rawpixel CC-0

10.2 STRENGTHS AND WEAKNESSES OF UNOBTRUSIVE RESEARCH

Learning Objectives
• Identify the major strengths of unobtrusive research • Identify the major weaknesses of unobtrusive research • Define the Hawthorne effect

As is true of the other research designs examined in this text, unobtrusive research has a number of strengths and weaknesses.

STRENGTHS OF UNOBTRUSIVE RESEARCH

Researchers who seek evidence of what people actually do, as opposed to what they say they do (as in survey and interview research), might wish to consider using unobtrusive methods. As we discussed in Chapter 8, researchers often, as a result of their presence, have an impact on the participants in their study simply because they measure and observe them. This effect is a type of reactivity threat to internal validity called the **Hawthorne effect.** As an example, compare how you would behave at work if you knew someone was watching you versus when you knew you were alone. Because researchers conducting unobtrusive research do not alert participants to their presence, they do not need to be concerned about the effect of their research on their subjects. The Hawthorne effect is not a concern for unobtrusive researchers because they do not interact directly with their research participants. In fact, this is one of the major strengths of unobtrusive research.

Another benefit of unobtrusive research is that it can be relatively low-cost compared to some of the other methods we've discussed. Because "participants" are generally inanimate objects (e.g., web journal entries, television shows, historical speeches) as opposed to human beings, researchers may be able to access data without having to worry about paying participants for their time (though certainly travel to or access to some documents and archives can be costly).

Unobtrusive research is also pretty forgiving. It is far easier to correct mistakes made in data collection when conducting unobtrusive research than when using any of the other methods described in this textbook. Imagine what you would do, for example, if you realized at the end of conducting 50 in-depth interviews that you'd accidentally omitted two critical questions from your interview guide. What are your options? Re-interview all 50 participants? Try to figure out what they might have said based on their other responses? Reframe your research question? Scratch the project entirely? Obviously, none of these options is ideal. The same problems arise if a mistake is made in survey research. Fortunately for unobtrusive researchers, going back to the source of the data to gather more information or correct some problem in the original data collection is a relatively straightforward prospect.

Finally, as described in the previous section, unobtrusive research is well suited to studies that focus on processes that occur over time. While longitudinal surveys and long-term field observations are also suitable ways of gathering such information, they cannot examine processes that occurred decades before data collection began. Unobtrusive methods, on the other hand, enable researchers to investigate events and processes that have long since passed. They also do not rely on retrospective accounts of participants, which may be subject to errors in memory.

In summary, the strengths of unobtrusive research include the following:

- There is no possibility for the Hawthorne effect.

- It is cost-effective.

- It is easier than other methods to correct mistakes in data collection.

- They are are conducive to examining processes that occur over time or in the past.

WEAKNESSES OF UNOBTRUSIVE RESEARCH

While there are many benefits to unobtrusive research, this method also comes with a unique set of drawbacks. Because unobtrusive researchers analyze data that may have been created or gathered for purposes entirely different from the researcher's aim, problems of validity sometimes arise in such projects. It may also be the case that data sources measuring whatever a researcher wishes to examine simply do not exist. This means that unobtrusive researchers may be forced to tweak their original research interests or questions to better suit the data that are available to them. Finally, it can be difficult in unobtrusive research projects to account for context. In an interview, for example, the researcher can ask what events lead up to some occurrence, but this level of personal interaction is impossible in unobtrusive research. So, while it can be difficult to ascertain why something occurred in unobtrusive research, we can gain a good understanding of what has occurred.

In sum, the weaknesses of unobtrusive research include the following:

- There may be problems with validity.

- The topics or questions that can be investigated are limited by data availability.

- It can be difficult to see or account for social context.

Key Takeaways

- Unobtrusive research is cost effective and allows for easier correction of mistakes than other methods of data collection do.
- The Hawthorne effect, which occurs when research subjects alter their behaviors because they know they are being studied, is not a risk in unobtrusive research as it is in other methods of data collection.
- Weaknesses of unobtrusive research include potential problems with validity, limitations in data availability, and difficulty in accounting for social context.

Glossary

- Hawthorne effect- a threat to internal validity in which participants in a study behave differently because they know they are being observed

Image attributions

man paris traffic by whitfieldink CC-0

10.3 UNOBTRUSIVE DATA COLLECTED BY THE RESEARCHER

Learning Objectives

- Define content analysis
- Describe the kinds of texts that content analysts analyze
- Describe the basics of analyzing unobtrusive data

This section focuses on how to gather data unobtrusively and what to do with those data once they have been collected. There are two main ways of gathering data unobtrusively: conducting a content analysis of existing texts and analyzing physical traces of human behavior. We'll explore both approaches.

CONTENT ANALYSIS

One way of conducting unobtrusive research is to analyze texts. Texts come in all kinds of formats. At its core, content analysis addresses the questions of "Who says what, to whom, why, how, and with what effect?" (Babbie, 2010, pp. 328–329). **Content analysis** is a type of unobtrusive research that involves the study of texts and their meaning. Here we use a more liberal definition of text than you might find in your dictionary. The text that content analysts investigate includes such things as actual written copy (e.g., newspapers or letters) and content that we might see or hear (e.g., speeches or other performances). Content analysts might also investigate more visual representations of human communication, such as television shows, advertisements, or movies. Table 10.1 provides a few specific examples of the kinds of data that content analysts have examined in prior studies. Which of these sources of data might be of interest to you?

Table 10.1 Content analysis examples

Data	Research question	Author(s) (year)
Spam e-mails	What is the form, content, and quantity of unsolicited e- mails?	Berzins (2009)
James Bond films	How are female characters portrayed in James Bond films, and what broader lessons can be drawn from these portrayals?	Neuendorf, Gore, Dalessandro, Janstova, and Snyder-Suhy (2010)
Console video games	How is male and female sexuality portrayed in the best-selling console video games?	Downs and Smith (2010)
Newspaper articles	How do newspapers cover closed-circuit television surveillance in Canada, and what are the implications of coverage for public opinion and policymaking?	Greenberg and Hier (2009)
Pro-eating disorder websites	What are the features of pro-eating disorder websites, and what are the messages to which users may be exposed?	Borzekowski, Schenk, Wilson, and Peebles (2010)

One thing you might notice about Table 10.1 is that the data sources represent primary sources. That is, they are the original documents written by people who observed the event or analyzed the data. Secondary sources, on the other hand, are sources that report on primary sources. Often, secondary sources are created by looking at primary sources and analyzing their contents.

Shulamit Reinharz (1992) offers a helpful way of distinguishing between these two types of sources in her methods text. She explains that while primary sources represent "the 'raw' materials of history," secondary sources are "the 'cooked' analyses of those materials" (p. 155). The distinction between primary and secondary sources is important for many aspects of social science, but it is especially important to understand when conducting content analysis. While there are certainly instances of content analysis in which secondary sources are analyzed, it is more common for content analysts to analyze primary sources.

In those instances where secondary sources are analyzed, the researcher's focus is usually on the process by which the original analyst or presenter of data reached his conclusions or on the choices that were made in terms of how and in what ways to present the data. For example, James Loewen (2007) conducted a content analysis of high school history textbooks. His aim was not to learn about history, but to understand how students are taught American history in high school. The results of his inquiry uncovered that the books often glossed over issues of racism, leaving students with an incomplete understanding of the trans-Atlantic slave trade, the extermination of Indigenous peoples, and the civil rights movement.

Sometimes students new to research methods struggle to grasp the difference between a content analysis of secondary sources and a literature review. In a literature review, researchers analyze theoretical, practical, and empirical sources to try to understand what we know and what we don't know about a particular topic. The sources used to conduct a scholarly review of the literature are typically peer-reviewed sources, written by trained scholars, published in some academic journal or press. These sources are culled in a literature review to arrive at some conclusion about our overall knowledge about a topic. Findings from sources are generally taken at face value.

Conversely, a content analysis of scholarly literature would raise questions not addressed in a literature review. A researcher who uses content analyst to examine scholarly articles would try to learn something about the authors (e.g., who publishes what and where), publication outlets (e.g., how well do different journals represent the diversity of the discipline), or topics (e.g., how has the popularity of topics shifted over time). A content analysis of scholarly articles would be a *"study* of the studies" as opposed to a *"review* of studies." Perhaps, for example, a researcher wishes to know whether more men than women authors are published in the top-ranking journals in the discipline. The researcher could conduct a content analysis of different journals and count authors by gender (though this may be a tricky prospect if relying only on names to indicate gender). Or perhaps a researcher would like to learn whether or how various topics of investigation go in and out of style. She could investigate changes over time in topical coverage in various journals. In these latter two instances, the researcher is not aiming to summarize the content of the articles, as in a literature review, but instead is looking to learn something about how, why, or by whom particular articles came to be published.

Content analysis can be qualitative or quantitative, and often researchers will use both strategies to strengthen their investigations. In qualitative content analysis, the aim is to identify themes in the text being analyzed and to identify the underlying meaning of those themes. For example, Alyssa Goolsby (2007) conducted qualitative content analysis in her study of national identity in the United States. To understand how the boundaries of citizenship were constructed in the United States, she conducted a qualitative content analysis of key historical congressional debates focused on immigration law.

Quantitative content analysis, on the other hand, involves assigning numerical values to raw data so that it can be analyzed statistically. Jason Houle (2008) conducted a quantitative content analysis of song lyrics. Inspired by an article on the connections between fame, chronic self-consciousness (as measured by frequent use of first-person pronouns), and self-destructive behavior (Schaller, 1997), Houle counted first-person pronouns in Elliott Smith song lyrics. Houle found that Smith's use of self-referential pronouns increased steadily from the time of his first album release in 1994 until his suicide in 2003. We'll elaborate on how qualitative and quantitative researchers collect, code, and analyze unobtrusive data in the final portion of this section.

INDIRECT MEASURES

Texts are not the only sort of data that researchers can collect unobtrusively. Unobtrusive researchers might also be interested in analyzing the evidence that humans leave behind that tells us something about who they are or what they do. This kind evidence includes the physical traces left by humans and the material artifacts that tell us something about their beliefs, values, or norms. Physical traces include such things as worn paths across campus, the materials in a landfill or in someone's trash can, indentations in furniture, or empty shelves in the grocery store. Examples of material artifacts include video games and video game equipment, sculptures, mementos left on gravestones, housing structures, flyers for an event, or even kitchen utensils.

One challenge with analyzing physical traces and material artifacts is that you generally don't have access to the people who left the traces or created the artifacts that you are analyzing. (And if you did find a way to contact them, then your research would no longer qualify as unobtrusive!) It can be especially tricky to analyze meanings of these materials if they come from some historical or cultural context other than your own. Situating the traces or artifacts you wish to analyze both in their original contexts and in your own is not always easy and can lead to problems during data analysis. How do you know that you are viewing an object or physical trace in the way that it was intended to be viewed? Do you have the necessary understanding or knowledge about the background of its original creators or users to understand where they were coming from when they created it?
Imagine an alien trying to understand some aspect of Western human culture simply by examining our artifacts. Cartoonist Mark Parisi (1989) demonstrates the misunderstanding that could ensue in his drawing featuring three very small aliens standing atop a toilet. One alien says, "Since water is the life-blood on this planet, this must be a temple of some sort...Let's stick around and see how they show their respect" (1989). Without a contextual understanding of Western human culture, the aliens misidentified the purpose of the toilet, and they will be in for quite a surprise when someone shows up to use it!

The point is that while physical traces and material artifacts make excellent sources of data, analyzing their meaning takes more than simply trying to understand them from your own contextual position. This can be challenging, but the good news is that social workers have been trained in cultural humility, and they strive for cultural competence. This means they recognize that their own cultural lenses may not provide accurate perspectives on situations. Social work researchers using physical traces and material artifacts must be aware of who caused the physical trace or created the artifact, when they created it, why they created, and for whom they created it. Answering these questions requires accessing materials in addition to the traces or artifacts themselves, such as historical documents or, if analyzing a contemporary trace or artifact, perhaps using another method of data collection such as interviews with its creators.

Key Takeaways

- Content analysts interpret texts.
- The texts that content analysts analyze include actual written texts such as newspapers or journal entries, as well as visual and auditory sources such as television shows, advertisements, or movies.
- Content analysts most typically analyze primary sources, though in some instances they may analyze secondary sources.
- Indirect measures that content analysts examine include physical traces and material artifacts.
- Content analysts may use code sheets to collect data.

Glossary

- Content analysis- a type of unobtrusive research that involves the study of texts and their meaning

10.4 SECONDARY DATA ANALYSIS

Learning Objectives

- Define secondary data analysis
- List the strengths and limitations of secondary data analysis
- Name at least two sources of publicly available quantitative data
- Name at least two sources of publicly available qualitative data

One type of unobtrusive research allows you to skip the data collection phase altogether. To many, skipping the data collection phase is preferable since it allows the researcher to proceed directly to answering their question through data analysis. When researchers analyze data originally gathered by another person or entity, they engage in **secondary data analysis**. Researchers gain access to data collected by other researchers, government agencies, and other unique sources by making connections with individuals engaged in primary research or accessing their data via publicly available sources.

Imagine you wanted to study whether race or gender influenced what major people chose at your college. You could do your best to distribute a survey to a representative sample of students, but perhaps a better idea would be to ask your college registrar for this information. Your college already collects this information on all of its students. Wouldn't it be better to simply ask for access to this information, rather than collecting it yourself? Maybe.

CHALLENGES IN SECONDARY DATA ANALYSIS

Some of you may be thinking, "I never gave my college permission to share my information with other researchers." Depending on the policies of your university, this may or may not be true. In any case, secondary data is usually **anonymized** or does not contain identifying information. In our example, students' names, student ID numbers, home towns, and other identifying details would not be shared with a secondary researcher. Instead, just the information on the variables—race, gender, and major—would be shared. *Techniques to make data anonymous are not foolproof*, however, and this is a challenge to secondary data analysis. Researchers have been able to identify individuals in "anonymized" data from credit card companies, Netflix, AOL, and online advertising companies have been able to be unmasked (Bode, 2017; de Montjoy, Radaelli, Singh, & Pentland, 2015).

Another challenge with secondary data stems from the *lack of control over the data collection process*. Perhaps your university made a mistake on their forms or entered data incorrectly. If this were your data, you could correct errors like this right away. With secondary data, you are less able to correct for any errors made by the original source during data collection. More importantly, you may not know these errors exist and reach erroneous conclusions as a result. Researchers using secondary data should evaluate the procedures used to collect the data wherever possible, and data that lacks documentation on procedures should be used with caution.

Secondary researchers, particularly those conducting quantitative research, must also ensure that their conceptualization and operationalization of variables matches that of the primary researchers. If your secondary analysis focuses on a variable that was not a major part of the original analysis, you may not have enough information about that variable to conduct a thorough analysis. For example, you want to study whether depression is associated with income for students and you found a dataset that included those variables. If depression was not a focus of the dataset, the original researchers may only have included a question like, "Have you ever been diagnosed with major depressive disorder?" While answers to this question will give you some information about depression, it will not give you the depth that a scale like Beck's Depression Inventory or the Hamilton Rating Scale for Depression would or provide information about severity of symptoms like hospitalization or suicide attempts. Without this level of depth, your analysis may lack validity. Even when operationalization for your variables of interest is thorough, researchers may conceptualize variables differently than you do. Perhaps they were interested in whether a person was diagnosed with depression anytime in their life, whereas, you are concerned with their current symptoms of depression. For these reasons, understanding the original study thoroughly by reading the study documentation is a requirement for rigorous secondary data analysis.

The lack of control over the data collection process also hamstrings the research process itself. While some studies are created perfectly, most are refined through pilot testing and feedback before the full study is conducted (Engel & Schutt, 2016). Secondary data analysis does not allow you to engage in this process. For qualitative researchers in particular, this is an important challenge. Qualitative research, particularly from the interpretivist paradigm, uses emergent processes in which research questions, conceptualization of terms, and measures develop and change over the course of the study. Secondary data analysis inhibits this process from taking place because the data are already collected. Because qualitative methods often involve analyzing the context in which data are collected, secondary researchers may have difficulty authentically and accurately representing the original data in a new analysis.

Another challenge for research using secondary data can be *getting access to the data*. Researchers seeking access to data collected by universities (or hospitals, health insurers, human service agencies, etc.) must have the support of the administration. It may be important for researchers to form a partnership with the agency or university whose data is included in the secondary data analysis. Administrators will trust people who they perceive as competent, reputable, and objective. They must trust you to engage in rigorous and conscientious research. Some secondary data are available in repositories where the researcher can have somewhat automatic access if she is able to demonstrate her competence to complete the analysis, shares her data analysis plan, and receives ethical approval from an IRB. Administrators of data that are often accessed by researchers, such as Medicaid or Census data, may fall into this category.

STRENGTHS OF SECONDARY DATA ANALYSIS

While the challenges associated with secondary data analysis are important, the strengths of secondary data analysis often outweigh these limitations. Most importantly, secondary data analysis is quicker and cheaper than a traditional study because the data are already collected. Once a researcher gains access to the data, it is simply a matter of analyzing it and writing up the results to complete the project. Data can take a long time to gather and be quite resource-intensive. So, avoiding this step is a significant strength of secondary data analysis. If the primary researchers had access to more resources, they may also be able to engage in data collection that is more rigorous than a secondary researcher could. In this way, outsourcing the data collection to someone with more resources may make your design stronger, not weaker. Finally, secondary researchers ask new questions that the primary researchers may not have considered. In this way, secondary data analysis deepens our understanding of existing data in the field. Table 10.3 summarizes the strengths and limitations of existing data.

Table 10.3 Strengths and limitations of existing data

Strengths	Limitations
Reduces the time needed to complete the project Cheaper to conduct, in many cases Primary researcher may have more resources to conduct a rigorous data collection than you Helps us deepen our understanding of data already in the literature Useful for historical research	Anonymous data may not be truly anonymous No control over data collection process Cannot refine questions, measures, or procedure or pilot tests May operationalize or conceptualize concepts diff primary researcher Missing qualitative context Barriers to access and conflicts of interest

Ultimately, you will have to weigh the strengths and limitations of using secondary data on your own. Engel and Schutt (2016, p. 327) propose six questions to ask before using secondary data:

1. What were the agency's or researcher's goals in collecting the data?

2. What data were collected, and what were they intended to measure?

3. When was the information collected?

4. What methods were used for data collection? Who was responsible for data collection, and what were their qualifications? Are they available to answer questions about the data?

5. How is the information organized (by date, individual, family, event, etc.)? Are there identifiers used to identify different types of data available?

6. What is known about the success of the data collection effort? How are missing data indicated and treated? What kind of documentation is available? How consistent are the data with data available from other sources?

SOURCES OF SECONDARY DATA

Many sources of quantitative data are publicly available. The General Social Survey (GSS), which was discussed in Chapter 7 , is one of the most commonly used sources of publicly available data among quantitative researchers. Data for the GSS have been collected regularly since 1972, thus offering social researchers the opportunity to investigate changes in Americans' attitudes and beliefs over time. Questions on the GSS cover an extremely broad range of topics, from family life to political and religious beliefs to work experiences.

Other sources of quantitative data include Add Health, a study that was initiated in 1994 to learn about the lives and behaviors of adolescents in the United States, and the Wisconsin Longitudinal Study, a study that has, for over 40 years, surveyed a panel of 10,000 people who graduated from Wisconsin high schools in 1957. Quantitative researchers interested in studying social processes outside of the United States also have many options when it comes to publicly available data sets. Data from the British Household Panel Study, a longitudinal, representative survey of households in Britain, are freely available to those conducting academic research (private entities are charged for access to the data). The International Social Survey Programme merges the GSS with its counterparts in other countries around the globe. These represent just a few of the many sources of publicly available quantitative data.

Unfortunately for qualitative researchers, far fewer sources of free, publicly available qualitative data exist. This is slowly changing, however, as technical sophistication grows and it becomes easier to digitize and share qualitative data. Despite comparatively fewer sources than for quantitative data, there are still a number of data sources available to qualitative researchers whose interests or resources limit their ability to collect data on their own. The Murray Research Archive, housed at the Institute for Quantitative Social Science at Harvard University, offers case histories and qualitative interview data. The Global Feminisms project at the University of Michigan offers interview transcripts and videotaped oral histories focused on feminist activism; women's movements; and academic women's studies in China, India, Poland, and the United States. At the University of Connecticut, the Oral History Office provides links to a number of other oral history sites. Not all the links offer publicly available data, but many do. Finally, the Southern Historical Collection at University of North Carolina–Chapel Hill offers digital versions of many primary documents online such as journals, letters, correspondence, and other papers that document the history and culture of the American South.

Keep in mind that the resources mentioned here represent just a snapshot of the many sources of publicly available data that can be easily accessed via the web. Table 10.4 summarizes the data sources discussed in this section.

Table 10.4 Sources of publicly available data

Organizational home	Focus/topic	Data	Web address
National Opinion Research Center	General Social Survey; demographic, behavioral, attitudinal, and special interest questions; national sample	Quantitative	http://www.norc.uchicago.edu/GSS+Website/
Carolina Population Center	Add Health; longitudinal social, economic, psychological, and physical well-being of cohort in grades 7–12 in 1994	Quantitative	http://www.cpc.unc.edu/projects/addhealth
Center for Demography of Health and Aging	Wisconsin Longitudinal Study; life course study of cohorts who graduated from high school in 1957	Quantitative	https://www.ssc.wisc.edu/wlsresearch/
Institute for Social & Economic Research	British Household Panel Survey; longitudinal study of British lives and well- being	Quantitative	https://www.iser.essex.ac.uk/bhps
International Social Survey Programme	International data similar to GSS	Quantitative	http://www.issp.org/
The Institute for Quantitative Social Science at Harvard University	Large archive of written data, audio, and video focused on many topics	Quantitative and qualitative	http://dvn.iq.harvard.edu/dvn/dv/mra
Institute for Research on Women and Gender	Global Feminisms Project; interview transcripts and oral histories on feminism and women's activism	Qualitative	http://www.umich.edu/~glblfem/index.html
Oral History Office	Descriptions and links to numerous oral history archives	Qualitative	http://www.oralhistory.uconn.edu/links.html
UNC Wilson Library	Digitized manuscript collection from the Southern Historical Collection	Qualitative	http://dc.lib.unc.edu/ead/archivalhome.php?CISOROOT=/ead

SPOTLIGHT ON UTA SCHOOL OF SOCIAL WORK

SECONDARY DATA ANALYSIS

Dr. Kathy Lee of the University of Texas at Arlington's School of Social Work is interested in mental health and quality of life among vulnerable and marginalized older adults and their family caregivers. Dr. Lee is particularly interested in social participation interventions and psychosocial intervention that promote their health and well-being outcomes. The majority of Dr. Lee's work has been conducted with panel survey data from the Health and Retirement Study (HRS). Some advantages of using secondary data includes building evidence based on high quality data (i.e., nationally representative data that are easily accessible) and allowing researchers to understand social trends over time. Although secondary analysis requires time and efforts to be familiar with the dataset due to its complexity and breadth, researchers can answer a wide range of research questions, particularly with knowledge of survey statistics and methods.

HRS is the first and the largest longitudinal study, consisting of over 37,000 individuals age 50 and over in 23,000 households in the United States. The purpose of HRS is to inform researchers and policymakers of important issues of retirement and health of aging populations and to promote discussion to respond to the rapidly aging society. Since 1992, a variety of content and data have been included, such as physical measures, biomarkers, and psychosocial factors, making the study multi-disciplinary. The data are collected through multiple modes: face-to-face, telephone, and mail. The survey is conducted biannually with support from the National Institute on Aging and the Social Security Administration. Panel survey data from publicly available databases, like HRS, are very essential for researchers to better understand opportunities and challenges to aging.

Dr. Lee's dissertation research (Lee, 2018) examined (1) the impact of volunteering on cognitive health among older adults with cognitive impairment, and (2) the complex relationships between volunteer behaviors, psychological well-being, and cognitive health. Using HRS data collected from 2004 to 2014, her study included older adults age 65 and older living with cognitive impairment based on the Telephone Interview for Cognitive Status (≤11 out of the total score of 27). With a focus on a description of change over time, Dr. Lee tested linear mixed effects models to examine growth or decline in cognitive health of older adults with cognitive impairment by volunteer and non-volunteer group. Dr. Lee also employed structural equation modeling to observe the snapshot of variables of interest – volunteer behaviors, psychological well-being, and cognitive health. The study data showed that (1) the level of cognitive functioning slightly increased over time only among those who volunteered, and (2) the relationship between psychological well-being and cognitive functioning was significantly greater than the relationship between volunteering and cognitive functioning, suggesting the importance of providing volunteer activities that can increase one's psychological well-being.

Research involving secondary data can be an important contribution to improving the lives of social work clients. The value of Dr. Lee's secondary data research was recognized by the

Gerontological Society of America who awarded her the Junior Scholar Award for Research Related to Disadvantaged Older Adults and the Emerging Scholar and Professional Organization Poster Award in 2018.

Dr. Lee is currently working on multiple other secondary analyses to broaden knowledge around social participation and depression among vulnerable aging populations.

Key Takeaways

- The strengths and limitations of secondary data analysis must be considered before a project begins.
- Previously collected data sources enable researchers to conduct secondary data analysis.

Glossary

- Anonymized data- data that does not contain identifying information
- Historical research-analyzing data from primary sources of historical events and proceedings
- Secondary data analysis- analyzing data originally gathered by another person or entity

Image attributions

anonymous by SplitShire CC-0

archive by Pexels CC-0

KathyLeePhoto by Tim Siepker CC BY-NC-ND

CHAPTER ELEVEN: REAL-WORLD RESEARCH

The previous chapters have focused on how social workers use social science research methods to understand the world. But what about social workers who aren't researchers? Social workers in practice may not have time or interest in conducting experiments or focus groups for the purposes of scholarly publication. While the preceding chapters should provide you the information you need to understand the research conducted by professional researchers, social workers in practice still must use research skills to help their clients. This chapter will review three approaches to research that social workers will use while in practice.

CHAPTER OUTLINE

- 11.1 Evaluation research
- 11.2 Single-subjects design
- 11.3 Action research

CONTENT ADVISORY

This chapter discusses or mentions the following topics: substance abuse and intimate partner violence.

11.1 EVALUATION RESEARCH

Learning Objectives

- Describe how to conduct evaluation research
- Define inputs, outputs, and outcomes
- Identify the three goals of process assessment

As you may recall from the definition provided in Chapter 1, evaluation research is research conducted to assess the effects of specific programs or policies. Evaluation research is often used when some form of policy intervention is planned, such as welfare reform or school curriculum change. The focus on interventions and social problems makes it natural fit for social work researchers. It might be used to assess the extent to which intervention is necessary by attempting to define and diagnose social problems in social workers' service areas, and it might also be used to understand whether their agencies' interventions have had their intended consequences. Evaluation research is becoming more and more necessary for agencies to secure and maintain funding for their programs. The main types of evaluation research are needs assessments, outcomes assessments, process assessments, and efficiency analyses such as cost-benefits or cost-effectiveness analyses. We will discuss two types in this section: *outcomes assessments* and *process assessments*.

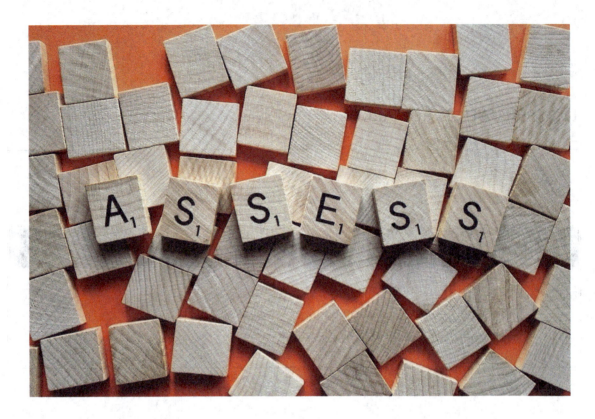

OUTCOMES ASSESSMENTS

An **outcomes assessment** is an evaluation designed to discover if a program achieved its intended outcomes. Much like other types of research, it comes with its own peculiar terminology. **Inputs** are the resources needed for the program to operate. These include physical location, any equipment needed, staff (and experience/knowledge of those staff), monetary funding, and most importantly, the clients. Program administrators pull together the necessary resources to run an intervention or program. The **program** is the intervention your clients receive—perhaps giving them access to housing vouchers or enrolling them in a smoking cessation class. The **outputs** of programs are tangible results of the program process. Outputs in a program might include the number of clients served, staff members trained to implement the intervention, mobility assistance devices distributed, nicotine patches distributed, etc. By contrast, *outcomes* speak to the purpose of the program itself. **Outcomes** are the observed changes, whether intended or unintended, that occurred due to the program or intervention. By looking at each of these domains, evaluation researchers can obtain a comprehensive view of the program.

Let's run through an example from the social work practice of the wife of Matt DeCarlo who wrote the source material for much of this textbook. She runs an after-school bicycling club called *Pedal Up* for children with mental health issues. She has a lot of inputs in her program. First, there are the children who enroll, the volunteer and paid staff members who supervise the kids (and their knowledge about bicycles and children's mental health), the bicycles and equipment that all clients and staff use, the community center room they use as a home base, the paths of the city where they ride their bikes, and the public and private grants they use to fund the program. Next, the program itself is a twice weekly after-school program in which children learn about bicycle maintenance and bicycle safety for about 30 minutes each day and then spend at least an hour riding around the city on bicycle trails.

In measuring the outputs of this program, she has many options. She would probably include the number of children participating in the program or the number of bike rides or lessons given. Other outputs might include the number of miles logged by the children over the school year, the number of bicycle helmets or spare tires distributed, etc. Finally, the outcomes of the programs might include each child's mental health symptoms or behavioral issues at school.

PROCESS ASSESSMENTS

Outcomes assessments are performed at the end of a program or at specific points during the grant reporting process. What if a social worker wants to assess earlier on in the process if the program is on target to achieve its outcomes? In that case a **process assessment** is recommended, which evaluates a program in its earlier stages. Faulkner and Faulkner (2016) describe three main goals for conducting a process evaluation.

The first is *program description*, in which the researcher simply tries to understand how the program looks like in everyday life for clients and staff members. In our Pedal Up example, assessing program description might involve measuring in the first few weeks the hours children spent riding their bikes, the number of children and staff in attendance, etc. This data will provide those in charge of the program an idea of how their ideas have translated from the grant proposal to the real world. If, for example, not enough children are showing up or if children are only able to ride their bikes for ten minutes each day, it may indicate that something is wrong.

Another important goal of process assessment is *program monitoring*. If you have some social work practice experience already, it's likely you've encountered program monitoring. Agency administrators may look at sign-in sheets for groups, hours billed by clinicians, or other metrics to track how services are utilized over time. They may also assess whether clinicians are following the program correctly or if they are deviating from how the program was designed. This can be an issue in program evaluations of specific treatment models, as any differences between what the administrators conceptualized and what the clinicians implemented jeopardize the internal validity of the evaluation. If, in our Pedal Up example, we have a staff member who does not review bike safety each week or does not enforce helmet laws for some students, we could catch that through program monitoring.

The final goal of process assessments is *quality assurance.* At its most simple level, quality assurance may involve sending out satisfaction questionnaires to clients and staff members. If there are serious issues, it's better to know them early on in a program so the program can be adapted to meet the needs of clients and staff. It is important to solicit staff feedback in addition to consumer feedback, as they have insight into how the program is working in practice and areas in which they may be falling short of what the program should be. In our example, we could spend some time talking with parents when they pick their children up from the program or hold a staff meeting to provide opportunities for those most involved in the program to provide feedback.

NEEDS ASSESSMENTS

A third type of evaluation research is a needs assessment. A needs assessment can be used to demonstrate and document a community or organizational need and should be carried out in a way to better understand the context in which the need arises. Needs assessments focus on gaining a better understanding of a gap within an organization or community and developing a plan to address that gap. They will often precede the development of a program or organization and are often used to justify the necessity of a program or organization to fill a gap. Needs assessments can be general, such as asking members of a community or organization to reflect on the functioning of a community or organization, or they can be specific in which community or organization members are asked to respond to an identified gap within a community or agency.

Needs assessments should respond to the following questions:

- What is the need or gap?
- What data exist about the need or gap?
- What data are needed in order to develop a plan to fill the gap?
- What resources are available to do the needs assessment?
- Who should be involved in the analysis and interpretation of the data?
- How will the information gathered be used and for what purpose?

- How will the results be communicated to community partners?

In order to answer these questions, needs assessments often follow a four-step plan. First, researchers must identify a gap in a community or organization and explore what potential avenues could be pursued to address the gap. This involves deciphering what is known about the needs within the community or organization and determining the scope and direction of the needs assessment. The researcher may partner with key informants within the community to identify the need in order to develop a method of research to conduct the needs assessment.

Second, the researcher will gather data to better understand the need. Data could be collected from key informants within the community, community members themselves, members of an organization, or records from an agency or organization. This involves designing a research study in which a variety of data collection methods could be used, such as surveys, interviews, focus groups, community forums, and secondary analysis of existing data. Once the data are collected, they will be organized and analyzed according to the research questions guiding the needs assessment.

Third, information gathered during data collection will be used to develop a plan of action to fill the needs. This could be the development of a new community agency to address a gap of services within the community or the addition of a new program at an existing agency. This agency or program must be designed according to the results of the needs assessment in order to accurately address the gap.

Finally, the newly developed program or agency must be evaluated to determine if it is filling the gap revealed by the needs assessment. Evaluating the success of the agency or program is essential to the needs assessment process.

CONCLUSION

Evaluation research is a part of all social workers' toolkits. It ensures that social work interventions achieve their intended effects. This protects our clients and ensures that money and other resources are not spent on programs that do not work. Evaluation research uses the skills of quantitative and qualitative research to ensure clients receive interventions that have been shown to be successful.

Key Takeaways

- Evaluation research is a common research task for social workers.
- Outcomes assessment evaluate the degree to which programs achieved their intended outcomes.
- Outputs differ from outcomes.
- Process assessments evaluate a program in its early stages, so changes can be made.

Glossary

- Inputs- resources needed for the program to operate
- Outcomes- the issues the program is trying to change
- Outcomes assessment- an evaluation designed to discover if a program achieved its intended outcomes
- Outputs- tangible results of the program process
- Process assessment- an evaluation conducted during the earlier stages of a program or on an ongoing basis
- Program- the intervention clients receive

Image attributions

assess by Wokandapix CC-0

11.2 SINGLE-SUBJECTS DESIGN

Learning Objectives

- Identify why social workers might use single-subjects design
- Describe the two stages of single-subjects design

Single-subjects design is distinct from other research methodologies in that, as its name indicates, only one person, group, policy, etc. (i.e., subject) is being studied. Because clinical social work often involves one-on-one practice, single-subjects designs are often used by social workers to ensure that their interventions are having a positive effect. While the results will not be generalizable, they do provide important insight into the effectiveness of clinical interventions. Single-subjects designs involve repeated measurements over time, usually in two stages. But what exactly are we measuring in single-subjects design? The behavior or outcome that we expect will change as a result of the treatment is the dependent variable in a single-subjects research design. The dependent variable is measured repeatedly during two distinct phases: the *baseline stage* and the *treatment stage*.

The **baseline stage** is the period of time before the intervention starts. During the baseline stage, the social worker is collecting data about the problem the treatment is hoping to address. For example, a person with substance use issues may binge drink on the weekends but cut down their drinking during the work week. A social worker might ask the client to record the number of drinks that they consume each day. By looking at this, we could evaluate the level of alcohol consumption. For other clients, the social worker might assess other indicators, such as the number of arguments the client had when they were drinking or whether or not the client blacked out as a result of drinking. Whatever measure is used to assess the targeted problem, that measure is the dependent variable in the single-subjects design.

The baseline stage should last until a pattern emerges in the dependent variable. This requires at least three different occasions of measurement, but it can often take longer. During the baseline stage, the social worker looks for one of three types of patterns (Engel & Schutt, 2016). The dependent variable may (1) be *stable* over time, (2) exhibit a *trend* where it is increasing or decreasing over time, or (3) have a *cycle* of increasing and decreasing that is repeated over time. Establishing a pattern can prove difficult in clients whose behaviors vary widely.

Ideally, social workers would start measurement for the baseline stage before starting the intervention. This provides the opportunity to determine the baseline pattern. Unfortunately, that may be impractical or unethical to do in practice if it entails withholding important treatment. In that case, a retrospective baseline can be attained by asking the client to recollect data from before the intervention started. The drawback to this is the information is likely to be less reliable than a baseline data recorded in real time. The baseline stage is important because with only one subject, there is no control group. Thus, we have to see if our intervention is effective by comparing the client before treatment to and during and after treatment. In this way, the baseline stage provides the same type of information as a control group — what it looks like when there is not treatment given.

The next stage is the **treatment stage**, and it refers to the time in which the treatment is administered by the social worker. Repeated measurements are taken during this stage to see if there is change in the dependent variable during treatment.

One way to analyze the data from a single-subjects design is to visually examine a graphical representation of the results. An example of a graph from a single-subjects design is shown in Figure 11.1. The x-axis is time, as measured in months. The y-axis is the measure of the problem we're trying to change (i.e., the dependent variable).

In Figure 11.1, the y-axis is caseload size. From 1998 to July of 1991, there was no treatment. This is the baseline phase, and we can examine it for a pattern. There is upward trend during the intervention phase, but it looks as if the caseloads began to decrease during the baseline (October 1989). Once the intervention occurred, there is a clear pattern of a downward trend, indicating the treatment may be associated with the reduction in caseload.

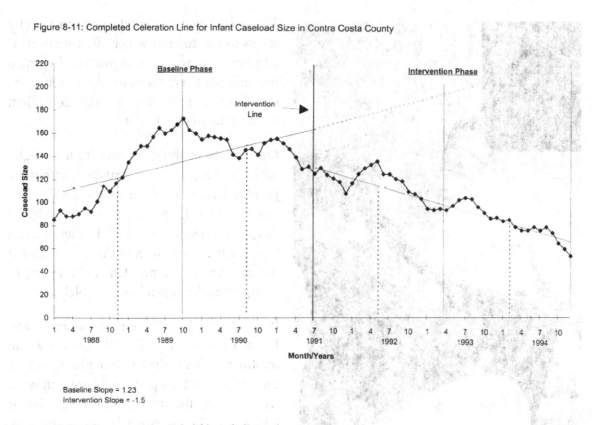

Figure 8-11: Completed Celeration Line for Infant Caseload Size in Contra Costa County

Baseline Slope = 1.23
Intervention Slope = -1.5

Figure 11.1 Example x-y graph for single subjects design

In single-subjects design, it is possible to begin a new course of treatment or add a new dimension to an existing treatment. This is called a a **multiple treatment design**. The graphing would continue as before, but with another vertical line representing the second intervention, indicating a new treatment began.

Another option would be to withdraw treatment for a specified time and continue to measure the client, establishing a new baseline. If the client continues to improve after the treatment is withdrawn, then it is likely to have lasting effects. This is called a **withdrawal design** and is represented as A-B-A or A-B-A-B.

Single-subjects designs, much like evaluation research in the previous section, are used to demonstrate that social work intervention has its intended effects. Single-subjects designs are most compatible with clinical modalities such as cognitive-behavioral therapy which incorporate as part of treatment client self-monitoring, clinician data analysis, and quantitative measurement. It is routine in this therapeutic model to track, for example, the number of intrusive thoughts experienced between counseling sessions. Moreover, practitioners spend time each session reviewing changes in patterns during the therapeutic process, using it to evaluate and fine-tune the therapeutic approach. Although researchers have used single-subjects designs with less positivist therapies, such as narrative therapy, the single-subjects design is generally used in therapies with more quantifiable outcomes. The results of single-subjects studies are not generalizable to the overall population, but they help ensure that social workers are not providing useless or counterproductive interventions to their clients.

Key Takeaways

- Social workers conduct single-subjects research designs to make sure their interventions are effective.
- Single-subjects designs use repeated measures before and during treatment to assess the effectiveness of an intervention.
- Single-subjects designs often use a graphical representation of numerical data to look for patterns.

Glossary

- Baseline stage- the period of time before the intervention starts
- Multiple treatment design- beginning a new course of treatment or add a new dimension to an existing treatment
- Treatment stage- the time in which the treatment is administered by the social worker
- Withdrawal design – a type of single-subjects research in which the treatment is discontinued and another baseline phase follows the treatment phase

Image attributions

counseling by tiyowprasetyo CC-0

11.3 ACTION RESEARCH

Learning Objectives

- Define and provide at least one example of action research
- Describe the role of stakeholders in action research

Action research is defined as research that is conducted for the purpose of creating social change. When conducting action research, scholars collaborate with community stakeholders at all stages of the research process with the aim of producing results that will be usable in the community and by scientists. Stakeholders are individuals or groups who have an interest in the outcome of your study. Social workers who engage in action research never just go it alone; instead, they collaborate with the people who are affected by the research at each stage in the process. In action research, stakeholders, particularly those with the least power, are consulted on the purpose of the research project, research questions, design, and reporting of results.

Action research also distinguishes itself from other research in that its purpose is to create change on an individual and community level. Kristin Esterberg (2002) puts it quite eloquently when she says, "At heart, all action researchers are concerned that research not simply contribute to knowledge but also lead to positive changes in people's lives" (p. 137). As you might imagine, action research is consistent with the assumptions of the critical paradigm, which focuses on liberating people from oppressive structures.

Action research has multiple origins across the globe, including Kurt Lewin's psychological experiments in the United States and Paulo Friere's literacy and education programs (Adelman, 1993; Reason, 1994). Over the years, action research has become increasingly popular among scholars who wish for their work to have tangible outcomes that benefit the groups they study.

Action research does not bring any new methodological tricks or terms, but it uses the processes of science in a different way from traditional research. What topics are important to study in a neighborhood or with a target population? A traditional scientist might look at the literature or use their practice wisdom to formulate a research question. An action researcher, on the other hand, would consult with the target population itself to see what they thought were the most pressing issues and best solutions. In this way, action research flips traditional research on its head. Scientists are more like consultants who provide the tools and resources necessary for a target population to achieve their goals and address social problems.

According to Healy (2001), the assumptions of participatory-action research are that (a) oppression is caused by macro-level structures such as patriarchy and capitalism; (b) research should expose and confront the powerful; (c) researcher and participant relationships should be equal, with equitable distribution of research tasks and roles; and (d) research should result in consciousness-raising and collective action. Coherent with social work values, action research supports the self-determination of oppressed groups and privileges their voice and understanding through the conceptualization, design, data collection, data analysis, and dissemination processes of research.

There are many excellent examples of action research. Some of them focus solely on arriving at useful outcomes for the communities upon which and with whom research is conducted.

Other action research projects result in some new knowledge that has a practical application and purpose in addition to the creation of knowledge for basic scientific purposes.

One example of action research can be seen in Fred Piercy and colleagues' (Piercy, Franz, Donaldson, & Richard, 2011) work with farmers in Virginia, Tennessee, and Louisiana. Together with farmers in these states, the researchers conducted focus groups to understand how farmers learn new information about farming. Ultimately, the aim of this study was to "develop more meaningful ways to communicate information to farmers about sustainable agriculture" (p. 820). This improved communication, the researchers and farmers believed, would benefit not just researchers interested in the topic but also farmers and their communities. Farmers and researchers were both involved in all aspects of the research, from designing the project and determining focus group questions to conducting the focus groups and finally to analyzing data and disseminating findings.

Perhaps one of the most unique and rewarding aspects of action research is that it is often interdisciplinary. Action research projects might bring together researchers from any number of disciplines, from the social sciences, such as sociology, political science, and psychology; to an assortment of physical and natural sciences, such as biology and chemistry; to engineering, philosophy, and history (to name just a few).

Anyone interested in social change can benefit from having some understanding of social scientific research methods. The knowledge you've gained from your methods course can be put to good use even if you don't have an interest in pursuing a career in research. As a member of a community, perhaps you will find that the opportunity to engage in action research presents itself to you one day. Your background in research methodology will no doubt assist you in making life better for yourself and those who share your interests, circumstances, or geographic region.

SPOTLIGHT ON UTA SCHOOL OF SOCIAL WORK

DR. MAXINE DAVIS SHARES EXPERIENCES WITH ACTION RESEARCH

There are various types of action research. Although the degree to which stakeholders are involved may vary across different stages of the research and dissemination process, each type is valuable and aims to accomplish shared decision-making, responsibility, and power between the researcher and the researched. I will share with you a few examples of recent research that I have had the pleasure of being involved in.

Case 1 (St. Louis, MO) Community based participatory research (CBPR)

As a community organizer, activist, and Missionary, Ms. Johnson is well connected to her community in North St. Louis city. She has worked in partnership with a number of clergy members throughout St. Louis on improving the overall well-being of African-Americans for a number of years. From education to political engagement, she has her pulse on the many issues of local residents and a wide network of clergy and ministers who trust her. In 2014, I partnered with Ms. Johnson to explore clergy perceptions on religious or spiritual (R/S) related abuse within intimate partner violence (IPV). Ms. Johnson conducted more than half of the interviews (many of which occurred only because of the trust clergy members had with her, not due to my recruitment efforts). We coded the data independently and analyzed it as a team. As a result, Ms. Johnson gained the skills to conduct basic qualitative data analysis that may be applicable to her other work. The study results revealed that R/S abuse in IPV was a serious issue that Black clergy often faced in ministry. Furthermore, they desired training to help them to better prepare in responding to this problem. The project did not end at manuscript development, rather the efforts to address this issue continue as we develop and plan to implement R/S specific IPV training for Black clergy in St. Louis.

Case 2 (Chicago, IL) Community-engaged research using a Community Collaborative/Advisory Board (CCB)

A colleague who knew of my interest in the intersection of religious faith and IPV connected me with a priest at St. Pius V parish who was looking for someone to evaluate a portion of the church's domestic violence program. The project combined evaluation research and action research. I sought and obtained funding tosupport the first step of a multi-phase project involving process evaluation in preparation for a longitudinal impact (i.e. outcome) evaluation. I convened a collaborative board of relevant stakeholders from different organizations and relocated to Chicago (Pilsen neighborhood) to embark upon the research. Over the course of one year, I lived in the

community and collected various types of data from a variety of sources while the CCB and I developed an evaluation plan that would meet the organization's needs. The primary research questions explored were: "What is The Men's Group (TMG)?" and "Why do participants attend and remain engaged in TMG?" We discovered that TMG was a trauma-informed, culturally-tailored (to Latino men), spirituality and group based partner abuse intervention program (PAIP) aiming to stop violence perpetration and help participants become self-aware. Men remained engaged in the PAIP because they were met with respect by staff/facilitators, reported gaining benefits because of participation, and connected with other group members through a brotherhood. A quasi-experimental design using quantitative data is currently underway.

Case 3 (Grand Prairie, TX) Youth-led CBPR

The Grand Prairie Storm Track & Field Association (GP Storm) reached out to me after their founders saw me present on the potential of hip-hop music influencing public perceptions about IPV. Our shared interest on increasing Black/African-American representation in health-related research careers brought us together. I invited high school students who were affiliated with the program to join me in examining this area, but also encouraged them to develop a set of their own research questions that they were excited to explore. We met weekly over the course of 3 months in the summer of 2019 and analyzed the lyrics of 7 hip-hop songs. The youth-led research team consisted of six Black/Multiracial young women (5 high school; 1 middle school), the organization founder/director, a PhD student, and myself. The findings revealed that hip-hop music brings awareness to IPV/A by discussing Death, Denial, Freedom, and Physical violence/various types of consequences. Partnering with the GP Storm and affiliated students (the community researchers) allowed the research team to examine research questions that were of interest to a wider audience and do so by drawing on multiple perspectives, thereby improving the rigor of the study. The research did not end here; rather next steps involve hosting a listening party as an intervention to reduce violence and acceptability thereof amongst youth and adults.

Lessons learned

I have learned a few lessons through conducting community-engaged research that I think are worth sharing. It is imperative that you are comfortable openly discussing race and diversity if you plan on engaging in action research with communities of color. This applies, regardless of your own identity, but is especially relevant for those who are an "outsider" in terms of gender or race/ethnicity. The second lesson is that trust need not be earned once, rather you must continuously build and maintain trust in order to conduct sound research. You must also plan to nurture and intend to maintain these relationships in a humanistic manner, beyond that of "a research product." If your intentions are genuine and you are honest with any trepidations, that plus meaningful project delivery will carry you far.

References

Refer to following articles for more exploration into this research:

Davis, M., ^Johnson, M., Bowland, S. (In Draft) "I hate it…but it's real": Black Clergy Perspectives on Intimate Partner Violence related Religious/Spiritual Abuse

Davis, M., ^Dahm, C., Jonson-Reid, M., Stoops, C., Sabri, B. (Revisions Submitted- Awaiting Final Decision). "The Men's Group" at St. Pius V: A Case Study of a Parish- Based Voluntary Partner Abuse Intervention Program.

^denotes community partners

Key Takeaways

- Action research is conducted by researchers who wish to create some form of social change.
- Stakeholders are true collaborators in action research.
- Action research is often conducted by teams of interdisciplinary researchers.

Glossary

- Action research- research that is conducted for the purpose of creating some form of social change in collaboration with stakeholders
- Stakeholders – individuals or groups who have an interest in the outcome of your study

Image attributions

protest by BruceEmmerling CC-0

Maxine Johnson and Maxine Davis by Maxine Davis CC BY-NC-ND

Community Researchers in Partnership by Maxine Davis CC BY-NC-ND

GP Storm by Maxine Davis CC BY-NC-ND

CHAPTER TWELVE: REPORTING RESEARCH

The previous chapters in this textbook described how to create a research question and answer it using the methods of social science. Once you've completed your analysis, your project is not over. In many ways, it is just beginning. In the beginning of this textbook, you were introduced to the idea that social work research as knowledge for action on behalf of target populations. Research that sits idle on your computer is not of use to anyone. Most social workers who conduct research hope their work will have relevance to others besides themselves. As such, research is a public activity. While the work may be conducted by an individual in a private setting, the knowledge gained from that work should be shared with peers and other parties who may have an interest. Understanding how to share your work is an important aspect of the research process.

CHAPTER OUTLINE

- 12.1 What to share and why we share
- 12.2 Disseminating your findings
- 12.3 The uniqueness of the social work perspective on science

CONTENT WARNING

This chapter discusses or mentions the following topics: sexual and domestic violence, poverty, mental health, the criminal justice system, and cancer.

12.1 WHAT TO SHARE AND WHY WE SHARE

Learning Objectives

- Identify the six questions researchers should be able to answer to ensure that their ethical obligations have been met
- Describe how social work roles might shape how a person shares research findings

When preparing to share your work with others you must decide what to share, with whom to share it, and in what format(s) to share it. In this section, we'll consider the former two aspects of sharing your work. In the section that follows, we'll consider the various formats through which social workers might share their work.

SHARING IT ALL: THE GOOD, THE BAD, AND THE UGLY

Because conducting social work research is a scholarly pursuit and because social work researchers generally aim to reach a true understanding of social processes, it is crucial that we share all aspects of our research—the good, the bad, and the ugly. Doing so helps ensure that others will understand, use, and effectively critique our work. We considered this aspect of the research process in Chapter 3, but it is worth reviewing here. We learned about the importance of sharing all aspects of our work for ethical reasons and for the purpose of replication. In preparing to share your work with others, and in order to meet your ethical obligations as a social work researcher, challenge yourself to answer the following questions:

- Why did I conduct this research?

- How did I conduct this research?

- For whom did I conduct this research?

- What conclusions can I reasonably draw from this research?

- Knowing what I know now, what would I do differently?

- How could this research be improved?

Understanding why you conducted your research will help you be honest—with yourself and your readers—about your own personal interest, investments, or biases with respect to the work. Being able to clearly communicate how you conducted your research is also important. This means being honest about your data collection methods, sample and sampling strategy, and data analysis.

The third question in the list is designed to help you articulate who the major stakeholders are in your research. Of course, the researcher is a stakeholder. Additional stakeholders might include funders, research participants, or others who share something in common with your research subjects (e.g., members of some community where you conducted research or members of the same social group, such as parents or athletes, upon whom you conducted your research). Professors for whom you conducted research as part of a class project might be stakeholders, as might employers for whom you conducted research. Understanding the answer to this question will allow you target formal and informal venues to share your research, which we will review in the next section.

The fourth question should help you think about the major strengths of your work. Finally, the last two questions are designed to make you think about potential weaknesses in your work and how future research might build from or improve upon your work. Presenting your research honestly requires admitting the limitations of your study but arguing why the results are important anyway. All scientific studies contain limitations and are open to questioning.

SOCIAL WORK ROLES

Sharing social work research is important to social workers across a variety of roles. Dubois and Krogsrud Miley (2005) describe generalist social work roles across three practice areas. The first practice area is resource management, and generalist social workers should understand that "resources are power" (p. 236). Organizations and individuals with money, knowledge, talent, staff, office space, technology, and other resources hold power in the social space and our ability to martial those resources on behalf of our clients can determine their treatment outcomes. The second practice area is education, and the authors emphasize that "knowledge is power," as well. Social work involves learning from and educating our clients, as well as sharing our knowledge where it is needed in the social service system. The final practice area is consultancy, recognizing that social workers bring expertise and resources and collaborate with clients to create solutions to problems. Let's think about how social workers on the micro, meso, and macro level might act within these roles to bring about change based on empirical research findings.

For social worker researchers engaged in macro social work, the *activist* role demands advocacy on behalf of target populations to individuals who control resources. Dissemination of social research findings can support this role by lobbying policy-makers directly through phone calls or letter campaigns which include research results. Another option would be to partner with service agencies who can use research results in grant applications for additional funding for their services. Sharing research–in the form of a journal article, conference presentation, editorial article, interview on local media, among countless others—contributes to what we know about the social problem addressed in the study as a society. The researcher may also engage in the role of a *planner*, using her research to help create new programs to address a problem in the community.

Meso-level social work roles are also compatible with disseminating social work research. As a *convener* or *mediator*, social workers can bring together community leaders and organizations to address problems as a team. Sharing their research, social work researchers highlight how the problems of individuals, communities, and society are intertwined. Perhaps the research could be a catalyst to creating a task force in the community. Or it could convince a variety of stakeholders such as anti-poverty organizations, anti-racist organizations, as well as police, to come together to address a problem jointly. It may also be used to propose trainings and outreach in the community.

Micro-level social workers can share the results of a study with their clients, which may make them feel less alone and contextualize their struggle within their home community. They can use research findings to advocate within the current system for their client's right to services, for exceptions to policies that block them from accessing necessary resources, and for the effective delivery of services. Research may also cue them to address the effects of racism and poverty in their clients' lives, providing a more comprehensive approach to intervention. Micro-level social workers also engage in educational practice and prevention roles, which can be informed and enhanced by research as well.

Social work research is research for action on behalf of target populations. Sharing results with the world is a necessary part of that mission.

Key Takeaways

- As they prepare to share their research, researchers must keep in mind their ethical obligations to their peers, their research participants, and the public.
- Social work roles across the ecosystem will shape how one's results are shared and for what purpose.

Image attributions

typing by StartupStockPhotos CC-0

hand by Myriams-Fotos CC-0

12.2 DISSEMINATING YOUR FINDINGS

Learning Objectives

- Define dissemination
- Describe how audience impacts the content and purpose of dissemination
- Identify the options for formally presenting your work to other scholars
- Explain the role of stakeholders in dissemination

Dissemination refers to "a planned process that involves consideration of target audiences and the settings in which research findings are to be received and, where appropriate, communicating and interacting with wider policy and...service audiences in ways that will facilitate research uptake in decision-making processes and practice" (Wilson, Petticrew, Calnan, & Natareth, 2010, p. 91). In other words, dissemination of research findings involves careful planning, thought, consideration of target audiences, and communication with those audiences. Writing up results from your research and having others take notice are two entirely different propositions. In fact, the general rule of thumb is that people will not take notice unless you help and encourage them to do so.

Disseminating your findings successfully requires determining who your audience is, where your audience is, and *how* to reach them. When considering who your audience is, think about who is likely to take interest in your work. Your audience might include those who do not express enthusiastic interest but might nevertheless benefit from an awareness of your research. Your research participants and those who share some characteristics in common with your participants are likely to have some interest in what you've discovered in the course of your research. Other scholars who study similar topics are another obvious audience for your work. Perhaps there are policymakers who should take note of your work. Organizations that do work in an area related to the topic of your research are another possibility. Finally, any and all inquisitive and engaged members of the public represent a possible audience for your work.

Where your audience is should be fairly obvious. You know where your research participants are because you've studied them. You can find interested scholars on your campus, at professional conferences, and via publications such as professional organizations' newsletters and scholarly journals. Policymakers include your state and federal representatives who, at least in theory, should be available to hear a constituent speak on matters of policy interest. Perhaps you're already aware of organizations that do work in an area related to your research topic, but if not, a simple web search should help you identify possible organizational audiences for your work. Disseminating your findings to the public more generally could take any number of forms: a letter to the editor of the local newspaper, a blog, or even a post or two on your social media channels.

Finally, determining how to reach your audiences will vary according to which audience you wish to reach. Your strategy should be determined by the norms of the audience. For example, scholarly journals provide author submission instructions that clearly define requirements for anyone wishing to disseminate their work via a particular journal. The same is true for newspaper editorials; check your newspaper's website for details about how to format and submit letters to the editor. If you wish to reach out to your political representatives, a call to their offices or a simple web search should tell you how to do so.

Disseminating findings involves the following three steps:

- Determine *who* your audience
- Identify *where* your audience
- Discover *how* best to reach your audience

TAILORING YOUR MESSAGE TO YOUR AUDIENCE

Once you are able to articulate with whom to you wish to share your research, you must decide what to share. While you would never alter your actual findings for different audiences, understanding who your audience is will help you frame your research in a way that is most meaningful to that audience. Certainly, the most obvious candidates with whom you'll share your work are other social scientists. If you are conducting research for a class project, your main "audience" will probably be your professor. Perhaps you'll also share your work with other students in the class.

What is more challenging, and possibly a little scary, is sharing your research with the wider world. Sharing with *professional audiences* is designed to bring your work to the attention of other social scientists and academics, but also other social workers or professionals who practice in areas related to your research. If you are sharing with other scientists, they are probably interested in your study's methods, particularly statistical tests or data analysis frameworks. Sharing your work with this audience will require you to talk about your methods and data in a different way than you would with other audiences. Professional social workers are more likely to want to hear about the practice and policy implications of your research.

PLAGIARISM

Scholars take extraordinary care not to commit **plagiarism**. Presenting someone else's words or ideas as if they are your own is among the most egregious transgressions a scholar can commit. Indeed, plagiarism has ended many careers (Maffly, 2011) [1] and many students' opportunities to pursue degrees (Go, 2008). [2] Take this very seriously. If you feel a little afraid

1. As just a single example, take note of this story about the pattern of plagiarism that cost a University of Utah scholar his job.
2. As a single example (of many) of the consequences for students committing plagiarism, see this article about two students kicked off semester at sea for plagiarism.

and paranoid after reading this warning, consider it a good thing— and let it motivate you to take extra care to ensure that you are not plagiarizing the work of others.

PEER-REVIEWED JOURNAL ARTICLES

Researchers commonly submit manuscripts to peer-reviewed academic journals. These journals are commonly read by other researchers, students, and practitioners. Peer review is a formal process in which other scholars review the work to ensure it is a high quality before publication. A manuscript may be rejected by a journal after being submitted. Often, this is an opportunity for the researchers to correct problems with the manuscript or find a journal that is a better fit for their research findings. Usually, even if a manuscript is accepted for publication, the peer reviewers will request improvements to it before it can be published. The process of peer review helps improve the quality of journal articles and research.

FORMAL PRESENTATIONS

Getting your work published in a journal is challenging and time-consuming, as journals receive many submissions but have limited room to publish. Researchers often seek to supplement their publications with formal presentations, which, while adhering to stringent standards, are more accessible and have more opportunities to share research. For researchers, presenting your research is an excellent way to get feedback on your work. Professional social workers often make presentations to their peers to prepare for more formal writing and publishing of their work. Presentations might be formal talks, either individually or as part of a panel at a professional conference; less formal roundtable discussions, another common professional conference format; or posters that are displayed in a specially designated area.

PRESENTATIONS TO STAKEHOLDERS

While it is important to let academics and scientists know about the results of your research, it is important to identify stakeholders who would also benefit from knowing the results of your study. Stakeholders are individuals or groups who have an interest in the outcome of the study you conduct. Instead of the formal presentations or journal articles you may use to engage academics or fellow researchers, stakeholders will expect a presentation that is engaging, understandable, and immediately relevant to their lives and practice. Informal presentations are no less rigorous than formal presentations, but they do not follow a strict format.

DISSEMINATING TO THE GENERAL PUBLIC

While there are a seemingly infinite number of informal audiences, there is one more that is worth mentioning—the general public. Part of our job as social workers is to shine a light towards areas of social injustice and raise the consciousness of the public as a whole. Researchers commonly share their results with popular media outlets to reach a broader audience with their study's conclusions. Unfortunately, journalism about scientific results can sometimes overstate the degree of certainty researchers have in their conclusions. Consequently, it's important to review the journalistic standards at the media outlet and reporter you approach by examining their previous work and clarifying the degree of control over the final product you will have.

Reports written for public consumption differ from those written for scholarly consumption. As noted elsewhere in this chapter, knowing your audience is crucial when preparing a report of your research. What are they likely to want to hear about? What portions of the research do you feel are crucial to share, regardless of the audience? What level of knowledge do they have about your topic? Answering these questions will help you determine how to shape any written reports you plan to produce. In fact, some outlets answer these questions for you, as in the case of newspaper editorials where rules of style, presentation, and length will dictate the shape of your written report.

CONCLUSION

Whoever your audience, don't forget what it is that you are reporting: social scientific evidence. Take seriously your role as a social scientist and your place among peers in your discipline. Present your findings as clearly and as honestly as you possibly can; pay appropriate homage to the scholars who have come before you, even while you raise questions about their work; and aim to engage your readers in a discussion about your work and about avenues for further inquiry. Even if you won't ever meet your readers face-to-face, imagine what they might ask you upon reading your report, imagine your response, and provide some of those details in your written report.

Key Takeaways

- Disseminating findings takes planning and careful consideration of your audiences.

- The dissemination process includes determining the who, where, and how of reaching your audiences.

- Plagiarism is among the most egregious academic transgressions a scholar can commit.

- In formal presentations, include your research question, methodological approach, major findings, and a few final takeaways.

- Reports for public consumption usually contain fewer details than reports for scholarly consumption.

- Keep your role and obligations as a social scientist in mind as you write research reports.

Glossary

- Dissemination- "a planned process that involves consideration of target audiences and the settings in which research findings are to be received and, where appropriate, communicating and interacting with wider policy and...service audiences in ways that will facilitate research uptake in decision-making processes and practice" (Wilson, Petticrew, Calnan, & Natareth, 2010, p. 91)

- Plagiarism- presenting someone else's words or ideas as if they are your own

Image attributions

microphone by Skitterphoto CC-0

woman man teamwork by rawpixel CC-0

audience by MariSmithPix CC-0

feedback by surdumihail CC-0

12.3 THE UNIQUENESS OF THE SOCIAL WORK PERSPECTIVE ON SCIENCE

Learning Objectives

- Describe how social workers contribute to social science

Social workers, by the nature of their work and their ethical orientation, have a lot of knowledge and expertise to contribute to social science. Social work research is, by its very nature, interdisciplinary. A social worker who wishes to understand how masculinity is impacting her adolescent male clients must become fluent in not only the social work literature on masculinity but also the literature from gender studies, sociology, and psychology. The synthesis of the insights from various social science disciplines, each representing a part of the person-in-environment framework, is a hallmark of strong social work research. Social work has, over time, established a substantial base of empirical and theoretical insights, represented in journals such as *Social Work* and *Social Service Review*. But its interdisciplinary roots remain. Given the recent direction in research and practice grant funding towards interdisciplinary projects, this is a significant strength.

Social workers are a pragmatic group. We use what is most useful to us in a given practice situation. This pragmatism also extends to the theories that social workers use. Social work education emphasizes theoretical fluency, or the ability to switch theoretical frames to understand the same situation in different ways. As social workers, we understand that as one of many different theoretical lenses through which to view a given situation. Each theory will lend itself to different testable propositions in quantitative research or jumping-off points for qualitative research. Because of this, social workers can see beyond disciplinary and theoretical blinders to produce a more comprehensive understanding of a phenomenon.

In addition to incorporating multiple theories, social work is an explicitly multi-paradigmatic discipline. It acknowledges not only the methods and assumptions of the positivist paradigm, which is almost universally accepted in all social science disciplines, but also the social constructionist, critical, and postmodern paradigms. Social workers understand the limitations of the positivist paradigm and have created new ways of knowing to respond to the unquantifiable and context-dependent aspects of the human experience. Social workers can challenge social science that is deemed to be "universally true" for all people because it understands the complexity and diversity of human life.

Social work is a values-oriented profession. When social workers examine theories, research, or social problems, they do so with an orientation towards social justice, self-determination, strengths and capacities, and interdependence between all peoples. These values are a strength, as they help social workers interpret and analyze research findings in terms of fighting oppression. At the same time, social work is action-oriented. Not only do social workers think in terms of social change, but they seek to create that change themselves. Social workers always ask the "so what" question. That is, "so what does this mean for my client?"

SPOTLIGHT ON UTA SCHOOL OF SOCIAL WORK

REPORTING RESEARCH ON TEXAN SURVIVORS OF INTIMATE PARTNER VIOLENCE

Dr. Rachel Voth Schrag of the UTA School of Social work always thinks about dissemination of her research findings at the beginning of a research project. Knowing at the outset who she wants to share her findings with, and how she hopes they will use them, means she will be able to ask the most helpful research questions.

Dr. Voth Schrag's team recently worked with the Texas Council on Family Violence on a research project which was all about generating information to share with intimate partner violence (IPV) service agencies, funders, and those who set IPV policy for the state of Texas (Voth Schrag, Ravi, & Robinson, 2019).

They wanted to learn about the experiences of Texan survivors who had *not* chosen to access IPV service agencies (like shelters, counseling, and advocacy programs). They believed that these survivors could share insights to help improve services access and delivery throughout Texas. They interviewed nearly 40 survivors, and combined their data with work from other Texan scholars.

A particularly strong finding was that many of the survivors they talked too had made attempts to access services, but had not had positive first experiences. Several survivors have identified feeling stymied by initial interactions with potential helpers, sharing that they began the process of disclosing aspects of their IPV experiences, but that the responses they received (including from law enforcement, health care, child protective, and IPV service staff) were not helpful. For some, an agency's inability to meet their initial needs (for example, for shelter or crisis intervention) created disconnects which disrupted the possibility of future interactions.

From the outset of the project, Voth Schrag and her team wanted to be able to share their findings — and the voices of the survivors who talked with them — with IPV agency staff, funders of IPV services across the state, and policy makers who set priorities for the IPV service sector. They worked with the Texas Council on Family Violence, their statewide IPV services coalition, to identify the most effective dissemination strategy for each of these groups.

By identifying who they wanted to share their findings with, and what they might be most interested in learning about, the team was able to tailor their research questions and methods to gather the sorts of data that both answer the questions they were interested in and generate the kinds of data that would capture the attention of influential individuals and groups. If you have the ability to answer a pressing question for someone, they'll usually keep listening to you when you add a little extra information. This allowed Voth Schrag and her team to share their findings more broadly. They spent several days in Austin giving presentations aimed at specific groups — inviting funders to one presentation, and agency executive directors to another. They also spent time answering questions about their findings in formal and informal meetings with stakeholders. The Texas Council on Family Violence was able to harness the power of their connections to reach leaders from across the state, increasing the spread and impact of the work, and allowing the team to underscore key steps, like expanding funding for and access to emergency shelter and transitional housing, that agencies, funders, and policy makers can take to address IPV and reach survivors who are not currently accessing services.

While it was great to be able to share their findings in person, Texas is a big state, and agency staff in particular are often not able to travel to Austin for research dissemination meetings. To reach this audience, the team recorded a webinar about the project and key findings, which is available on the Texas Council on Family Violence's website. They also participated in the development of a website that provides information on their study methods, findings, and conclusions, and also has lots of other useful data and tools that can support IPV service agencies across Texas in using data in their work.

Key Takeaways

- Social work contributes to social science through its orientation towards interdisciplinary knowledge, multiple theories and paradigms, and action on behalf of clients.

Image attributions

social media by geralt CC-0

GLOSSARY

A-

Acquiescence bias – when respondents say yes to whatever the researcher asks (5.5)

Action research – research that is conducted for the purpose of creating some form of social change in collaboration with stakeholders (11.3)

Aggregate matching – when the comparison group is determined to be similar to the experimental group along important variables (8.2)

Anonymity – when the identity of research participants is not known to researchers (3.2)

Anonymized data – data that does not contain personally identifying information (10.4)

Attributes – the characteristics that make up a variable (5.5)

Authenticity – the degree to which researchers capture the multiple perspectives and values of participants in their study and foster change across participants and systems during their analysis (5.4)

Authority – learning by listening to what people in authority say is true (1.1)

B-

Baseline stage – the period of time before the intervention starts (11.2)

Bivariate analysis – quantitative analysis that examines relationships among two variables (8.4)

C-

Categorical measures – a measure with attributes that are categories (5.5)

Causality – the idea that one event, behavior, or belief will result in the occurrence of another, subsequent event, behavior, or belief (4.2)

Classic experimental design – a type of experimental design that uses random assignment, an experimental and control group, as well as pre- and posttesting (8.1)

Closed-ended questions – questions for which the researcher offers response options (7.4)

Cluster sampling – a sampling approach that begins by sampling groups (or clusters) of population elements and then selects elements from within those groups (6.3)

Code – a shorthand representation of some more complex set of issues or ideas (9.5)

Codebook – a document that outlines how a survey researcher has translated her data from words into numbers (8.4)

Coding – identifying themes across qualitative data by reading transcripts (9.5)

Cognitive biases – predictable flaws in thinking (1.1)

Cohort survey – describes how people with a defining characteristic change over time (7.3)

Comparison group – a group in quasi-experimental design that does not receive the experimental treatment; it is similar to a control group except assignment to the comparison group is not determined by random assignment (8.2)

Concept – notion or image that we conjure up when we think of some cluster of related observations or ideas (5.2)

Conceptualization – writing out clear, concise definitions for key concepts, particularly in quantitative research (5.2)

Concurrent validity – if a measure is able to predict outcomes from an established measure given at the same time (5.4)

Confidentiality – when identifying information about research participants is known to the researchers but is not divulged to anyone else (3.2)

Confirmability – the degree to which the results reported are linked to the data obtained from participants (5.4)

Confirmation bias – observing and analyzing information in a way that confirms what you already think is true (1.1)

Constructs – are not observable but can be defined based on observable characteristics (5.1)

Content analysis – a type of unobtrusive research that involves the study of texts and their meaning (10.3)

Content validity – if the measure includes all of the possible meanings of the concept (5.4)

Contingency table – shows how variation on one variable may be contingent on variation on another (8.4)

Continuous measures – a measure with attributes that are numbers (5.5)

Control group – the group in an experiment that does not receive the intervention (8.1)

Control variables – potential "third variables" effects that are controlled for mathematically in the data analysis process to highlight the relationship between the independent and dependent variable (4.2)

Convenience sample – when a researcher gathers data from whatever cases happen to be convenient (6.2)

Convergent validity – if a measure is conceptually similar to an existing measure of the same concept (5.4)

Covariation – the degree to which two variables vary together (4.2)

Credibility – the degree to which the results are accurate and viewed as important and believable by participants (5.4)

Critical paradigm – a paradigm in social science research focused on power, inequality, and social change (2.2)

Cross-sectional surveys – surveys that are administered at just one point in time (7.3)

D-

Data saturation – the point in the qualitative research data collection process when no new information is being discovered

Deductive approach – when a researcher studies what others have done, reads existing theories of whatever phenomenon she is studying, and then tests hypotheses that emerge from those theories (2.3)

Dependability – ensures that proper qualitative procedures were followed during the research process and that any changes that emerged during the research process are accounted for, justified, and described in the final report (5.4)

Dependent variable – a variable that depends on changes in the independent variable (4.2)

Descriptive research – research that describes or defines a particular phenomenon (4.1)

Direct experience – learning through informal observation (1.1)

Discriminant validity – if a measure is not related to measures to which it shouldn't be statistically correlated (5.4)

Dissemination – "a planned process that involves consideration of target audiences and the settings in which research findings are to be received and, where appropriate, communicating and interacting with wider policy and…service audiences in ways that will facilitate research uptake in decision-making processes and practice" (Wilson, Petticrew, Calnan, & Natareth, 2010, p. 91) (12.2)

Double-barreled question – a question that asks two different questions at the same time, making it difficult for a research participant to respond accurately (7.4)

Double-blind – when researchers interact with participants are unaware of who is in the control or experimental group (8.3)

Dunning-Kruger effect – when unskilled people overestimate their ability and knowledge (and experts underestimate their ability and knowledge)

E-

Ecological fallacy – claims about one lower-level unit of analysis are made based on data from some higher-level unit of analysis (4.3)

Emphasis – in a mixed methods study, refers to the priority that each method is given (4.4)

Epistemology – a set of assumptions about how we come to know what is real and true (1.1)

Evaluation research – research that evaluates the outcomes of a policy or program (1.3)

Evidence-based practice– making decisions on how to help clients based on the best available evidence (1.3)

Ex post facto control group – a control group created when a researcher matches individuals after the intervention is administered (8.2)

Exclusion criteria – characteristics that disqualify a person from being included in a sample (6.1)

Exempt review – lowest level of IRB review for studies with minimal risk or human subject involvement (3.1)

Exhaustiveness – when all possible attributes are listed (5.5)

Expedited review – middle level of IRB review for studies with minimal risk but greater human subject involvement (3.1)

Experiment – a method of data collection designed to test hypotheses under controlled conditions (8.1)

Experimental group – the group in an experiment that receives the intervention (8.1)

Explanatory research – explains why particular phenomena work in the way that they do; answers "why" questions (4.1)

Exploratory research – conducted during the early stages of a project, usually when a researcher wants to test the feasibility of conducting a more extensive study (4.1)

External validity – the degree to which experimental conclusions generalize to larger populations and different situations (8.3)

F-

Face validity – if it is plausible that the measure measures what it intends to (5.4)

Fairness – the degree to which "different constructions, perspectives, and positions are not only allowed to emerge, but are also seriously considered for merit and worth" (Rodwell, 1998, p. 107) (5.4)

False negative – when a measure does not indicate the presence of a phenomenon, when in reality it is present (5.5)

False positive – when a measure indicates the presence of a phenomenon, when in reality it is not present (5.5)

Fence-sitters – respondents who choose neutral response options, even if they have an opinion (7.4)

Field notes – written notes produced by the researcher during the data collection process (9.2)

Filter question – a question that identifies some subset of survey respondents who are asked additional questions that are not relevant to the entire sample (7.4)

Floaters – respondents that choose a substantive answer to a question when really, they don't understand the question or don't have an opinion (7.4)

Focus groups – planned discussions designed to elicit group interaction and "obtain perceptions on a defined area of interest in a permissive, nonthreatening environment" (Krueger & Casey, 2000, p. 5) (9.4)

Focused coding – collapsing or narrowing down codes, defining codes, and recoding each transcript using a final code list (9.5)

Frequency distribution – summarizes the distribution of responses on a single survey question (8.4)

Full board review – highest level of IRB, for studies with greater than minimal risk to participants (3.1)

G-

Generalizability – the idea that a study's results will tell us something about a group larger than the sample from which the findings were generated (10.3)

Generalize– to make claims about a larger population based on an examination of a smaller sample (7.2)

Gray literature – research and information released by non-commercial publishers, such as government agencies, policy organizations, and think-tanks (2.2)

H-

Hawthorne effect – a threat to internal validity in which participants in a study behave differently because they know they are being observed (10.2)

Hypothesis – a statement describing a researcher's expectation regarding what she anticipates finding (4.2)

I-

Idiographic research – attempts to explain or describe the phenomenon exhaustively, based on the subjective understandings of the participants (4.2)

Inclusion criteria – the characteristics a person must possess in order to be included in a sample (6.1)

In-depth interviews – interviews in which researchers hear from respondents about what they think is important about the topic at hand in the respondent's own words (9.2)

Independence – when there is no relationship between the two variables in question (8.4)

Independent variable – a variable that causes a change in the dependent variable (4.2)

Index – a measure that contains several indicators and is used to summarize a more general concept (5.3)

Indicators – represent the concepts that a researcher is interested in studying (5.3)

Indirect observables – things that require indirect observation and inference to measure (5.1)

Individual matching – pairing participants with similar attributes for the purpose of assignment to groups (8.2)

Inductive approach – when a researcher starts with a set of observations and then moves from particular experiences to a more general set of propositions about those experiences (2.3)

Informed consent – a research subject's voluntary agreement to participate in a study based on a full understanding of the study and of the possible risks and benefits involved (3.2)

Inputs – resources needed for the program to operate (11.1)

Instrumentation – a threat to internal validity when measures do not accurately measure participants or are implemented in a way that biases participant responses

Internal consistency reliability – the degree to which scores on each question of a scale are correlated with each other (5.4)

Internal validity – the confidence researchers have about whether their intervention produced variation in their dependent variable (8.3)

Inter-rater reliability – the degree to which different observers agree on what happened (5.4)

Interval level – a level of measurement that is continuous, can be rank ordered, is exhaustive and mutually exclusive, and for which the distance between attributes is known to be equal (5.5)

Interview guide – a list of questions or topics that the interviewer hopes to cover during the course of an interview (9.2)

Interview schedules – when a researcher poses questions verbally to respondents (7.3)

Interviews – a method of data collection that involves two or more people exchanging information through a series of questions and answers (9.1)

Intuition – your "gut feeling" about what to do

J-

Journaling – making notes of emerging issues and changes during the research process (9.2)

L-

Leading question – a question with wording that influences how a participant responds (5.5)

Likert scales – ordinal measures that use numbers as a shorthand (e.g., 1=highly likely, 2=somewhat likely, etc.) to indicate what attribute the person feels describes them best (5.5)

Longitudinal surveys – surveys in which a researcher makes observations over an extended period of time (7.3)

M-

Macro-level – examining social structures and institutions (1.1)

Matrix question – lists a set of questions for which the answer categories are all the same (7.4)

Mean – also known as the average, this is the sum of the value of all responses on a given variable divided by the total number of responses (8.4)

Measurement – the process by which researchers describe and ascribe meaning to the key facts, concepts, or other phenomena they are investigating (5.1)

Median – the value that lies in the middle of a distribution of responses (8.4)

Meso-level – examining interaction between groups (1.1)

Micro-level – examining the smallest levels of interaction, usually individuals (1.1)

Mode – the most common response given to a question (8.4)

Moderator – the researcher tasked with facilitating the conversation in the focus group (9.4)

Multiple treatment design – beginning a new course of treatment or adding a new dimension to an existing treatment (11.2)

Multivariate analysis – quantitative analysis that examines relationships among more than two variables (8.4)

Mutual exclusivity – when a person cannot identify with two different attributes simultaneously (5.5)

Multi-dimensional concepts – concepts that are comprised of multiple elements (5.2)

N-

Natural experiments – situations in which comparable groups are created by differences that already occur in the real world (8.2)

Nominal – a level of measurement that is categorical and for which those categories cannot be mathematically ranked, though they are exhaustive and mutually exclusive (5.5)

Nomothetic research – a type of research that provides a more general, sweeping explanation that is universally true for all people (4.2)

Nonequivalent comparison group design – a quasi-experimental design similar to a classic experimental design but without random assignment (8.2)

Nonprobability sampling – sampling techniques for which a person's likelihood of being selected for membership in the sample is unknown (6.2)

Nonresponse bias – bias reflected in differences between people who respond to a survey and those who do not respond (8.4)

O-

Objective truth – a single truth, observed without bias, that is universally applicable

Observational terms – things that can be seen with the naked eye simply by looking at them (5.1)

One-group pre-/posttest design – a type of pre-experimental design that applies an intervention to one group and administers a pretest and posttest (8.2)

One-shot case study – a pre-experimental design that applies an intervention to only one group without a pretest (8.2)

Ontology – a set of assumptions about what is real (1.1)

Open coding – reading through each transcript, line by line, and makes a note of whatever categories or themes seem to jump out (9.5)

Open-ended questions – questions for which the researcher does not include response options (7.4)

Operationalization – a process by which researchers conducting quantitative research spell out precisely how a concept will be measured and how to interpret that measure (5.3)

Ordinal – a level of measurement that is categorical, has categories that can be rank ordered, and those categories are exhaustive and mutually exclusive (5.5)

Outcomes – in the context of program evaluation, outcomes are the issues the program is trying to change (11.1)

Outcomes assessment – an evaluation designed to discover if a program achieved its intended outcomes (11.1)

Outputs – tangible results of the program process (11.1)

Overgeneralization – using limited observations to make assumptions about broad patterns (1.1)

P-

Panel survey – describes how people in a specific group change over time, asking the same people each time the survey is administered (7.3)

Paradigm – a way of viewing the world and a framework from which to understand the human experience (2.2)

Periodicity – the tendency for a pattern to occur at regular intervals (6.3)

Placebo effect – when a participant feels better, despite having received no intervention at all (8.3)

Plagiarism – presenting someone else's words or ideas as if they are your own (12.2)

Plausibility – in order to make the claim that one event, behavior, or belief causes another, the claim has to make sense (4.2)

Population – the cluster of people about whom a researcher is most interested (6.1)

Positivism – a paradigm guided by the principles of objectivity, knowability, and deductive logic (2.2)

Postmodernism – a paradigm focused on the historical and contextual embeddedness of scientific knowledge and a skepticism towards certainty and grand explanations in social science (2.2)

Posttest – a measurement taken after the intervention (8.1)

Posttest-only control group design – a type of experimental design that uses random assignment and an experimental and control group, but does not use a pretest (8.1)

Practice wisdom – "learning by doing" that guides social work intervention and increases over time (1.1)

Predictive validity – if a measure predicts things, it should be able to predict in the future (5.4)

Pre-experimental designs – a variation of experimental design that lacks the rigor of experiments and is often used before a true experiment is conducted (8.2)

Pretest – a measurement taken prior to the intervention (8.1)

Process assessment – an evaluation conducted during the earlier stages of a program or on an ongoing basis (11.1)

Program – the intervention clients receive (11.1)

Probability proportionate to size – in cluster sampling, giving clusters different chances of being selected based on their size so that each element within those clusters has an equal chance of being selected (6.3)

Probability sampling – sampling approaches for which a person's likelihood of being selected from the sampling frame is known (6.3)

Probe – a request for more information in qualitative research (9.3)

Process assessment – an evaluation conducted during the earlier stages of a program or on an ongoing basis

Purposive sample – when a researcher seeks out participants with specific characteristics (6.2)

Q-

Qualitative methods – examine words or other media to understand their meaning (1.2)

Quantitative methods – examine numerical data to precisely describe and predict elements of the social world (1.2)

Quasi-experimental design – a variation of experimental design that lacks random assignment to experimental and control groups (8.2)

Quota sample – when a researcher selects cases from within several different subgroups (6.2)

R-

Random assignment – using a random process to assign people into experimental and control groups (8.1)

Random error – unpredictable error that does not consistently result in scores that are consistently higher or lower on a given measure (5.5)

Random selection – using a randomly generated numbers to determine who from the sampling frame gets recruited into the sample (6.3)

Ratio level – a level of measurement in which attributes are mutually exclusive and exhaustive, attributes can be rank ordered, the distance between attributes is equal, and attributes have a true zero point (5.5)

Recruitment – the process by which the researcher informs potential participants about the study and attempts to get them to participate (6.1)

Reductionism – when claims about some higher-level unit of analysis are made based on data from a lower-level unit of analysis (4.3)

Reification – assuming that abstract concepts exist in some concrete, tangible way (5.2)

Reliability – a measure's consistency (5.4)

Replication – conducting another researcher's experiment in the same manner and seeing if it produces the same results (8.3)

Representative sample – a sample that resembles the population from which it was drawn in all the ways that are important for the research being conducted (6.3)

Research methods – an organized, logical way of knowing based on theory and observation (1.1)

Response rate – the number of people who respond to a survey divided by the number of people to whom the survey was distributed (8.4)

Retrospective surveys – a type of survey that describes changes over time but are administered only once (7.3)

S-

Sample – the group of people who are successfully recruited from the sampling frame to participate in a study (6.1)

Sampling error – a statistical calculation of the difference between results from a sample and the actual parameters of a population (6.3)

Sampling frame – a real or hypothetical list of people from which a researcher will draw her sample (6.1)

Scale – a composite measure designed in a way that accounts for the possibility that different items on an index may vary in intensity (5.3)

Science – a particular way of knowing that attempts to systematically collect and categorize facts or knowledge (1.2)

Secondary data analysis – analyzing data originally gathered by another person or entity (10.4)

Selection bias – when the elements selected for inclusion in a study do not represent the larger population from which they were drawn due to sampling method or thought processes of the researcher (6.4);

Self-administered questionnaires – when a research participant is given a set of questions, in writing, to which they are asked to respond (7.3)

Semi-structured interviews – questions that are open ended and may not be asked in exactly the same way or in exactly the same order to each and every respondent (9.2)

Sequence – in a mixed methods study, refers to the order that each method is used, either concurrently or sequentially (4.4)

Simple random sampling – selecting elements from a list using randomly generated numbers (6.3)

Snowball sample – when a researcher relies on participant referrals to recruit new participants (6.2)

Social constructionism – a paradigm based on the idea that social context and interaction frame our realities (2.2)

Social desirability bias – when respondents answer based on what they think other people would like, rather than what is true (5.5)

Solomon four-group design – a type of experimental design that uses random assignment, two experimental and two control groups, pretests for half of the groups, and posttests for all (8.1)

Spurious relationship – when an association between two variables appears to be causal but can in fact be explained by some third variable (4.2)

Stakeholders – individuals or groups who have an interest in the outcome of the study a researcher conducts (11.3)

Static group design – uses an experimental group and a comparison group, without random assignment and pretesting (8.2)

Strata – the characteristic by which the sample is divided (6.3)

Stratified sampling – dividing the study population into relevant subgroups and then drawing a sample from each subgroup (6.3)

Subjective truth – one truth among many, bound within a social and cultural context

Survey research – a quantitative method whereby a researcher poses some set of predetermined questions to a sample (7.1)

Systematic error – when measures consistently output incorrect data, usually in one direction and due to an identifiable process (5.5)

Systematic sampling – selecting every kth element from a list (6.3)

T-

Temporality – whatever cause a researcher identifies must happen before the effect (4.2)

Testing effects – when a participant's scores on a measure change because they have already been exposed to it (8.1)

Test-retest reliability – if a measure is given multiple times, the results will be consistent each time (5.4)

Theory – "a systematic set of interrelated statements intended to explain some aspect of social life" (Rubin & Babbie, 2017, p. 615) (2.2)

Theory building – the creation of new theories based on inductive reasoning (4.2)

Theory testing – when a hypothesis is created from existing theory and tested mathematically (4.2)

Time series design – a quasi-experimental design that uses multiple observations before and after an intervention (8.2)

Transcript – a complete, written copy of the recorded interview or focus group containing each word that is spoken on the recording, noting who spoke which words (9.5)

Treatment stage – the time in which the treatment is administered by the social worker (11.2)

Trend – a pattern in the data of a single-subjects design (11.2)

Trend survey – describes how people in a specific group change over time, asking different people each time the survey is administered (7.3)

True experiments – a group of experimental designs that contain independent and dependent variables, pretesting and post testing, and experimental and control groups (8.1)

Trustworthiness – the "truth value, applicability, consistency, and neutrality" of the results of a research study (Rodwell, 1998, p. 96) (5.4)

Typology – a measure that categorizes concepts according to particular themes (5.3)

U-

Unit of analysis – an entity that a researcher wants to say something about at the end of her study (4.3)

Unit of observation – the item that a researcher actually observes, measures, or collects in the course of trying to learn something about her unit of analysis (4.3)

Univariate analysis – quantitative analysis that describes patterns across just one variable (8.4)

Unobtrusive research – methods of collecting data that don't interfere with the subjects under study (10.1)

V-

Validity – a measure's accuracy (5.4)

Variable – refers to a grouping of several characteristics (5.5)

Vulnerable populations – groups of people who receive additional protection during IRB review (3.1)

W –

Withdrawal design – a type of single-subjects research in which the treatment is discontinued and another baseline phase follows the treatment phase

PRACTICE BEHAVIOR INDEX

Educational Policy and Accreditation Standards	Chapters Referenced
Competency 1- Demonstrate Ethical and Professional Behavior:	
a. Make ethical decisions by applying the standards of the NASW Code of Ethics, relevant laws and regulations, models for ethical decision-making, ethical conduct of research, and additional codes of ethics as appropriate to context	1, 3
b. Use reflection and self-regulation to manage personal values and maintain professionalism in practice situations	
c. Demonstrate professional demeanor in behavior; appearance; and oral, written, and electronic communication	
d. Use technology ethically and appropriately to facilitate practice outcomes	1, 11
e. Use supervision and consultation to guide professional judgment and behavior	
Competency 2- Engage Diversity and Difference in Practice:	
a. Apply and communicate understanding of the importance of diversity and difference in shaping life experiences in practice at the micro, mezzo, and macro levels	3
b. Present themselves as learners and engage clients and constituencies as experts of their own experiences	1, 11
c. Apply self-awareness and self-regulation to manage the influence of personal biases and values in working with diverse clients and constituencies	
Competency 3- Advance Human Rights and Social, Economic, and Environmental Justice:	
a. Apply their understanding of social, economic, and environmental justice to advocate for human rights at the individual and system levels	1, 3, 11, 12
b. Engage in practices that advance social, economic, and environmental justice	1, 3, 11, 12
Competency 4- Engage in Practice-informed Research and Research-informed Practice:	
a. Use practice experience and theory to inform scientific inquiry and research	1, 2, 11
b. Apply critical thinking to engage in analysis of quantitative and qualitative research methods and research findings	1, 2, 3, 4, 5, 6, 7, 8, 9, 10, 11, 12
c. Use and translate research evidence to inform and improve practice, policy, and service delivery	1, 2, 3, 4, 5, 6, 7, 8, 9, 10, 11, 12
Competency 5- Engage in Policy Practice:	
a. Identify social policy at the local, state, and federal level that impacts well-being, service delivery, and access to social services	
b. Assess how social welfare and economic policies impact the delivery of and access to social services	8, 11, 12
c. Apply critical thinking to analyze, formulate, and advocate for policies that advance human rights and social, economic, and environmental justice	
Competency 6-Engage with Individuals, Families, Groups, Organizations, and Communities:	
a. Apply knowledge of human behavior and the social environment, person-in-environment, and other multidisciplinary theoretical frameworks to engage with clients and constituencies	2

b. Use empathy, reflection, and interpersonal skills to effectively engage diverse clients and constituencies	
Competency 7- Assess Individuals, Families, Groups, Organizations, and Communities:	
a. Collect and analyze data, and apply critical thinking to interpret information from clients and constituencies	1, 2, 5, 6, 7, 8, 9, 10, 11, 12
b. Apply knowledge of human behavior and the social environment, person-in-environment, and other multidisciplinary theoretical frameworks in the analysis of assessment data from clients and constituencies	2, 4, 5, 8
c. Develop mutually agreed-on intervention goals and objectives based on the critical assessment of strengths, needs, and challenges within clients and constituencies	
d. Select appropriate intervention strategies based on the assessment, research knowledge, and values and preferences of clients and constituencies	1, 11
Competency 8- Intervene with Individuals, Families, Groups, Organizations, and Communities:	
a. Critically choose and implement interventions to achieve practice goals and enhance capacities of clients and constituencies	1, 11
b. Apply knowledge of human behavior and the social environment, person-in-environment, and other multidisciplinary theoretical frameworks in interventions with clients and constituencies	1, 11
c. Use inter-professional collaboration as appropriate to achieve beneficial practice outcomes	
d. Negotiate, mediate, and advocate with and on behalf of diverse clients and constituencies	
e. Facilitate effective transitions and endings that advance mutually agreed-on goals	
Competency 9- Evaluate Practice with Individuals, Families, Groups, Organizations, and Communities:	
a. Select and use appropriate methods for evaluation of outcomes	1, 2, 3, 5, 6, 7, 8, 9, 10, 11, 12
b. Apply knowledge of human behavior and the social environment, person-in-environment, and other multidisciplinary theoretical frameworks in the evaluation of outcomes	1, 2, 5, 11
c. Critically analyze, monitor, and evaluate intervention and program processes and outcomes	1, 3, 4, 5, 6, 7, 8, 9, 10, 11, 12
d. Apply evaluation findings to improve practice effectiveness at the micro, mezzo, and macro levels	1, 8, 11, 12

BIBLIOGRAPHY

Adelman, C. (1993). Kurt Lewin and the origins of action research. *Educational Action Research, 1*, 7-24.

Adler, E. S., & Clark, R. (2008). How it's done: An invitation to social research (3rd ed.). Belmont, CA: Thomson Wadsworth

Agar, M., & MacDonald, J. (1995). Focus groups and ethnography. *Human Organization, 54,*78–86

Ainsworth, M., Blehar, M., Waters, E., & Wall, S. (1978). Patterns of attachment: A psychological study of the Strange Situation. Hillsdale, NJ: Erlbaum.

Alexander, B. (2010). Addiction: The view from rat park. Retrieved from: http://www.brucekalexander.com/articles-speeches/rat-park/148-addiction-the-view-from-rat-park

Allen, K. R., Kaestle, C. E., & Goldberg, A. E. (2011). More than just a punctuation mark: How boys and young men learn about menstruation. *Journal of Family Issues, 32,* 129–156.

American Sociological Association. (2011). Study: Negative classroom environment adversely affects children's mental health. Retrieved from: https://www.sciencedaily.com/releases/2011/03/110309073717.htm

Arnett, J. J. (2008). The neglected 95%: Why American psychology needs to become less American. *American Psychologist, 63,* 602–614.

Arnold, D. S., O'Leary, S. G., Wolff, L. S., & Acker, M. M. (1993). The parenting scale: A measure of dysfunctional parenting in discipline situations. *American Psychological Association, 5,* 137–144

Babbie, E. (2010). The practice of social research (12th ed.). Belmont, CA: Wadsworth

Baicker, K., Taubman, S. L., Allen, H. L., Bernstein, M., Gruber, J. H., Newhouse, J. P., ... & Finkelstein, A. N. (2013). The Oregon experiment—effects of Medicaid on clinical outcomes. *New England Journal of Medicine, 368*, 1713-1722

Baiden, P., Mengo, C., Boateng, G. O., & Small, E. (2018). Investigating the association between age at first alcohol use and suicidal ideation among high school students: Evidence from the youth risk behavior surveillance system. *Journal of Affective Disorders, 242*(2019), 60-67. doi: 10.1016/j.jad.2018.08.078

Baiden, P., Stewart, S. L., & Fallon, B. (2017). The role of adverse childhood experiences as determinants of non-suicidal self-injury among children and adolescents referred to community and inpatient mental health settings. *Child Abuse & Neglect, 69*, 163-176. doi: 10.1016/j.chiabu.2017.04.011

Bateman, P. J., Pike, J. C., & Butler, B. S. (2011). To disclose or not: Publicness in social networking sites. *Information Technology & People, 24*, 78–100.

Begley, S. (2010). What's really human? The trouble with student guinea pigs. *Newsweek*. Retrieved from http://www.newsweek.com/2010/07/23/what-s-really- human.html

Belkin, L. (2003, October 26). The opt-out revolution. *New York Times*. Retrieved from https://www.nytimes.com/2003/10/26/magazine/the-opt-out-revolution.html

Berger, P. L., & Luckman, T. (1966). *The social construction of reality: A treatise in the sociology of knowledge*. New York, NY: Doubleday.

Berger, P. L. (1990). Nazi science: The Dachau hypothermia experiments. *New England Journal of Medicine, 322*, 1435–1440.

Berk, R., Campbell, A., Klap, R., & Western, B. (1992). The deterrent effect of arrest in incidents of domestic violence: A Bayesian analysis of four field experiments. *American Sociological Review, 57*, 698–708.

Berzins, M. (2009). Spams, scams, and shams: Content analysis of unsolicited email. *International Journal of Technology, Knowledge, and Society, 5*, 143–154

Best, S., & Kellner, D. (1991). *Postmodern theory: Critical interrogations*. New York, NY: Guilford.

Bhattacherjee, A. (2012). *Social science research: Principles, methods, and practices*. Textbook Collection. Retrieved from http://scholarcommons.usf.edu/oa_textbooks/3

Bode, K. (2017, January 26). One more time with feeling: 'Anonymized' user data not really anonymous. *Techdirt*. Retrieved from: https://www.techdirt.com/articles/20170123/08125136548/one-more-time-with-feeling-anonymized-user-data-not-really-anonymous.shtml

Bowlby, J. (1969). *Attachment and loss: Volume 1*. New York, NY: Basic Books.

Borzekowski, D. L. G., Schenk, S., Wilson, J. L., & Peebles, R. (2010). e-Ana and e-Mia: A content analysis of pro-eating disorder Web sites. *American Journal of Public Health, 100*, 1526–1534

Broderick, C.B. (1971). Beyond the five conceptual frameworks: A decade of development in family theory. *Journal of Marriage and Family, 33*(1), 139-159.

Bronfenbrenner, U. (1986). Ecology of the family as a context for human development: Research perspectives. *Developmental Psychology, 22*, 723-742.

Burnett, D. (2012). Inscribing knowledge: Writing research in social work. In W. Green & B. L. Simon (Eds.), *The Columbia guide to social work writing* (pp. 65-82). New York, NY: Columbia University Press.

Burns, G. L., & Patterson, D. R. (1990). Conduct problem behaviors in a stratified random sample of children and adolescents: New standardization data on Eyberg Child Behavior Inventory. *Psychological Assessments, 2*, 391–397

Buysse, J. A. M., & Embser-Herbert, M. S. (2004). Constructions of gender in sport: An analysis of intercollegiate media guide cover photographs. *Gender & Society, 18*, 66–81

Calhoun, C., Gerteis, J., Moody, J., Pfaff, S., & Virk, I. (Eds.). (2007). *Classical sociological theory* (2nd ed.). Malden, MA: Blackwell.

Campbell, D., & Stanley, J. (1963). *Experimental and quasi-experimental designs for research*. Chicago, IL: Rand McNally

Carroll, J. (2005). Who supports marijuana legalization? Retrieved from http://www.gallup.com/poll/19561/who-supports-marijuana-legalization.aspx

Charmaz, K. (2006). *Constructing grounded theory: A practical guide through qualitative analysis*. Thousand Oaks, CA: Sage

Cheung, J. C. S. (2016). Researching practice wisdom in social work. Journal of Social Intervention: *Theory and Practice, 25*(3), 24-38

Curtin, R., Presser, S., & Singer, E. (2000). The effects of response rate changes on the index of consumer sentiment. *Public Opinion Quarterly, 64*, 413–428

Davis, M., Johnson, M., Bowland, S. (In Draft) "I hate it…but it's real": Black Clergy Perspectives on Intimate Partner Violence related Religious/Spiritual Abuse

Davis, M., Dahm, C., Jonson-Reid, M., Stoops, C., Sabri, B. (Revisions Submitted-Awaiting Final Decision). "The Men's Group" at St. Pius V: A Case Study of a Parish-Based Voluntary Partner Abuse Intervention Program.

de Montjoy, Y. A., Radaelli, L., & Singh, V. K. (2015). Unique in the shopping mall: On the reidentifiability of credit card metadata. *Science, 347*(6221), 536-539

DeCoster, S., Estes, S. B., & Mueller, C. W. (1999). Routine activities and sexual harassment in the workplace. *Work and Occupations, 26*, 21–49.

Delgado, R., & Stefancic, J. (2001). *Critical race theory: An introduction.* New York: New York University Press.

Devault, M. (1990). Talking and listening from women's standpoint: Feminist strategies for interviewing and analysis. *Social Problems, 37*, 96–116

Dillman, D. A. (2000). *Mail and Internet surveys: The tailored design method* (2nd ed.). New York, NY: Wiley

Downs, E., & Smith, S. L. (2010). Keeping abreast of hypersexuality: A video game character content analysis. *Sex Roles, 62*, 721–733

Dubois, B. L., & Miley, K. K. (2005). *Social work: An empowering profession*, 5th ed. Boston, MA: Pearson.

Elliott, W., Jung, H., Kim, K., & Chowa, G. (2010). A multi-group structural equation model (SEM) examining asset holding effects on educational attainment by race and gender. *Journal of Children & Poverty, 16*, 91–121.

Ellwood, D., & Kane, T. (2000). Who gets a college education? Family background and growing gaps in enrollment. Securing the Future: Investing in Children from Birth to College.

Engel, R. J. & Schutt, R. K. (2016). *The practice of research in social work* (4th ed.). Washington, DC: SAGE Publishing

Esterberg, K. G. (2002). *Qualitative methods in social research.* Boston, MA: McGraw-Hill.

Faden, R. R., & Beauchamp, T. L. (1986). *A history and theory of informed consent.* Oxford, UK: Oxford University Press.

Faris, R., & Felmlee, D. (2011). Status struggles: Network centrality and gender segregation in same- and cross-gender aggression. *American Sociological Review, 76,* 48–73.

Faulkner, S. S. & Faulkner, C. A. (2016). *Research methods for social workers: A practice-based approach.* New York, NY: Oxford University Press.

Ferguson, K. M., Kim, M. A., & McCoy, S. (2011). Enhancing empowerment and leadership among homeless youth in agency and community settings: A grounded theory approach. *Child and Adolescent Social Work Journal, 28,* 1–22.

Frankfort-Nachmias, C. & Leon-Guerrero, A. (2011). *Social statistics for a diverse society.* Washington, DC: Pine Forge Press.

Fraser, N. (1989). *Unruly practices: Power, discourse, and gender in contemporary social theory.* Minneapolis, MN: University of Minnesota Press.

Gallagher, J. R., & Nordberg, A. (2016). Comparing and contrasting White and African American participants' lived experiences in drug court. *Journal of Ethnicity in Criminal Justice, 14,* 100-119. doi: 10.1080/15377938.2015.1117999

Giorgi, A. and Giorgi, B. (2003). Phenomenology. In J. A. Smith (Ed.) *Qualitative Psychology: A Practical Guide to Research Methods.* London: Sage Publications.

Glaser, B. G., & Strauss, A. L. (1967). *The discovery of grounded theory: Strategies for qualitative research.* Chicago, IL: Aldine

Go, A. (2008). Two students kicked off semester at sea for plagiarism. *U.S. News & World Report.* Retrieved from http://www.usnews.com/education/blogs/paper-trail/2008/08/14/two-students-kicked-off-semester-at-sea-for-plagiarism

Goolsby, A. (2007). U.S. immigration policy in the regulatory era: Meaning and morality in state discourses of citizenship (Unpublished master's thesis). Department of Sociology, University of Minnesota, Minneapolis, MN

Graaf, G. and Snowden, L. (2019). State approaches to funding home and community-based mental health care for non-Medicaid youth: Alternatives to Medicaid waivers. *Administration and Policy in Mental Health and Mental Health Services Research*. https://doi.org/10.1007/s10488-019-00933-2

Greenberg, J., & Hier, S. (2009). CCTV surveillance and the poverty of media discourse: A content analysis of Canadian newspaper coverage. *Canadian Journal of Communication, 34*, 461–486

Greene, V. W. (1992). Can scientists use information derived from the concentration camps? Ancient answers to new questions. In A. L. Caplan (Ed.), *When medicine went mad: Bioethics and the Holocaust* (p. 169–170). Totowa, NJ: Humana Press.

Guba, E. G. (1990). *The paradigm dialog.* Newbury Park, CA: Sage Publications

Healy, K. (2001). Participatory action research and social work: A critical appraisal. *International Social Work, 44*, 93-105

Heckathorn, D. D. (2012). Snowball versus respondent-driven sampling. *Sociological Methodology, 41*(1), 355-366. doi: 10.1111/j.1467-9531.2011.01244.x

Henrich, J., Heine, S. J., & Norenzayan, A. (2010). The weirdest people in the world? *Behavioral and Brain Sciences, 33*, 61–135

Hesse-Biber, S. N., & Leavy, P. L. (Eds.). (2007). *Feminist research practice: A primer.* Thousand Oaks, CA: Sage

Hoefer, R., Black, B., & Ricard, M. (2015). The impact of state policy on teen dating violence prevalence. Journal of Adolescence, 44, 88-96. doi: 10.1016/j.adolescence.2015.07.006

Hoefer, R. & Bryant, D. (2017). A quantitative evaluation of the Multi-Disciplinary Approach to Prevention Services (MAPS) program to protect children and strengthen families, *Journal of Social Service Research, 43*, 459-469, doi: 10.1080/01488376.2017.1295009

Hoefer, R., & Silva, S. M. (2010). Assessing and augmenting administration skills in nonprofits: An exploratory mixed methods study. *Human Service Organizations: Management, Leadership & Governance, 38*, 246-257. doi: 10.1080/23303131.2014.892049

Hollander, J. A. (2004). The social context of focus groups. *Journal of Contemporary Ethnography, 33*, 602–637.

Holt, J. L., & Gillespie, W. (2008). Intergenerational transmission of violence, threatened egoism, and reciprocity: A test of multiple psychosocial factors affecting intimate partner violence. *American Journal of Criminal Justice, 33*, 252–266.

Hopper, J. (2012, February 15). Rules of thumb for survey length. [blog post]. Versta Research. Retrieved from https://verstaresearch.com/blog/rules-of-thumb-for-survey-length/

Houle, J. (2008). Elliott Smith's self-referential pronouns by album/year. Prepared for teaching SOC 207, Research Methods, at Pennsylvania State University, Department of Sociology

Huff, D. & Geis, I. (1993). *How to lie with statistics*. New York, NY: W. W. Norton & Co.

Hughes, M. E., Waite, L. J., Hawkley, L. C., & Cacioppo, J. T. (2004). A short scale for measuring loneliness in large surveys: Results from two population-based studies. *Research on Aging, 26*, 655-672. doi: 10.1177/0164027504268574

Humphreys, L. (1970). *Tearoom trade: Impersonal sex in public places*. London, UK: Duckworth.

Humphreys, L. (2008). *Tearoom trade: Impersonal sex in public places, enlarged edition with a retrospect on ethical issues*. New Brunswick, NJ: Aldine Transaction.

Jakobsson, S., Horvath, G., & Ahlberg, K. (2005). A grounded theory exploration of the first visit to a cancer clinic—strategies for achieving acceptance. *European Journal of Oncology Nursing, 9*(3), 248-257.

James, D., Schumm, W., Kennedy, C., Grigsby, C., & Shectman, K. (1985). Characteristics of the Kansas Parental Satisfaction Scale among two samples of married parents. *Psychological Reports, 57*(1), 163–169

Jaschik, S. (2009, December 4). Protecting his sources. *Inside Higher Ed.* Retrieved from: http://www.insidehighered.com/news/2009/12/04/demuth

Jenkins, P. J., & Kroll-Smith, S. (Eds.). (1996). *Witnessing for sociology: Sociologists in court*. Westport, CT: Praeger.

Johnson, P. S., & Johnson, M. W. (2014). Investigation of "bath salts" use patterns within an online sample of users in the United States. *Journal of Psychoactive Drugs, 46*(5), 369-378

Kaplan, A. (1964). *The conduct of inquiry: Methodology for behavioral science*. San Francisco, CA: Chandler Publishing Company.

Keeter, S., Dimock, M., & Christian, L. (2008). Calling cell phones in '08 pre-election polls. The Pew Research Center for the People and the Press. Retrieved from https://assets.pewresearch.org/wp-content/uploads/sites/5/legacy-pdf/cell-phone-commentary.pdf

Keeter, S., Kennedy, C., Dimock, M., Best, J., & Craighill, P. (2006). Gauging the impact of growing nonresponse on estimates from a national RDD telephone survey. *Public Opinion Quarterly, 70,* 759–779;

Kezdy, A., Martos, T., Boland, V., & Horvath-Szabo, K. (2011). Religious doubts and mental health in adolescence and young adulthood: The association with religious attitudes. *Journal of Adolescence, 34,* 39–47

Kimmel, M. (2000). The gendered society. New York, NY: Oxford University Press; Kimmel, M. (2008). Masculinity. In W. A. Darity Jr. (Ed.), *International encyclopedia of the social sciences* (2nd ed., Vol. 5, p. 1–5). Detroit, MI: Macmillan Reference USA

Kimmel, M. (2008). *Guyland: The perilous world where boys become men.* New York, NY: Harper Collins

Kimmel, M. (2008). Masculinity. In W. A. Darity Jr. (Ed.), *International encyclopedia of the social sciences* (2nd ed., Vol. 5, p. 1–5). Detroit, MI: Macmillan Reference USA

Kimmel, M. & Aronson, A. B. (2004). *Men and masculinities*: A-J. Denver, CO: ABL-CLIO.

King, R. D., Messner, S. F., & Baller, R. D. (2009). Contemporary hate crimes, law enforcement, and the legacy of racial violence. *American Sociological Review, 74,* 291–315.

Kogan, S. M., Wejnert, C., Chen, Y., Brody, G. H., & Slater, L. M. (2011). Respondent-driven sampling with hard-to-reach emerging adults: An introduction and case study with rural African Americans. *Journal of Adolescent Research, 26,* 30–60.

Krueger, R. A., & Casey, M. A. (2000). *Focus groups: A practical guide for applied research* (3rd ed.). Thousand Oaks, CA: Sage

Kuhn, T. (1962). *The structure of scientific revolutions.* Chicago, IL: University of Chicago Press.

LaBrenz, C. & Fong, R. (2016). Outcomes of family centered meetings for families referred to Child Protective Services. *Children and Youth Services Review, 71,* 93-102. doi: 10.1016/j.childyouth.2016.10.032

Langer, G. (2003). About response rates: Some unresolved questions. Public Perspective, May/June, 16–18. Retrieved from: https://www.aapor.org/AAPOR_Main/media/MainSiteFiles/Response_Rates_-_Langer.pdf

Lee, K. (2018). Older adults and volunteering: A comprehensive study on physical and psychological well-being and cognitive health (Doctoral dissertation). Proquest Dissertations Publishing. 11005225.

Lenza, M. (2004). Controversies surrounding Laud Humphreys' tearoom trade: An unsettling example of politics and power in methodological critiques. *International Journal of Sociology and Social Policy, 24,* 20–31.

Liamputtong, P. (2011). *Focus group methodology: Principles and practice.* Washington, DC: Sage.

Lisk, J. (2011). Addiction to our electronic gadgets. Retrieved from: https://www.youtube.com/watch?v=9lVHZZG5qvw

Loewen, J. W. (2007). *Lies my teacher told me: Everything your American history textbook got wrong.* Grenwich, CT: Touchstone.

MacKinnon, C. 1979. *Sexual harassment of working women: A case of sex discrimination.* New Haven, CT: Yale University Press.

Maffly, B. (2011, August 19). "Pattern of plagiarism" costs University of Utah scholar his job. *The Salt Lake Tribune.* Retrieved from http://www.sltrib.com/sltrib/cougars/52378377-78/bakhtiari-university-panel-plagiarism.html.csp?page=1

Markham, A., & Buchanan, E. (2012). Ethical decision-making and internet research: Recommendations from the AoIR ethics working committee (version 2.0). Retrieved from http://www.aoir.org/reports/ethics.pdf

Markham, A., & Buchanan, E. (2017). Research ethics in context decision-making in digital research in M. T. Schäfer and K. van Es (Eds.), *The Datafied Society* (pp. 201-210). Amsterdam University Press. Retrieved from https://www.jstor.org/stable/j.ctt1v2xsqn.19

McCoy, S. K., & Major, B. (2003). Group identification moderates emotional response to perceived prejudice. *Personality and Social Psychology Bulletin, 29,* 1005–1017.

Merkle, D. M., & Edelman, M. (2002). Nonresponse in exit polls: A comprehensive analysis.

In M. Groves, D. A. Dillman, J. L. Eltinge, & R. J. A. Little (Eds.), *Survey nonresponse* (pp. 243–258). New York, NY: John Wiley and Sons.

Messner, M. A. (2002). *Taking the field: Women, men, and sports.* Minneapolis: University of Minnesota Press.

Messner, M. A., Duncan, M. C., & Jensen, K. (1993). Separating the men from the girls: The gendered language of televised sports. *Gender & Society, 7,* 121–137

Milkie, M. A., & Warner, C. H. (2011). Classroom learning environments and the mental health of first grade children. *Journal of Health and Social Behavior, 52,* 4–22.

Milgram, S. (1974). *Obedience to authority: An experimental view.* New York, NY: Harper & Row.

Miyawaki, C. E., Mauldin, R. L., & Carman, C. R. (2019). Optometrists' referrals to community-based exercise programs: Finding from a mixed-methods feasibility study. *Journal of Aging and Physical Activity.* doi: 10.1123/japa.2018-0442

Milkie, M. A., & Warner, C. H. (2011). Classroom learning environments and the mental health of first grade children. *Journal of Health and Social Behavior, 52,* 4–22.

Moe, K. (1984). Should the Nazi research data be cited? *The Hastings Center Report, 14,* 5–7.

Morgan, D. L. (1997). *Focus groups as qualitative research* (2nd ed.). Thousand Oaks, CA: Sage.

Morgan, P. A. (1999). Risking relationships: Understanding the litigation choices of sexually harassed women. *The Law and Society Review, 33,* 201–226.

Mortimer, J. T. (2003). *Working and growing up in America.* Cambridge, MA: Harvard University Press.

National Commission for the Protection of Human Subjects in Biomedical and Behavioral Research. (1979). The Belmont report: Ethical principles and guidelines for the protection of human subjects of research. Retrieved from https://www.hhs.gov/ohrp/regulations-and-policy/belmont-report/index.html

National Research Act of 1974, Pub. L. no. 93-348 Stat 88. (1974). The act can be read at https://history.nih.gov/research/downloads/PL93-348.pdf

Neuendorf, K. A., Gore, T. D., Dalessandro, A., Janstova, P., & Snyder-Suhy, S. (2010). Shaken and stirred: A content analysis of women's portrayals in James Bond films. *Sex Roles, 62,* 747–761.

Neuman, W. L. (2003). *Social research methods: Qualitative and quantitative approaches* (5th ed.). Boston, MA: Pearson

Neuman, W. L. (2007). *Basics of social research: Qualitative and quantitative approaches* (2nd ed.). Boston, MA: Pearson

Nordberg, A., Crawford, M. R., & Praetorius, R. T. (2016). Exploring minority youths' police encounters: A qualitative interpretive meta-synthesis. *Child and Adolescent Social Work Journal, 33,* 137-149. doi: 10.1007/s10560-015-0415-3

Oakley, A. (1981). Interviewing women: A contradiction in terms. In H. Roberts (Ed.), *Doing feminist research* (pp. 30–61). London, UK: Routledge & Kegan Paul

Ogden, R. (2008). Harm. In L. M. Given (Ed.), *The SAGE encyclopedia of qualitative research methods* (p. 379–380). Los Angeles, CA: Sage.

Open Science Collaboration. (2015). Estimating the reproducibility of psychological science. *Science,* 349(6251), aac4716.

Padgett, D. K. (2016). *Qualitative methods in social work research* (Vol. 36). Thousand Oaks, CA: Sage Publications.

Padilla-Medina, D., Rodríguez, E., & Vega, G. (2019). Gender Role Beliefs and Puerto Rican Adolescents intention to use abusive behaviors in romantic relationships: A consideration of developmental and gender variations. Manuscript under review

Padilla-Medina, D., Rodríguez, E., Vega, G., & Williams, J. (2019). Understanding the behavioral determinants Influencing Puerto Rican adolescents' decision to engage in romantic relationship violence. Manuscript under review.

Parisi, M. (1989). Alien cartoon 6. Off the Mark. Retrieved from: http://www.offthemark.com/System/2006-05-30

Pate, A., & Hamilton, E. (1992). Formal and informal deterrents to domestic violence: The Dade county spouse assault experiment. *American Sociological Review, 57,* 691–697.

Percheski, C. (2008). Opting out? Cohort differences in professional women's employment rates from 1960 to 2005. *American Sociological Review, 73,* 497–517

Petrie, B. F. (1996). Environment is not the most important variable in determining oral morphine consumption in Wistar rats. *Psychological Reports, 78*(2), 391-400

Pew Research (n.d.) *Sampling.* Retrieved from: http://www.pewresearch.org/methodology/u-s-survey-research/sampling/

Piercy, F. P., Franz, N., Donaldson, J. L., & Richard, R. F. (2011). Consistency and change in participatory action research: Reflections on a focus group study about how farmers learn. *The Qualitative Report, 16,* 820–829

Pozos, R. S. (1992). Scientific inquiry and ethics: The Dachau data. In A. L. Caplan (Ed.), *When medicine went mad: Bioethics and the Holocaust* (p. 104). Totowa, NJ: Humana Press.

Reason, P. (1994). *Participation in human inquiry.* London, UK: Sage

Reinharz, S. (1992). *Feminist methods in social research.* New York, NY: Oxford University Press

Reverby, S. M. (2009). *Examining Tuskegee: The infamous syphilis study and its legacy.* Chapel Hill, NC: University of North Carolina Press

Rodwell, M. K. (1998). *Social work constructivist research.* New York, NY: Garland Publishing

Rothman, D. J. (1987). Ethics and human experimentation. *The New England Journal of Medicine, 317,* 1195–1199.

Rubin, C. & Babbie, S. (2017). *Research methods for social work* (9th edition). Boston, MA: Cengage

Rubin, A., and Babbie, E. R. (2017). *Research methods for social work* (9th ed.). Belmont: Wadsworth.

Sadker, M., & Sadker, D. (1994). *Failing at fairness: How America's schools cheat girls.* New York, NY: Maxwell Macmillan International.

Schaller, M. (1997). The psychological consequences of fame: Three tests of the self-consciousness hypothesis. *Journal of Personality, 65,* 291– 309

Shakur, S. (1993). *Monster: The autobiography of an L.A. gang member.* New York, NY: Atlantic Monthly Press.

Schriver, J. M. (2011). *Human behavior and the social environment: Shifting paradigms in essential knowledge for social work practice* (5th ed.) Boston, MA: Pearson.

Schutt, R. K. (2006). *Investigating the social world: The process and practice of research*. Thousand Oaks, CA: Pine Forge Press.

Sheikh, J. I., & Yesavage, J. A. (1986). 9/Geriatric Depression Scale (GDS): Recent evidence and development of a shorter version. *Clinical Gerontologist, 5*(1/2), 165-172. doi: 10.1300/J018v05n01_09

Sherman, L. W., & Berk, R. A. (1984). The specific deterrent effects of arrest for domestic assault. *American Sociological Review, 49,* 261–272.

Simons, D. A., & Wurtele, S. K. (2010). Relationships between parents' use of corporal punishment and their children's endorsement of spanking and hitting other children. *Child Abuse & Neglect, 34,* 639–646.

Slater, H. M., & Mitschke, D.B. (2015). *Evaluation of the Crossroads Program in Arlington, TX: Findings from an Innovative Teen Pregnancy Prevention Program,* Arlington, TX: University of Texas at Arlington.

Slater, A., & Tiggemann, M. (2010). "Uncool to do sport": A focus group study of adolescent girls' reasons for withdrawing from physical activity. *Psychology of Sport and Exercise, 11,* 619–626

Smith, L. T. (2013). *Decolonizing methodologies: Research and indigenous peoples* (2nd edition). London: Zed Books, Ltd.

Smith, T. W. (2009). Trends in willingness to vote for a black and woman for president, 1972–2008. *GSS Social Change Report No. 55.* Chicago, IL: National Opinion Research Center

Solinas, M., Thiriet, N., El Rawas, R., Lardeux, V., & Jaber, M. (2009). Environmental enrichment during early stages of life reduces the behavioral, neurochemical, and molecular effects of cocaine. *Neuropsychopharmacology, 34,* 1102

Stacey, J. (1988). Can there be a feminist ethnography? *Women's Studies International Forum, 11,* 21–27

Stratmann, T. & Wille, D. (2016). *Certificate-of-need laws and hospital quality.* Mercatus Center at George Mason University, Arlington, VA. Retrieved from: https://www.mercatus.org/system/files/mercatus-stratmann-wille-con-hospital-quality-v1.pdf

Substance Abuse and Mental Health Services Administration (2007). *Pathways' housing first program*. Retrieved from: https://pathwaystohousingpa.org/sites/pathwaystohousingpa.org/files/Pathways%20Housing%20First%20Evidence-based.pdf

Trucco, E.M. (2012). *Contextual factors in substance use: How neighborhoods, parents, and peers impact substance use in an early adolescent sample*. ProQuest Dissertation Publishing (3541306).

Uggen, C., & Blackstone, A. (2004). Sexual harassment as a gendered expression of power. *American Sociological Review, 69*, 64–92.

US Department of Health and Human Services. (1993). Institutional review board guidebook glossary. Retrieved from https://ori.hhs.gov/education/products/ucla/chapter2/page00b.html

US Department of Health and Human Services. (2009). Code of federal regulations (45 CFR 46).

Venkatesh, S. (2008). *Gang leader for a day: A rogue sociologist takes to the streets*. New York, NY: Penguin Group.

von Hoffman, N. (1970, January 30). Sociological snoopers. *The Washington Post*, p. B1.

Voth Schrag, R., Ravi, K., & Robinson, S. (2019). *Understanding the needs of non-service seeking survivors*. Austin, TX: Texas Council on Family Violence

Wal-Mart Stores, Inc. v. Dukes, 564 U.S. (2011)

Warwick, D. P. (1973). Tearoom trade: Means and ends in social research. *Hastings Center Studies*, 1, 39–49.

Warwick, D. P. (1982). Types of harm in social research. In T. L. Beauchamp, R. R. Faden, R. J. Wallace Jr., & L. Walters (Eds.), *Ethical issues in social science research*. Baltimore, MD: Johns Hopkins University Press

Weiner, M. (2010). *Power, protest, and the public schools: Jewish and African American struggles in New York City*. Piscataway, NJ: Rutgers University Press

Wilson, P. M., Petticrew, M., Calnan, M. W., & Natareth, I. (2010). Disseminating research findings: What should researchers do? A systematic scoping review of conceptual frameworks. *Implementation Science, 5,* 91.

Wong, W. (2007). The top 10 hand gestures you'd better get right. Retrieved from http://www.languagetrainers.co.uk/blog/2007/09/24/top-10-hand-gestures

Ylanne, V., & Williams, A. (2009). Positioning age: Focus group discussions about older people in TV advertising. *International Journal of the Sociology of Language, 200,* 171–187.

DERIVATIVE NOTES

This open textbook is primarily based on the open textbook, *Scientific Inquiry in Social Work* by Matthew DeCarlo with additional open source material used from *Social Science Research: Principles, Methods, and Practices* by Anol Bhattacherjee; *Ethical Decision-Making and Internet Research* (2012); and *Research Ethics in Context Decision-Making in Digital Research* (2017) by Annette Markham and Elizabeth Buchanan. Licensing information can be found in the front matter. The following index details where content from each source was used in this manuscript. New content (as noted below) indicates major additions, such as chapters, sections, subsections, or key concepts that I created or solicited contributions for from faculty at the University of Texas at Arlington's School of Social Work.

Minor revisions not noted below include editing language for clarity, length, and flow as well as corrections to hyperlinks and citations.

CHAPTER 1

Content from DeCarlo

- Chapter 1

Major revisions/New content

- Section 1.3: New text and a figure (Figure 1.1) on evidence-based practice
- Section 1.3: *Spotlight on UTA School of Social Work: An Evidence-Based Program to Prevent Child Maltreatment* contributed by Richard Hoefer

CHAPTER 2

Content from DeCarlo

- Chapter 6 with the exception of some of the material from the Complementary approaches subsection in 6.3

Major revisions/New content

- Section 2.1: New examples of micro-, meso-, and macro-level research were contributed by Brooke Troutman
- Section 2.2: *Spotlight on UTA School of Social Work: Catherine LaBrenz connects social theory and child welfare research* was contributed by Catherine LaBrenz

CHAPTER 3

Content from DeCarlo

- Chapter 5

Content from Markham & Buchanan, 2012, 2017

- Section 3.2 subsection *Internet Research* was derived from these materials

CHAPTER 4

Content from DeCarlo

- Chapter 7

Major revisions/New content

- Section 4.4: Provided a new example of mixed methods research

CHAPTER 5

Content from DeCarlo

- Chapter 9 except for the "Trustworthiness and authenticity" subsection of 9.4

Major revisions/New content

- Figure 5.2 was revised to exclude "Valid but not reliable" with the rationale that this text wishes to present reliability as a requirement for validity; therefore an instrument could not be valid if it were not reliable

- Section 5.3: information on Levels of measurement were moved into this section
- Section 5.5: restructured validity section to include subheadings for types of validity
- Section 5.5: added and revised information about criterion and construct validity
- Section 5.6: added headings to levels of measurement, additional explanations for mutual exclusivity,
- Added a line to Table 5.1
- Section 5.4: *Spotlight on UTA School of Social Work: Are interactions with a social robot associated with changes in depression and loneliness?* contributed by Ling Xu and Noelle Fields

CHAPTER 6

Content from DeCarlo

- Chapter 10 except several paragraphs from 10.1 "Applying sampling terms"

Content from Bhattacherjee

- Content from Chapter 12 was used in Sections 6.1, 6.2, and 6.4 with references to interpretative research replace with the term qualitative research and information about overarching interpretative research paradigm removed to better align with the introductory nature of this new textbook

Major revisions/New content

- Section 6.1: added headers, re-ordered the presentation of inclusion and exclusion criteria
- Section 6.2: changed the section name to *Nonprobability sampling* and included reference to its use in quantitative research as well as qualitative research
- Section 6.2: clarified that Kogan et al. used respondent-driven sampling which is similar, but different from snowball sampling
- Section 6.3: changed the section name to *Probability sampling*, added information about proportionate and disproportionate stratified random sampling, added headings for subsections
- Section 6.4: changed the section name to Critical thinking about samples

CHAPTER 7

Content from DeCarlo

- Chapter 11
- Portions of Chapter 12.4

Major revisions/New content

- Section 7.2: changed the name of the section to "assessing survey research" and added a subsection on response rate
- Section 7.4: created new content about using standardized instruments
- Section 7.1: *Spotlight on UTA School of Social Work: Diana Padilla-Medina conducts survey research* contributed by Diana Padilla-Medina

CHAPTER 8

Content from DeCarlo

- Chapter 12: 12.1, 12.2, and 12.3 (some information from 12.2 was moved to 8.1 under a new heading "Experimental Design in Macro-level Research")

Major revisions/New content

- Section 8.1: New organization and headings, revised material changing comparison groups to control groups, added some new material in the subsection Experimental Design in Macro-level Research
- Section 8.2: Added headers to subsections, new material about the one-group pretest post-test design, reorganized material about pre-experiments
- Section 8.3: Added additional types of threats to internal validity; *Spotlight on UTA School of Social Work: Assessing a teen pregnancy and STI prevention program* contributed by Holli Slater and Diane Mitschke

CHAPTER 9

Content from DeCarlo

- Chapter 9: subsection *Trustworthiness and authenticity* from 9.4

- Chapter 13, with minor deletions from the sections on Focus Groups and moderate deletions from Analyzing Qualitative Data

Major revisions/New content

- Section 9.4 Added a new *Grounded Theory* section contributed by Erin Roark Murphy
- Section 9.5 *Spotlight on UTA School of Social Work: Dr. Genevieve Graf conducts research using interviews and focus groups* contributed by Genevieve Graf

CHAPTER 10

Content from DeCarlo

- Chapter 14 Sections 14.1-14.4, with the exception of some content from 14.3 *Indirect measures* and *Analysis of unobtrusive data collected by you* subsections, and 14.4 *Challenges in secondary data analysis*

Major revisions/New content

- Section 10.3: Added a short reflection on cultural humility and cultural competence in *Indirect measures* subsection; added brief information about analyzing photographs in *Analysis of unobtrusive data collected by you* subsection
- Section 10.4: *Spotlight on UTA School of Social Work: Secondary data analysis* subsection contributed by Kathy Lee

CHAPTER 11

Content from DeCarlo

- Chapter 15, with some deletions from section 15.2

Major revisions/New content

- Section 11.1: Added a new section on *Needs Assessment* contributed by Sarah R. Robinson
- Section 11.2: New content written to describe single-subjects design
- Section 11.3: *Spotlight on UTA School of Social Work: Dr. Maxine Davis shares experiences with action research* contributed by Maxine Davis

CHAPTER 12

Content from DeCarlo

- Chapter 16 with moderate deletions from Section 16.2

Major revisions/New content

  ◦ Section 12.2: Added a subsection on peer-reviewed journal articles
  ◦ Section 12.3: *Spotlight on UTA School of Social Work: Reporting research on Texan survivors of intimate partner violence* contributed by Rachel Voth Schrag

GLOSSARY

Content from DeCarlo

- Glossary

PRACTICE BEHAVIOR INDEX

Content from DeCarlo

- Practice behavior index with chapter numbers revised to reflect new organization

LINKS BY CHAPTER

FRONT MATTER

Mavs Open Press (https://library.uta.edu/scholcomm/mavs-open-press)

Creative Commons licenses (https://creativecommons.org/licenses/)

OER (https://library.uta.edu/scholcomm/open-education/oer)

Pressbooks Accessibility Policy (https://pressbooks.org/blog/2018/05/01/our-accessibility-policy-and-forthcoming-accessibility-improvements)

Open Education at UTA (http://libguides.uta.edu/utacares)

OER Adoption Form (https://uta.qualtrics.com/jfe/form/SV_8HTkgCym5Q6Mk7j)

BCcampus Open Education (https://open.bccampus.ca/)

CHAPTER 1

Wikipedia entry on cognitive biases (https://en.wikipedia.org/wiki/List_of_cognitive_biases)

Louis Cuff (https://www.snopes.com/fact-check/high-steaks/)

this comic (http://www.smbc-comics.com/?id=2475)

Culture-bound syndromes (https://en.wikipedia.org/wiki/Culture-bound_syndrome)

National Public Radio article (https://www.npr.org/2018/11/01/663012390/survey-suggests-manels-all-male-panels-are-still-the-norm)

New Yorker cartoon (https://condenaststore.com/featured/are-you-just-pissing-and-moaning-edward-koren.html)

Ted talk on homelessness (https://youtu.be/HsFHV-McdPo)

Cochrane Reviews digital library (http://www.cochranelibrary.com/)

Campbell Collaboration (https://campbellcollaboration.org/)

Richard Hoefer (https://mentis.uta.edu/explore/profile/dr-richard-hoefer)

CHAPTER 2

Philip Baiden (https://mentis.uta.edu/explore/profile/phillip-baiden)

Eusebius Small (https://mentis.uta.edu/explore/profile/eusebius-small)

Anne Nordberg (https://mentis.uta.edu/explore/profile/anne-bain)

Regina Praetorius (https://mentis.uta.edu/explore/profile/regina-praetorius)

Richard Hoefer (https://mentis.uta.edu/explore/profile/dr-richard-hoefer)

CC-BY-NC-SA 3.0 (https://creativecommons.org/licenses/by-nc-sa/3.0/)

National Gang Crime Research Center (NGCRC) (http://www.ngcrc.com/)

CHAPTER 3

The Truman Show (http://www.imdb.com/title/tt0120382)

President Clinton publicly apologized (https://www.cdc.gov/tuskegee/clintonp.htm).

Scholars for Academic Justice (http://sajumn.wordpress.com

Ethical Decision-Making and Internet Research (https://aoir.org/reports/ethics2.pdf)

New Yorker cartoon (https://www.art.com/products/p15063407512-sa-i6847806/dana-fradon-filing-cabinets-labeled-our-facts-their-facts-neutral-facts-disput-new-yorker-cartoon.htm?upi=PGQTTQ0

CHAPTER 4

University of Maryland (http://withoutmedia.wordpress.com

CHAPTER 5

New Yorker cartoon (https://condenaststore.com/featured/it-all-depends-on-how-you-define-chop-tom-cheney.html)

well-being (http://www.well-beingindex.com/)

searched directly (https://eds-b-ebscohost-com.ezproxy.uta.edu/ehost/search/advanced?vid=0&sid=ddac6185-1131-453a-85d2-5640c42e09ca%40pdc-v-sessmgr01)

viewed online (https://uta.alma.exlibrisgroup.com/discovery/openurl?institution=01UTAR_INST&rfr_id=info:sid%2Fsummon&rft_dat=ie%3D611331596 20004911,language%3DEN&svc_dat=CTO&u.ignore_date_coverage=true&vid=01UTAR_IN ST:Services)

Noelle Fields (https://mentis.uta.edu/explore/profile/noelle-fields)

Ling Xu (https://mentis.uta.edu/explore/profile/ling-xu)

Reliability and validity (https://commons.wikimedia.org/wiki/File:Reliability_and_validity.svg)

CHAPTER 6

The first measured century (http://www.pbs.org/fmc/timeline/e1948election.htm)

Random.org (https://www.random.org)

CHAPTER 7

General Social Survey (http://www.norc.uchicago.edu/GSS+Website)

Diana Padilla-Medina (https://mentis.uta.edu/explore/profile/diana-padilla)

Monitoring the Future Study (http://www.monitoringthefuture.org/)

Youth Development Study (https://cla.umn.edu/sociology/graduate/collaboration-opportunities/youth-development-study)

SurveyMonkey (https://www.surveymonkey.com)

Qualtrics (https://www.qualtrics.com/)

CC-BY-NC-SA 3.0 (https://creativecommons.org/licenses/by-nc-sa/3.0/)

David Elkind's theory (https://en.wikipedia.org/wiki/Imaginary_audience)

CHAPTER 8

Diane Mitschke (https://mentis.uta.edu/explore/profile/diane-mitschke)

Holli Slater (https://mentis.uta.edu/explore/profile/holli%20-slater)

CHAPTER 9

Guyland (https://www.harpercollins.com/9780062885739/guyland/)

CC-BY-NC-SA 3.0 (https://creativecommons.org/licenses/by-nc-sa/3.0/)

CHAPTER 10

his drawing (http://www.offthemark.com/System/2006-05-30)

General Social Survey (gss.norc.org)

Add Health (http://www.cpc.unc.edu/projects/addhealth)

Wisconsin Longitudinal Study (https://www.ssc.wisc.edu/wlsresearch)

British Household Panel Study (https://www.iser.essex.ac.uk/bhps)

International Social Survey Programme (http://www.issp.org)

Murray Research Archive (http://dvn.iq.harvard.edu/dvn/dv/mra)

The Global Feminisms project (https://globalfeminisms.umich.edu/contact)

Oral History Office (https://ovpr.uconn.edu/services/rics/irb/researcher-guide/oral-histories/)

Southern Historical Collection (https://library.unc.edu/wilson/shc/)

Dr. Kathy Lee (https://mentis.uta.edu/explore/profile/k-lee)

Health and Retirement Study (http://hrsonline.isr.umich.edu/)

CHAPTER 11

Maxine Davis (https://mentis.uta.edu/explore/profile/maxine-davis)

CC BY-NC-ND (https://creativecommons.org/licenses/by-nc-nd/4.0/legalcode)

CHAPTER 12

Rachel Voth Schrag (https://mentis.uta.edu/explore/profile/rachel-voth-schrag)

this story (https://archive.sltrib.com/article.php?id=52378377&itype=CMSID&page=1)

this article (https://www.usnews.com/education/blogs/paper-trail/2008/08/14/two-students-kicked-off-semester-at-sea-for-plagiarism)

Texas Council on Family Violence's website (https://tcfv.org/)